**WITHDRAWN
UTSA LIBRARIES**

DATE DUE

The American Garden City
and the New Towns Movement

Architecture and Urban Design, No. 13

Stephen C. Foster, Series Editor

Associate Professor of Art History
University of Iowa

Other Titles in This Series

No. 8	*The Development of the American Modern Style*	Deborah Frances Pokinski
No. 9	*The Inland Architect: Chicago's Major Architectural Journal, 1883-1908*	Robert Prestiano
No. 10	*Business Architectural Imagery in America, 1870-1930*	Kenneth Turney Gibbs
No. 11	*Changing Ideas on Architecture in the* Encyclopédie, *1750-1776*	Kevin Harrington
No. 14	*Hitler's Berlin: The Speer Plans for Reshaping the Central City*	Stephen D. Helmer
No. 15	*Frederick Law Olmsted and the Philosophic Background to the City Planning Movement in the United States*	Irving David Fisher
No. 16	*Berlin's Housing Revolution: German Reform in the 1920s*	Ronald V. Wiedenhoeft
No. 17	*William Le Baron Jenney: A Nineteenth-Century Architect*	Theodore Turak

The American Garden City and the New Towns Movement

by
Carol A. Christensen

UMI RESEARCH PRESS
Ann Arbor, Michigan

Copyright © 1986, 1978
Carol Ann Christensen
All rights reserved

Produced and distributed by
UMI Research Press
an imprint of
University Microfilms International
A Xerox Information Resources Company
Ann Arbor, Michigan 48106

Library of Congress Cataloging in Publication Data

Christensen, Carol A., 1946-
  The American garden city and the new towns movement.

  (Architecture and urban design ; no. 13)
  Revision of author's thesis (Ph.D.—University of Minnesota, 1977)
  Bibliography: p.
  Includes index.
  1. Garden cities—United States. 2. Garden cities—United States—Case studies. 3. New towns—United States. 4. City planning—United States. I. Title. II. Series.
HT164.U6C47 1986   307.7'68'0973   85-20866
ISBN 0-8357-1684-8 (alk. paper)

For Phillip

The future is not a result of choices among alternative paths offered by the present, but a place that is created—created first in mind and will, created next in activity. The future is not some place we are going to, but one we are creating. The paths to it are not found but made, and the activity of making them changes both the maker and the destination.
—John Schaar

Contents

List of Figures   *ix*

Acknowledgments   *xi*

Introduction   *1*

1 The City in American Thought   *9*

2 Nature, Community, and the Birth of Urban Planning   *29*

3 Ebenezer Howard and the Garden City Idea   *45*

4 Radburn, New Jersey: "A Town for the Motor Age"   *55*

5 Greendale and the Greenbelt Program   *71*

6 Levittown, New Jersey: "More House for the Money"   *95*

7 Columbia, Maryland: "A Garden for People to Grow In"   *105*

8 New Towns as Social Inventions   *127*

Figures   *137*

Notes   *157*

Bibliography   *179*

Index   *191*

Figures

Figures following page 135

1. An Underpass at Radburn, New Jersey, 1985

2. Interior Park within a Superblock at Radburn, New Jersey, 1985

3. Houses Turned to Face the Interior Park, Radburn, New Jersey, 1985

4. Multifamily Housing, Radburn, New Jersey, 1985

5. The Elementary School and Its Surrounding Park, Radburn, New Jersey, 1985

6. Swimming Pool within the Superblock and near the Elementary School, Radburn, New Jersey, 1985

7. Underpass at Greenbelt, Maryland, 1942

8. Aerial View of Greenbelt, Maryland, during Early Construction, 1936

9. Aerial View, Greenhills, Ohio, 1938

10. Housing and Open Space, Greenbelt, Maryland, 1942

11. Greendale, Wisconsin, 1939

12. Tree-lined Streets in Levittown (Willingboro), New Jersey, 1985

Figures

13. Housing in Levittown (Willingboro), New Jersey, 1985

14. Neighborhood School and Recreation Center, Levittown (Willingboro), New Jersey, 1985

15. Downtown Columbia, Maryland, 1985

16. Fishing in Downtown Columbia, Maryland, 1985

17. Columbia, Maryland, 1985

18. The Neighborhood Concept at Columbia, Maryland

19. Open Space, Columbia, Maryland, 1985

20. Open Space and Condominium Housing, Columbia, Maryland, 1985

Acknowledgments

One of the pleasures of seeing my early research materialize in book form is the opportunity it presents to again express my deep gratitude to Mulford Sibley and Mary Turpie. Less concerned with finding the "right" answers than with clarifying the questions and asking new ones, they opened the spaces between disciplines and fields for exciting new challenges. My intellectual debt to them will always be large. They encouraged me to weave threads from American studies, urban studies and future studies, which this work reflects, but which has also provided the foundation for my professional life. Their retirement from the University of Minnesota in recent years is an incalculable loss for current and future graduate students in the American studies program there. Mary and Mulford: thank you.

So many colleagues have carried my weight and suffered my divided attention these past months. You know who you are and how much I appreciate your forbearance.

Thank you, too, David Ames and Barry Cullingworth of the University of Delaware's College of Urban Affairs and Public Policy for your assistance with resources in updating this work.

Revising the manuscript under pressure of deadlines and other obligations would have not been possible but for my colleague and loving friend Linda Kovan whose commitment to the project at times exceeded my own. Linda, this book is for you too.

My first and final thanks are due my son who has been patient and long-suffering beyond any mother's expectation for a seven-year-old on summer vacation. His flowers and backrubs, popsicles and faith that it would soon be done saw me through to the end. This book is for you, dear, dear Phillip.

Introduction

Since the Industrial Revolution, one of the most potent forces in shaping urban life has been an association linking the reform of society with the reform of the city. This linkage brought about astonishing changes in a very few decades as late-nineteenth century urban reformers changed the face of the American city and with it the fabric of American life. Their efforts gave rise to zoning, of course, but they also led to settlement houses, modern sociology, and social work. They resulted in the merit system of civil service, at-large representation, and the city manager and commission forms of government. The urban reform movement was responsible for regulatory legislation in housing standards, the workplace, and urban services.

The emergence during this period of a new group of reformers collectively oriented to reforming society through reforming the city was the combined result of Enlightenment ideas about the perfectability of society, social Darwinian philosophy which no longer regarded the old inevitables as eternal and unchanging, and rapid and massive urbanization which made the city the visible symbol of poverty, vice, disease, inequity, ignorance, and radicalism. Progressive reformers widely feared that democracy and the very foundations of American society were imperiled by the persistence and alarming growth of conditions then seen so clearly in urban settings. Their efforts paved the way for the modern planning premise that urban and societal reform were fundamentally related.

One of the outcomes of this association was the new towns movement, an effort to build entire new cities from scratch and to remake society through the deliberate creation of new models for urban *life* as well as urban form.

Modern new towns trace their origins to Ebenezer Howard who originated the garden city concept in England with the 1898 publication of *Garden Cities of Tomorrow: A Peaceful Path to Real Reform*.[1] Howard's treatise, together with the two garden cities he actually brought into being, led directly to Britain's extensive involvement in new towns as an instrument of national urban policy in the post-World War II years. The concept was brought to the United States by the Regional Planning Association of America in the 1920s; and, through Radburn, New Jersey, the first American attempt at garden city building, it led to the flowering of new towns in the 1960s. By the middle of that decade, the Urban Land Institute counted no fewer than 160 new communities either planned or in the construction stage.[2] Since the days of Radburn, the garden city idea has been an enduring theme in urban planning, albeit one that has reflected uniquely American beliefs and practices.

What follows is an exploration of how the garden city has been interpreted in the design of American new towns. The study focuses on four well known and highly regarded experiments in urban planning: Radburn, New Jersey, built in 1928 and clearly the most influential model for subsequent American new communities; Greendale, Wisconsin and the New Deal's greenbelt town program, undertaken during the Great Depression and atypical in its close kinship with Howard's ideas; Columbia, Maryland, the most famous of American new cities and illustrative of the 1960s new town renaissance; and Levittown, New Jersey, an example of postwar, large-scale suburban development. Of course Levitt & Sons did not intend Levittown to be a "garden city," but the town is included here to indicate how American new towns, despite their variety, are remarkably more alike than different. Philosophically most are closer to one another than they are to Howard's conception of the garden city.

The cities examined in detail here are not representative of American new towns building; indeed, they are generally considered among the finest examples of their respective types. Yet they all express a similar interpretation of the garden city, suggesting that *cultural* values have been an influential if neglected determinant of urban planning theory. In comparing these towns with one another and with Howard's garden city proposal, several dominant cultural themes emerge which are of particular importance for understanding urban planning history and which apply to new towns in general. This book considers these as well as other influences on the modern new towns movement.

My analysis yokes perspectives from the fields of American studies, urban studies and also future studies, for it is in the nature of these towns as models for *future* American urbanization that their current significance lies. These cities have an importance that extends beyond their small numbers. As models, their *demonstration* function is particularly valuable. By physically embodying alternative social visions, by conceptualizing the future as potentially different from that which presently exists, they serve an important social purpose. Demonstration projects such as these enlarge and enrich the "imaging stock" from which new directions may be taken; they free the future from dominance by present trendlines and so "open" it to new possibilities. As more of the future comes within the realm of conscious design and choice, generating new visions increasingly becomes a social *responsibility*—as does the need to make explicit those values and premises on which such visions rest. This study contributes to this "futures creation" process by exploring the assumptions which undergird and define "the good city" for many twentieth-century American planners. It asks, what have been the decisive guiding images for planners? What are their basic assumptions about society, economy, technology, and polity? About cause and effect? What are their perceptions of human nature? What are the values and purposes that guide the design? How are people related to institutions, to nature, to spirit, to each other? What are the limits of change? What is the view of the future?

The Dutch sociologist Frederick Polak once wrote,

> Through his images of the future, we come to know man, who he is and how he wishes to be, what his thoughts are, what he values most highly, what he thinks is worth striving for, and whether he thinks it is attainable.... Certain types of men hold certain types of visions, subject to their temper and spirit; tell me what your vision of the future is and I will tell you what you are.[3]

Such visions are as latent in artifacts as they are in words. This book is an attempt to elucidate the basic assumptions and future images contained within the new communities movement in America, and these cannot be separated from the new towns' kinship with utopianism.

New Towns and Utopian Traditions

America's garden cities are descended from the Progressive reform movement and reflect the values of that period, but they are also heirs of the utopian tradition. This utopian heritage is important for understanding the potentiality as well as the actuality of the new town experience.

To label the new town "utopian" is by no means to discredit the concept. Quite the contrary. Utopianism has fallen on very hard times and bears some defense here, for if correctly understood the concept has much to teach us.

Utopianism has been unfairly misinterpreted. The word has its origins in Sir Thomas More's sixteenth-century depiction of an imaginary society to which he gave the name "Utopia." Translated from the Greek, "utopia" meant "no place"—but it also meant "good place." (Sir Thomas deliberately punned with the prefix.) It is this former association of "no place" that has endured, defining utopia as foolish, childish, and unattainable. Yet utopia's real contribution is as "good place," for utopia is concerned with improvement, not with perfection. In its long history as a literary form, the utopian tradition has been secular, concerned with creating the good life *on earth* and in the here-and-now. Utopia is very much related to the present reality against which the utopist is writing. Each utopia is an implicit criticism of the civilization that serves as its background, as Lewis Mumford has said. Each is an attempt to uncover potentialities that existing institutions have either ignored or buried under an ancient crust of custom and habit.[4]

Utopia not only pictures a good world; it pictures a *whole* world. And it faces every part of it at the same time. In each utopia we see a mind in the act of creating a complete hypothetical society, each made up of many institutions and situations, all bound together, each conditioning the other.[5]

Contrary to popular belief, the utopist does not view social problems in personal or moral terms. Social improvement is sought through changing the social structure from *without*, not through changing the individual from *within*. The utopian tradition is an environmental one: it holds the manipulation of institutions to be possible and worthwhile and believes the good person to be a reflection of a healthy environment. The utopian tradition rests firmly on the rationalistic assumption that reason alone is sufficient to change society from what it is to what it should be.[6] I cannot think of a more demanding task than constructing a utopia, for the utopist must first clarify his or her goals and determine the axioms around which the social system is organized. Then a relatively whole system must be constructed involving the interaction of work, people and place, and the interrelationships between functions, institutions and human purposes. The utopist must do this all while relating means to ends.

True utopianism is not escapist. It is constructive. Taken as a whole, the literature of utopianism enriches the sense of human possibility. As George Kateb has written:

> It makes vivid the fact that any given society does not—cannot—exploit the full richness of human nature; each society, obviously, elicits and develops some qualities, while ignoring or suppressing others. Each society does not—cannot—contain all possible character types, all possible social roles, and all possible varieties of human experience. Utopianism does its share of reminding society that society is limited, and that, although society may be, to some degree, pleased with itself, other forms and ways of life are imaginable.[7]

Today the literary utopia is in virtual eclipse. We have dystopias—not visions of better societies, but warnings of worse ones to come. Yet through the nineteenth century, the literary utopia was a prominent form of social criticism and invention, and one in which the city figured prominently.

Long before massive urbanization had brought the city to the forefront of social life, utopists were carefully attending to the city in their writings, clearly linking the reform of society with the city. Just as they examined polity, economy, technology, family, religion, law, education, and the like, so they examined the city. In fact, attention to the city is so strong in utopian writing that the idea of utopia appears to be inextricably entwined with the idea of the city. This emphasis cannot be explained merely as attention to "a problem." It is instead related to the city's historic identifications with human achievement as well as the nature of the utopian genre itself.

The evils associated with the city throughout history cannot be denied. War is foremost among them. But the city is also a monument to, and symbolic of, human culture. Etymologically and historically, "city" is synonymous with "civilization." The city has been the home of science and art, culture, learning, and writing. It was the birthplace of democracy. Law arose in cities, as did trade, government and protection. According to Jane Jacobs, even domesticated agriculture was born in cities and later exported to the countryside.[8] All the great religions are identified with cities, and in Christianity the city has special significance. As it emerged from its preurban form, the city was a symbolic representation of the universe itself. Initially it represented cosmological or divine order.[9] Later it came to represent social order.[10] Over time the city has been viewed as the great nurturer of humankind, essential for moral development and human growth. Only in the city could one confront the idea of difference and so enlarge one's understanding of the human family.[11]

The reformist character of the literary utopia also explains why the city figures so importantly in the genre. Utopia is a *social* form, addressing the relations between and among people within *society*. The "natural state" for the utopist is one of interdependence and community; the settlement, as the locus of human interdependence, is therefore appropriately emphasized. Further, the utopian purpose is inherently social and political, addressing the reordering of society and its institutions and the restructuring of relationships among its members. Is it even possible to accomplish this purpose without attending to the city, the very embodiment of social relations and goals? For most of the classical utopists, the city was perceived as *society* itself, and the community, not the individual, was considered to be at the heart of social change.

The connection between utopia and the city became more explicit in the nineteenth century as utopia increasingly was brought into time. "Nowhere" became "somewhere." The material strain in utopia, present at least since Bacon's *New Atlantis*, did not become dominant until the Industrial Revolution directed the utopist's attention to either the inequities or the promises of the new order. While the genre itself is strongly environmental, assuming the manipulation of the environment to be the means through which society was changed, judged by nineteenth-century utopian writings and experiments, "environment" was more tangibly expressed in space and place than ever before.

As utopianism came into time, it found expression in the communitarian movement which flowered throughout the United States, with hundreds of intentional societies self-consciously yoking their community experiments to a vision of a new social order.[12] As Arthur Bestor defines the significance of this nineteenth-century movement, communitarianism was reformist and nonrevolutionary, concerned with *inventing* solutions to social problems. It stressed voluntary action, assuming human beings could remake institutions by reasoned choice. Its practitioners applied their procedures on a small scale rather than on the whole; their idea was to serve as a model for the larger society. Communitarianism presumed the *community* to be at the heart of social change.[13]

Communitarianism was an important social movement in its own right, but it was also influential for the garden city as Howard outlined it.

The decline of the literary utopia was further paralleled by the rise to prominence of the "spatial utopia" or ideal city. First noticeable as a phenomenon in the mid-1900s, the spatial utopia became dominant by the turn of the century. This more literal interpretation of utopia was no doubt influenced by the environmental determinism of Marx and Darwin. It was also affected by the "land question," very much in the air and explored by numerous reformers. A new connection of land reform with social reform, coupled with the clear presence of urban problems, reinforced a more material definition of environment. This paved the way for a deemphasis on institutional reform as a means to a reordered society and increasing attention to artifacts, space, and structure as vehicles for social reform. This in turn led to the view, infrequently articulated but nonetheless present, that society could be reordered through restructuring urban structures and space. Such a premise has strongly affected American new town planning—particularly as it relates to "community."

"Community" has always been at the heart of utopia and remains so with the new towns. They reflect an effort to fashion a city in which mutual support and fraternal concern are givens. In its pursuit, however, "community" has proved a highly elusive ideal. Is it to be attained through institutional means or through the rearrangement of space and the material environment? If both, how and to what extent?

For the early spatial utopists, the ideal was pursued through institutions as well as artifacts. A changed physical environment was vital, but so were innovations in social, political, and economic institutions. (Fourier devoted much of his attention to new work and sexual relationships and Owen puzzled over social and family organization.) Such an approach of "institutions-plus-artifacts" was commonly adopted by communitarian groups, but most importantly for this study, it was the approach taken by Ebenezer Howard. The bright and fair future Howard sought for England, through garden cities in careful relationship to one another, was predicated upon an *institutional* change—the municipal ownership of land. In contrast, American garden cities reflect an overriding emphasis on landscape and the physical environment and scant attention to institutions. They are descended less from the communitarian movement than from Frank Lloyd Wright's Broadacre City, a scheme premised on social change through *technical* means.

From Land Reform to Landscape

American new towns reflect aims and philosophies quite different from Howard's. The institutional restructuring central to his scheme has been supplanted by other objectives: to create "contemporary cities" responsive to current economic, social, and technological trends; and to design communities that support neighborhood and family life.[14] To this "new" conception of the new town Howard had something to contribute, but the most singular influence on American new communities has been "The Radburn Idea." Radburn introduced the elementary school-based neighborhood, the park as the heart of the city, separation of traffic types which safely integrated the automobile into the design, and the concept of the leisure city. These innovations permitted planners to respond to perceived defects in urban *life* as well as urban form, and so became vehicles for *social* as well as physical planning.

New towns reflect arcadian premises more than utopian ones. Whereas utopia is a *social* genre dealing with institutional change, the arcadian tradition emphasizes rural peace and simplicity, spontaneous innocence, artless equality and harmony with nature.[15] Absent are institutions, complexity, conflict, evil—and cities. Indeed, the single most striking feature of the new towns (and one that bespeaks their arcadian premises) is the attempt to design cities in which disorder does not exist—either spatially, aesthetically, socially, or interpersonally. The democratic neighborhood central to their plans is seen as a harmonious unit, not as one of diverse values.

In this context, the garden city as planners have interpreted it continues a long-standing intellectual tradition of suspicion of the city which is closely related to a cultural belief in the superiority of physical nature. A persistent strain in American art, literature and intellectual history, this belief is one where nature as landscape and nature as natural law are presumed to cohere, giving manmade institutions an artificial (and therefore negative) function. This identifies the "natural" basis of community as that which resides in physical nature. Social planning in the new cities is intimately connected with this cultural legacy which helps illuminate why new town planners have emphasized the "garden" at the expense of the "city." Thus individualism, autonomy, unfettered freedom, instinctive moral behavior, self-reliance, simplicity in accord with a divine plan—all "natural" values associated with "nature"—have been assumed jeopardized by an encroaching urban civilization commanding restraint, interdependence, impersonality, complexity, and requiring Americans to come to terms with community and diversity. The American attitude toward the city is very much related to an ambivalent attitude toward community and those values associated with it. This ambivalence becomes especially problematic in the new towns where a communal ideal is sought—but often manifested in ways that do not seriously challenge personal freedom or those social forces that create and perpetuate injustice and inequity.

Consistent with this attitude toward "natural community," new town planners have diminished the importance of institutions in their designs. The urban economy is downplayed and the urban polity is virtually absent. In most new towns the city as an independent legal entity does not exist. Planners have strongly emphasized the democratic city, but the concept of the *political* city is frequently missing. And with institutions so minimized, what remains of "the city" is an environment for individual growth, intense family living, and convivial social interaction—all within an abundance of green open space where nature dominates and where hours of leisure time may be wholesomely spent. This is the "good city" as new town planners have created it.

Planners have further defined the individual and the primary group as the building block of the community. In Columbia, Maryland, this has found its purest expression as "a garden for people to grow in." In all cases, the "family neighborhood" has been identified as the nucleus of the community. The overall image is not of a familistic city, however, but a city of discrete nuclear families—which again reveals the ambivalence toward community as interpreted by garden city planners.

1

The City in American Thought

Rapid and massive urbanization is one of the most striking features of American history. Within a mere 300 years, the United States has undergone a startling transformation from a nation without cities to an almost entirely urbanized nation. The earliest settlers in this country necessarily banded together for mutual protection against the hostile and unknown territory, but dispersion followed shortly. When the first federal census was taken in 1790, only five percent of the population was urban. From this time forward, the numbers of American urban dwellers steadily increased. By 1810, one of every twenty Americans lived in cities; by 1840, one in twelve; by 1860, one in six; by 1880, one in four; by 1900, one in three; by 1920, one in two.[1] Today roughly three quarters of the American population is urban, and urban influences are so profound that even the nonurbanite is daily affected by metropolitan life.

During the formative years of the Republic, the American continent was sparsely settled. The line of settlement extended only to the Alleghenies, and most of the population concentrated along the Eastern seaboard. The wilderness here was less wild and savage than the earliest colonists had known. Settlers had domesticated it, and under these simple agrarian conditions our political institutions were formed. There were cities in those early days, to be sure, but it was not *cities* that left a lasting favorable imprint on the American mind—it was physical nature. For generations the American has revered nature and has denigrated cities, for cities were considered the very obverse of nature, whether nature was defined as physical landscape or as natural law. Americans generally lack a tradition of attachment to the city; "nature" on the other hand has carried important metaphysical meanings. Independence, autonomy, economic freedom and opportunity, simplicity, harmony, democracy—all have been associated more with physical nature and deemed threatened by cities. The strong yet subtle power of this American attitude toward nature has pervaded American art, literature, historical writings, philosophy, public policy, and even the most *urban* of activities, urban planning. It is in terms of "nature" that the American attitude toward the city is best understood.

The City in American History

Perhaps the most important expression of the allure of physical nature for Americans was Frederick Jackson Turner's famous and highly influential thesis, "The Significance of the Frontier in American History." When Turner presented this paper before a meeting of the American Historical Association in 1893, the modern city had already appeared throughout America. Turner feared that the virtues created by frontier conditions were under threat by the new urban-industrial order. Had the American ideals, derived from the experience with the West, gained sufficient momentum "to sustain themselves under conditions so radically unlike those in the days of their origin,"[2] he wondered?

The immediate inspiration for Turner's paper was a Census Bureau bulletin, issued in 1890, which announced that the frontier had passed:

> Up to and including 1889, the country had a frontier of settlement, but at present the unsettled area has been so broken into by isolated bodies of settlement that there can hardly by said to be a frontier line. In the discussion of its extent, its westward movement, etc., it cannot, therefore, any longer have a place in the census report.[3]

Turner argued that the frontier was the major, if not the decisive, determinant of American culture and civilization. His central theme was the "transforming influence of the American wilderness," which had meant a "steady movement away from the influence of Europe, a steady growth of independence on American lines." He held that "free lands promoted individualism, economic equality, freedom to rise, democracy."[4] Since land was free and abundant, even the most oppressed and the poorest could advance themselves. The frontier thus served as a "safety valve," alleviating social conflict and industrial strife. Turner also believed the frontier was the major force behind the nationalizing of the country. The frontiersman's common problems and special needs for transportation, markets, and protection could be better resolved through national governments than through state or local ones, and the frontier was thus instrumental in fostering an effective national democracy over a vast area of land—an accomplishment hitherto unprecedented.

The city was given scant attention in the development of American institutions. The transformation of the American continent from primitive wilderness to civilization, he argued, was the work of the frontiersman through a series of successive stages of settlement and advance. First was the explorer's frontier, and then the frontier of the hunter, trapper, fur trader, and miner. This was followed by the frontier of trade, manufacturing, and organized government. From totally unsettled virgin land to the city—this was the progression of American history. The city would not have been possible, in Turner's view, without the frontier.

The influence of this thesis on subsequent historians has been immense—so immense, in fact, that there was no interpretation of American history which included the striking importance of the city and its considerable role in shaping American development until 1949. Pioneering in *urban* history was Arthur Schlesinger who asserted that "the city, no less than the frontier, has been a major factor in American civilization. Without an appreciation of both, the story is only half told."[5] Other urban historians followed Schlesinger and it is now possible to appreciate the influence cities have had on many national events, including economic development, political policy, intellectual and cultural life, westward expansion, and the Revolutionary and Civil Wars.

From the very beginning, cities played a far greater role in national development than their small numbers warranted. In all periods of American history they have served as an organizing force first for their regions and then for American life as a whole. This was as true in colonial times as it is now. Cities were the economic, social, political, and cultural centers of their regions.

This early dominance has its foundation in the commercial basis of urbanism. Colonial cities were fiercely competitive for the resources surrounding them. Those cities well-situated in relation to waterways and rich hinterlands dominated colonial life: Boston, New York, Philadelphia, Newport, and Charleston. They were not without challenge, however, from Augusta, Savannah, Norfolk, Salem, Portsmouth, and Providence. The economic rivalry between and among the primary cities, and the challenges of the secondary ones for supremacy over a hinterland's resources, accounts for much of the speed and other characteristics of American development. Recent scholarship has shown that this rivalry ("urban imperialism,"[6] as Miller has called it) is related in no small measure to westward expansion, early industrialization, the nationalizing of the country, and even to the drive for American independence.

The story of the city's role in the Revolutionary conflict has been well told by Richard Wade, Zane Miller, and others. When the colonies revolted, the cities provided the impetus. While less than five percent of the population was urban, it was in the cities that "the coincidence of people, events, ideas and leadership forged both a sense of American nationalism and a revolution."[7] Notions of the Enlightenment which undergirded the Revolution came here through cities, and the cities alone had the books and newspapers with which to spread them.[8] Resistance to imperial reorganization policies found its leadership first in the urban business classes and only later in radical politicians.[9] By 1750, an urban elite had emerged in the major cities. This group was most threatened by Britain's new revenue policy after 1763, and initially asserted provincial "rights" against British authorities by strengthening assemblies and councils. The period was one of "protracted guerilla warfare" between urban protestors and imperial authorities.[10]

Wade and Miller view Boston's special place in revolutionary history as related to the city's declining economic fortunes. Bounded almost entirely by water, Boston had a limited hinterland and suffered most from coercive legislation which further restricted her commercial growth. Continued interurban competition for resources and stronger successful challenges from other cities meant that urban primacy, once Boston's province, was passing to New York and Philadelphia. An urban interpretation of the American revolt shows that the Revolution was born in the streets of Boston, and not on the rolling greens of Lexington.[11]

Not only was the Revolution itself initiated by urban business and creditor classes jealous of their prosperity, but the framing and ratification of the Constitution reflected their influence as well. Urban interests favored a strong central government to protect economic and commercial growth and ensure stability. Howard Chudacoff notes that New York City and surrounding counties threatened to secede from the state if it did not ratify the Constitution.[12]

Cities too must be recognized for their significant role in the country's great westward expansion between 1800 and 1860. Recent scholarship casts doubt on Turner's contention that cities climaxed a settlement sequence of mining, pastoral, and farming frontiers. Wade notes that in 1890, the Far West, although the most sparsely populated area, was the most highly urbanized region of the country; and that towns existed in *advance* of the line of settlement—they were spearheads of the frontier and held the West for the approaching population.[13]

Urban imperialism also quickened the westward movement. An aggressive, interurban competition for markets and resources was the root cause of the midnineteenth century transportation revolution. It is generally agreed that the national railroad network between 1840 and 1880 was the dynamic element in the first stage of industrialization, but what fostered this network was *not* pressures from farmers for better routes to markets—it was the ambitions of *cities* that accounted for the railroad system. As resources in the more immediate hinterland were mined, cities became dependent on more outlying areas. Commercial rivalry for these new markets, and then for transportation routes to the resource-rich interior, speeded up the transformation of the continent from a wilderness to an industrial civilization. The railroad system then stimulated manufacturing by cutting production and transportation costs and opening up new markets and demands. These in turn provided incentives for managerial and manufacturing innovations.[14] It was this transportation network that cemented the country together. The cities, more than the West, were nationalizing agents. Not only did cities hold together regional diversity, but urban magnates alone had tangible national interests, and this group favored measures which would unify the nation.[15] Urban interests also advocated a common national currency, federal spending for internal transport, the protective tariff, and the standardization of railroad tracks. While intended to stimulate commerce and manufacturing throughout the country, these measures also served to nationalize and unify the diverse sections and regions.

The role of cities in the Civil War also suggests how interurban rivalry influenced important national events. Schlesinger notes how leading Southern towns and cities strongly supported the movement for separation. "It was no mere coincidence that Charleston, dropping rapidly behind the northern ports, initiated every secessionist movement in the entire South from Jackson's time onward."[16] Given withdrawal from the Union and free trade with England, it was believed that within ten years Charleston would become another New York. Other southern cities shared similar hopes.[17]

Interurban competition for commercial hegemony ultimately influenced the outcome of the Civil War. In the West, St. Louis and Chicago vied for midwestern supremacy, a contest won by Chicago who by 1860 had become the midcontinent's railroad center. The economy of the West then tilted to the East, where Chicago's connections lay, rather than to the South and border areas, where St. Louis was oriented. As trade went West-East, rather than West-South, Southern urban centers entered a period of relative decline. Had St. Louis "won," with her economic ties to New Orleans, then the West might have been neutralized, thereby enhancing the South's chances for independence.[18]

Turner hailed the frontier as an equalizing force, but it is surely significant that slavery first declined in the cities. Wade argues that slavery was disintegrating in southern cities by 1860, and that the outcome of the slavery question was more importantly affected by the ambitions of cities than by the ideological issues involved. Slavery, and the patriarchal system it rested upon, required an agricultural economy with unskilled labor dispersed over the land. With slavery the South was locked into an agricultural economy; as such, it could not support the concentrated life nor amass the capital of cities. In southern cities, moreover, the control needed to maintain slavery broke down and discipline grew more difficult. The system of slavery was unconsciously abandoned in southern cities, Wade says, but new institutions, like segregation, arose to replace it. He argues that segregation had its origins in southern cities even before the Civil War since slavery could not be reconciled with urban life.[19]

Of all Turner's contentions, none has been challenged so forcefully as his "safety valve" theory. Turner had hypothesized that no one would "accept inferior wages and a permanent position of social subordination [in cities] when this promised land of freedom and equality was theirs for the taking. Who would rest content under oppressive legislative conditions when with a slight effort he might reach a land wherein to become a co-worker in the building of free cities and free states on the lines of his own ideal?"[20]

The answer is that many did because the effort was more than slight. Migration studies have shown that internal migration after 1800 was relatively rarely from city to farm, and that European migration, even in the 1840s, tended to be from European to American city, and from rural Europe to rural America. There has always been a close relationship between economics and migration, with most migration occurring during prosperous times, and even then only by those with the means to afford the considerable costs involved. The passage of the Homestead Act in 1863 did not appreciably affect the social and economic status of the mass of the poor. What spoiled the dream was the land speculator who was always one step ahead of the farmer and who bought up the best farmlands and sites—parting with them, of course, for a good price.

For many nineteenth-century Americans, westward movement was not even within wildest possibility. As Stephan Thernstrom has shown, the poorest of the poor, the uncounted, were downwardly mobile.[21] Social mobility for the laboring classes tended to be generational, and even though steady, it was always slow. It was to *cities* that the poor migrated in search of opportunity.[22]

If the frontier was less instrumental in American economic development than Turner believed, if it was not the decisive factor in the nationalizing of the country he thought it to be, if it served only poorly as a safety valve fostering social and economic equality, was Turner totally wrong about the frontier's significance for American life? I suggest its greatest influence has been on American values and beliefs. The frontier fostered independence, as Turner clearly showed. Certainly *cities* did not encourage autonomy. They meant *inter*dependence, and urban life mandated an interest in others. This interest could be purely functional, reflecting a recognition that one was perforce dependent upon others for services, or it could be more positive, reflecting an active and fraternal concern for others. Urban life has given rise to both recognitions of the collective, the first in public health concerns, paved streets, waterworks, and much of what falls under the rubric of "the public welfare," and the second in genuine social reform. Schlesinger notes that:

> Under urban stimulus arose the movement for free schools, for public libraries, for married women's property rights, for universal peace, for prison reform, for a better deal for the insane. The new conditions of city life begot a social conscience on the part of the townsfolk which would be of lasting effect and which increasingly differentiated them from their brethren on the farm and frontier.[23]

Antiurbanism in American Art and Architecture

American antiurbanism covers a complex set of attitudes. The long tradition of distrust of the city in American thought cannot be explained simply by ignorance or prejudice. Some of our nation's finest minds have been suspicious of the city. Nor is the antiurban bias related to one system of thought. Those who have disagreed widely and fundamentally have found themselves in accord in their distrust of the city.

There are a host of reasons for this attitude. Historically, cities were suspect because alien and disturbing influences were there—radicals, Jews, Catholics, and always immigrants with their strange ways. Informal social control was impossible in the city. Diversity thrived there. The city had room for sin and vice, for theater, prostitution, drink, and crime. To many an observer, the presence of deviance in cities meant that cities *caused* moral decay.

Sometimes antiurbanism was a legitimate and understandable response to problems that seemed indigenously urban and hopeless of solution in populous settings. Thus the suspicion of the city following smallpox epidemics in Boston and Charleston was understandable. Urban problems have always been with us—indeed, compared to earlier days, the modern American city is relatively problem-free [24]—and some distrust of the city has been a response to those problems.

Economic reasons account for much distrust of the city, particularly in the nineteenth century. Imperialistic urban centers had dominated economic life from the earliest days, often to the detriment of the farmer. Growing discontent over urban dominance took political form early in the century, gained momentum as an industrial economy first threatened and then supplanted an agricultural one, and flowered in the Populist movement toward the century's close. The view that cities were parasites on the land, stealing their wealth and power from the very farmers who had earned it, found its purest expression in William Jennings Bryan, *the* voice of American antiurbanism. In his thunderous 1896 "Cross of Gold" speech, Bryan threatened the urban East: "Burn down your cities and leave our farms, and your cities will spring up again as if by magic; but destroy our farms and the grass will grow in the streets of every city in the country."[25]

Intellectuals in particular have distrusted the city—frequently because it seemed inimical to democracy. Political democracy was born in cities, but Americans have had great difficulty in reconciling democracy with urbanism. When de Tocqueville visited the United States in 1831, he was hopeful that democracy would succeed in America because there were no great cities here. The absence of a dominating metropolis, he believed, would help maintain a democratic republic and counteract the potential tyranny of the majority. Other observers feared that centralization, sheer size, so visible a disparity between rich and poor—all implied in cities—dangerously threatened democratic society. So fearful was Thomas Jefferson that the urban peril would undermine the democratic experiment that he viewed Philadelphia's yellow fever epidemic as a blessing in disguise:

> When great evils happen, I am in the habit of looking out for what good may arise from them as consolation to us, and Providence has in fact so established the order of things, as that most evils are the means of producing some good. The yellow fever will discourage the growth of great cities in our nation.[26]

What is most striking about the American suspicion of the city is not its direct attack on cities per se but its expression in praise of physical nature and the values associated with it. The endurance of this "pronature" attitude is related to two powerful traditions in American thought, the "agrarian utopia," and the "arcadian utopia." The agrarian tradition stresses economics; the arcadian tradition does not. Arcadia emphasizes rural peace and simplicity, spontaneous innocence, artless equality, and harmony with nature. In the arcadian tradition, organized society and nature are antithetical terms. Both arcadian and agrarian traditions have coexisted throughout American history, but the second became the more dominant with industrialization. Neither tradition is truly "utopian," however, since the utopian is an inherently social form. Utopia deals with people *in* society, not removed from it, and alienation from society has been one of the strongest themes in American intellectual history.

Nature in Art and Architecture

The long tradition in praise of agriculture and nature is seen most frequently in written documents, but it appears in American art forms as well. Even a casual observer cannot help but note the striking predominance of landscape painting in the nineteenth century and the almost total neglect of urban subject matter. After the aping of continental styles and subject matter had lost its power, the American artist painted virtually nothing but nature subjects and landscapes. No major painter made the city his or her subject before the 1890s, and even then the depiction of urban life was largely romanticized by the Ash Can School.

Barbara Novak has argued persuasively that American *landscape* painting is American *history* painting: America's grand past was resident in physical nature, and the artist celebrated it.[27] Thomas Cole, father of the Hudson River School, lamented that he had to meet the public's demand for "accurate" native landscapes in order to support himself. The American Art Union, painting's nineteenth-century counterpart to the Book of the Month Club, sold thousands of engravings of landscape scenes in keeping with the public's insatiable demand for them. The average American preferred one of Bierstadt's or Church's western scenes to Vanderlyn's "Ariadne Asleep on the Isle of Naxos"—not merely because Vanderlyn's nude required an educated taste and an appreciation of classical history, but because "The Rocky Mountains" or "Catopaxi" were considered more "natural."[28]

An enormously popular nineteenth-century art form was the panorama, precursor to the modern motion picture. Imported from Europe at the turn of the century, it reached its heyday in America between 1840 and 1870, enjoying far greater popularity here than on the continent. The earliest panoramas depicted the wonders of civilization and brought European *cities* to American viewers. Eventually the form became a vehicle for sermons and allegories, but panoramas were never so popular as when they brought native scenery like Niagara and views of the west before the eyes of captivated Americans. Both in form and in subject matter, the panorama gave visual expression to a unique American feeling for space. The panoramist attempted to create the effect of being in the actual presence of the scene, and the broad sweep of the enveloping canvas suggested the vastness and grandeur of the American landscape.

As comment on the city was defined by its antithesis in painting, so too was it expressed in architecture. After the classical revival of the early nineteenth century and its associations with the civilizations of Greece and Rome, American architects turned to forms and motifs inspired by the romantic rural villas and country estates of Italy, France, and England. The result was a profusion of styles—Italianate, Renaissance, Queen Anne, Gothic, Eclectic—all in keeping with the century-long debate over what the national style should be.

Landscape architect Andrew Jackson Downing was one of the most influential tastemakers of the period and his 1842 publication, *Cottage Residences*, provided a practical handbook for the design of "proper" homes. A best seller and printed in several editions, the book spread the rural gothic cottage throughout the country and with it Downing's message that a home should be fitted to the natural environment in which it appeared. In his insistence that houses be adapted to the trees and plants, rocks and grounds where they stood, he prefigured the design philosophy of Frank Lloyd Wright.

Downing believed that nature was spiritually redemptive and socially beneficial. He eschewed classicism, which he associated with mastery of nature and with raw power, and favored instead the gothic, which symbolized *harmony* with nature. Under the "enchanting influence" of the gothic cottage, he believed the "too great hustle and excitement of our commercial cities [would] be happily counterbalanced by the more elegant and quiet enjoyments of a country life."[29]

A similar political and aesthetic statement was made years later by Frank Lloyd Wright, first in his housing designs and later in his conception of

Broadacre City. Wright believed that a building must be integral with nature. Horizontal and low, his houses were constructed of native materials left unaltered and exposed. No clear distinction was made between structure and nature. Even as his houses extended into the garden, the garden was brought into the house.

Rich in wood and stone, Wright's houses were in stark contrast to the brilliant chrome, steel, and glass of Le Corbusier's structures. Unlike European architecture, late-nineteenth-century American architects appear to have been oblivious to the new technology which underlay the country's new wealth; and with few exceptions, other than occasional ornament and bric-a-brac, these architects made little use of this new potential in materials and design. The school for the American architect was instead "nature." Even for Louis Sullivan, the father of modern architecture and ostensibly an *urban* architect, Nature was the great teacher. Sullivan's philosophy of functionalism was discovered in, and demanded by, Nature herself. In *Autobiography of an Idea*, Sullivan ecstatically recalled his discovery of this "universal principle":

> And, inquiring more deeply, he discovered that in truth it was not simply a matter of form expressing function, but the vital idea was this: That the function *created* or organized its form. Discernment of this idea threw a vast light upon all things within the universe, and condensed with astounding impressiveness upon mankind, upon all civilizations, all institutions, every form and aspect of society, every mass-thought and mass-result, every individual thought and individual result... it was the application to man's thoughts and deeds; to his inherent powers and the results of the application of these powers, mental, moral, physical, that thrilled Louis to the depths as he realized... a universal law admitting of no exception in any phrase or application whatsoever.[30]

The Literary Hero in Nature

Americans have never shared the Aristotelian view of the city as the fundamental political and social unit. "The natural unit" has instead been the autonomous individual in contact with physical nature. Certainly what is common to many criticisms of the city is the belief that cities imply a diminished role for the individual. Cities are identified with interdependence and restraint. Individualism and autonomy are identified with nature. The congruence of nature as landscape, nature as natural law, and nature as freedom has been a strong theme in our intellectual history—so strong, in fact, that it has taken on the character of a unifying "myth" fusing concept and emotion and explaining the origins and the destiny of the American people. The metaphysical meanings associated with nature have been examined by many historians. Richard Hofstadter has called this set of attitudes "the Agrarian Myth," and R. W. B. Lewis, "the Adamic Myth." Perhaps none has explored so completely those dimensions of American attitudes forged from a confrontation with the land as David Noble, who in many books has written of the "American covenant with nature."[31] Noble argues that the American experience is best understood as an escape from "medievalism," from institutions which are time- and culture-bound, humanly created and therefore imperfect. The American experience has been one of repeated attempts to preserve individualism from a variety of feudal obligations and restraints. He argues that Americans have never really come to terms with community and the problems of mutual interdependence, nor seen community as a set of positive relationships between individuals. The crucial environment for the American has been physical nature, not culture.

The literary artist has illuminated these tensions well. American literary heroes, Walter Allen says, differ from their British counterparts in one important way. They "are characters not in process of discovering the nature of society and of themselves in and through society, but are, on the contrary, characters profoundly alienated from society."[32] The *solitary* hero dominates American fiction.

Richard Chase believes this accounts for the absence of tragedy in American fiction since true tragedy involves the individual in conflict with *fate*, not in conflict with *society*. It also explains the dominance of romance and allegory in American fiction. The American novelist has been more concerned with the radical alienation of the individual *from* society than his or her reconciliation *with* society, which the tradition of the novel implies.[33]

R. W. B. Lewis has written of the fictional hero as "the American Adam," and others have pointed to the solitary hero, isolated, orphaned, unmarried, unattached, who finds freedom in space. Huckleberry Finn, true child of nature, spoke for many an American character when he said "I reckon I got to light out for the territory ahead of the rest, because Aunt Sally she's going to adopt me and civilize me, and I can't stand it. I been there before."[34] For Huck, freedom lay in the territory, as it once had on the raft. Freedom was found in the forest for Hester Prynne, in the wilds for Natty Bumppo, at sea for Ishmael, on the island for Jay Gatsby, in the woods for Nick Adams.

For the American novelist, nature has been identified with moral freedom, autonomy, innocence, and natural law, while the city has been associated with moral restraint, interdependence, experience, artificial law. The tension between these two sets of values has been one of the most enduring themes in American literature.

These radical dualisms became most explicit in transcendentalism, where veneration of nature and distrust of the city were combined into a formalized philosophical system exalting the solitary individual in communion with nature. The transcendentalists believed that physical nature mirrored the currents of higher law emanating from God,[35] and the wilderness, not the city, was the environment where spiritual truths were revealed most clearly. Revelation of truth was through the individual in direct confrontation with nature.

The transcendental attitude toward nature was closely related to luminist vision in American painting. In luminist painting, Novak writes, there is no sense of the artist as intermediary. The viewer confronts the image directly. The ultra-clarity, and dazzling, almost palpable, light which bathes the entire scene, unites matter and spirit in a single image. Luminism was an attitude toward light, but it was also an attitude toward *things* in nature. The luminist painter looked at nature with a supernatural eye.[36]

Enlightenment Philosophy and the Image of the City

Transcendentalism did not spring full blown. Many of its strains were prefigured in the Puritan sensibility and Enlightenment thought, both of which paved the way for the transcendentalist's radical distinction between nature and cities. Certainly the Puritans did not venerate physical nature and vilify the city. They associated wilderness with Satanic darkness and followed the Biblical mandate to build a heavenly city on earth. The Puritans did not exalt the individual. They believed the community was important to an individual's religious life and feared when someone strayed from its fellowship. Theirs was a sensibility which uniquely blended individual and communal values, as evidenced by land ownership and land use in Puritan settlements. Nevertheless, the Puritan mind was Manichean, seeing an inherent dualism between the natural and the divine, the real and the ideal, the secular and the sacred. This paved the way for dualistic metaphysics which placed nature and cities in diametrical opposition.

While the transcendentalist believed nature was the medium through which God spoke, the Puritan clearly did not. Puritans saw the natural world as distinct from the divine world. The yoking of the natural with the divine was derived from the congruence of Enlightenment ideas and the settlement of a new continent where those ideas might be tested. The Puritan vision of a divine order on earth, would humanity but follow God, was secularized by later generations who believed that a new setting made possible the reestablishment of the "natural" order if men and women would but follow natural law.

American political and social institutions were based on the Enlightenment premise that the good society would exist if it were constructed in accord with natural laws. Because the political state was resident in nature, it was necessary to peel back the layers of civilization to discover nature. Lockean beliefs that natural law could be discerned if one went back prior to the beginnings of civilization combined with an intellectual disdain for civilization, articulated by Rousseau. Rousseau asserted that civilization had corrupted the harmonious natural state where individuals were free and self-reliant. This was a divinely ordained state, whereas civilization was not.

Such ideas were current with the discovery of the American continent, and the primitive land here gave a new excitement—and even urgency—to them. In Europe the feudal system was breaking down and wealth and power were increasingly concentrated in the hands of landowners. While the Old World slipped further from the natural state, America, the New Eden, became a concrete embodiment of what in Europe could only be a utopian dream. America was to serve as an example for all humanity. This was to be a redeemed land. Nature, not civilization, would be the common denominator of the new order.

Nothing succeeds like success, and the abundance of land "proved" the Enlightenment hope correct. Physical nature wed metaphysical nature, geography mated morality. The abundance of land fostered and exalted a belief in individualism and a conception of land as a civil liberty. A way of life necessarily based on self-reliance exalted self-reliance and equated autonomy with natural law. Human institutions, consequently, were given a negative function. Land—"nature"—came to represent social freedom, literally affirming the Lockean dictum that the political state was resident in nature.

The abundance of land also morally sanctioned the view that space was not a mere resource, but a commodity to be bought and sold. For thousands of years, land had been the primary source of individual opportunity. Here it was no different. Land was not regarded as belonging to the group and transferred to the individual, but was perceived instead as properly belonging to the individual. A person's property represented that person's free status, and property ownership conferred the right to vote and to belong to a political community. Private ownership of land became an avenue of escape from constraints imposed by the village, the church, and the king. Ownership of land meant freedom *from* meddling, and freedom *for* autonomy. This proprietary attitude toward land led to an individualistic land law, the "fee simple" system, where land could be bought and sold, leased and bequeathed, with great ease; and to a federal policy which made land distribution simple and unsupervised with unlimited freedom to buy as much as one chose.[37] The idea that private land is not to be tampered with lightly endures today even in the right of eminent domain. Land may not be taken unless it is to be used for an *important public purpose*, and only after a *hearing* and just *compensation*. This view of land as a fundamental civil liberty, a private "right," is the crux of the American city's problems today.[38]

When Thomas Jefferson denounced cities and spoke of the superiority of the simple yeoman farmer, he gave expression to this constellation of economic and metaphysical values associated with the land. Jefferson consistently derided the "artificial" dependencies and lordship patterns which existed where land was scarce, and he believed that political independence rested on economic security provided by ownership of land. He believed that ownership of land made equality possible, and without equality, democracy could not work. Hence his conviction that the simple yeoman farmer made the best citizen. It is difficult to overstate the importance Jefferson attached to property as defining freedom. He believed that *only* a propertied individual was truly free, and *land* defined property.

In his preference for nature, Jefferson was highly representative of his age. Daniel Boorstin, in an impressive study of the Jeffersonian world view,[39] has documented how everything the Jeffersonian believed was derived from his perception of and proximity to physical nature. The Jeffersonian perceived God as the Supreme Workman, the Great Architect. Since nature mirrored natural law, to discover the Creator's plan one studied the natural world. Everything one needed to know was to be found in the Creation, and everything that was ever to be was determined at the time of the Creation. To admit of change or spontaneous generation was to admit waste or transience in the divine economy. Institutions were given a negative role because they were not part of the natural Creation. Cities especially did not conform to natural law because dependent relationships (which cities implied) did not exist in nature. The only community the Jeffersonian recognized was through creaturehood. Community was biological, not cultural. Men and women were bound together not by their need for one another but by their common membership in the species.

Transcendentalism and the Image of the City

With the possible exception of late-nineteenth-century populism, the period of Jacksonian democracy was probably the most explicitly antiurban of any in American history. This attitude appeared in direct attack upon cities themselves and also in high praise for physical nature. The idea that physical nature had redemptive power came to be widely shared and was given new fuel by the romantic movement, earlier transported from Europe and in full flower here by 1850. The explicit antiurban mood was strengthened by the rapid change and social dislocation during those years.

The mid-nineteenth century was the most dynamic period in all American history. These were expansionist years geographically, technologically, demographically, and economically. Many far reaching changes took place in a few short decades: the rise of manufacturing, an effective transportation network linking the East with the interior, the emergence of the "common man" as a political force, and the first major wave of European immigration. The country witnessed an "urban explosion" between 1820 and 1860 unmatched by any since as phenomenal urban growth took place. Urban population rose by 797 percent while the national population as a whole increased only by 226 percent.[40] Cities themselves began to expand physically as the new transportation technology broke down the old walking city. The vast and growing numbers in cities made for many new problems, but urban governments, modelled after the unwieldy federal system of checks and balances, were unable to cope. The city was virtually ungovernable—even by bosses and machines which first appeared at this time.

Nationally, the conflict between the urban East and rural West became the major political issue it remained throughout the century. Farmers lost economically to urban interests as cities continued insatiable in their imperialistic desires. The "Monster Bank" became the rallying point for this rural-urban contest. To Andrew Jackson, the anti-Bank campaign symbolized the resentment of the agrarian debtor West against the creditor urban East.

Antiurbanism during this period reflected more than economic conflict between urban and agrarian factions, as John Ward has shown. Like the Jeffersonian before him, the Jacksonian believed that self-reliance and self-determination were natural virtues, and that God's will was revealed through physical nature—with the important difference that it was discerned through *intuition*, not through reason. And as the Jeffersonian had understood it, "reason" implied training and experience, both of which the Jacksonian discounted. It was through the promptings of one's *heart* that wisdom was attained. Because human intuition was God's word mediated through the book of Nature, the forest was the surest guide to wisdom. Learning *corrupted* true wisdom. The Jacksonian presumed a dynamic relationship between physical nature and human character, believing that instinctive moral behavior was found in physical nature. The contemporary view was that movement away from nature was a measure of moral and spiritual decline.[41]

This complex of attitudes towards nature and civilization was codified intellectually by the transcendentalists. Thoreau and Emerson in particular gave antiurbanism a systematized philosophical base. A common theme was that divinity exists in everyone and could be realized only in nature, not in society. In Thoreau especially the spirit of independence became a way of life. Thoreau admonished his contemporaries to cut through "the mud and slush of opinion and prejudice and tradition and delusion...through Paris and London, through New York and Boston...till we come to a hard bottom and rocks in place, which we call reality."[42] He urged them to simplify, for nature was simple; he urged them to be independent, for "all good things are wild and free."[43] If he was tireless in his celebration of nature and natural virtues, he was equally tireless in his derision of the city. Discontented with the emerging technological civilization, and convinced that "the commercial spirit" was a virus infecting his age,[44] Thoreau remarked that "the only room in Boston which I visit with alacrity is the Gentlemen's Room at the Fitchburg Depot, where I wait for cars sometimes for two hours, in order to get out of town."[45]

Emerson serves as a better spokesman for transcendental thought. A man of urban tastes, he respected others of culture and enjoyed the advantages the city offered in opera, art, and intellectual clubs. But he had conflicting feelings towards the city: "I wish to have rural strength and religion for my children, and I wish city facility and polish," he wrote. "I find with chagrin that I cannot have both."[46] Emerson praised civilization and wrote much about it; but he did not identify the city with civilization and so he could criticize the city while yet lauding the values of civilized life.[47]

For Emerson, the city was an artificial and corrupting influence, degrading because it magnified trifles. With Thoreau, he contrasted the natural state of simplicity with the artificial state of cities where speculation, calculation, and conspiracy thrived. "That uncorrupted behavior which we admire in animals and in young children belongs to him ... who lives in the presence of Nature," he wrote. "Cities force growth and make men talkative and entertaining, but they make them artificial."[48]

Emerson's suspicion of the city went to the very heart of transcendental philosophy, which distinguished between the faculties of "Reason" and "Understanding." "Understanding" was the inferior faculty; it was identified with empiricism and scientists and also with cities. "Reason" was considered the highest faculty because it "never proves; it simply perceives; it is vision."[49] Reason was inherent in everyone, and realized in Nature, *not* in cities.

> The city delights the Understanding. It is made up of finites: short, sharp, mathematical lines, all calculable. It is full of varieties, of successions, of contrivances. The country, on the contrary, offers an unbroken horizon, the monotony of the endless road, of vast uniform plains, of distant mountains, the melancholy of uniform and infinite vegetation; the objects on the road are few and worthless, the eye is invited ever to the horizon and the clouds. It is the school of Reason.[50]

Progressivism and Urban Interdependence

Unabashed enthusiasm for nature and wilderness was largely a nineteenth-century phenomenon, increasing with industrialization and urbanization, and peaking toward the end of the century. Yet conflict between the values associated with nature and those associated with cities intensified during the last decades of the century as the "natural" values of autonomy, economic opportunity, freedom and self-reliance were increasingly challenged by the conditions and demands of urban life. The tension between communal interdependence and individual self-determination had always been a problem in America, but reconciling the individual and the group took on new urgency as the frontier closed, as one third of the populace lived in cities, and as thousands of Blacks and displaced farmers migrated to urban centers and thousands of others emigrated from Southern and Eastern Europe.

The years between 1880 and 1917 represented an age of tremendous and sweeping reform. The resounding defeat of Bryan in 1896, plus increasing regulation in government, business, and labor practices, suggested that "community" was taking precedence over individualism and autonomy. And this, in fact, has been the conventional interpretation of the age of reform. But of those historians who have treated this period in recent years, none agrees that a positive embracing of community occurred. Reconciling the individual with the group was at heart a distributional problem involving justice and restraint, yet those "solutions" which surfaced during this period reflect more a concern for *functional* or structural interdependence than for *fraternal* interdependence. Cleaning up the political machine, for example, was long regarded as a major step forward in responsibility for the poor and ignorant who were presumably exploited by the boss and his organization. Recent scholarship questions this interpretation. It is not necessary to romanticize the boss to realize that he represented a constituency whose needs were otherwise unattended. The boss filled a void for the immigrant. He responded to the newcomer's needs for a job, for housing, for food, for fellowship. The machine also represented the only avenue for social mobility open to many Americans with surnames like Berczynskas and Rudkus. It was the boss more than the reformer who represented communal values, responding, as he did, to the immediate and personal needs of the immigrant. Progressive reformers represented values which were more abstract, formal, future-oriented, impersonal.

Historians of the age differ widely in their interpretations of the motivations behind these many reform efforts. Even so, none believes that autonomy and individualism were seriously challenged during the period. Hays' analysis suggests that reform efforts, despite the rhetoric which lay behind them, were not community-oriented. They did not *extend* the circle of democracy but actually *restricted* it.[51] While justified as helping the poor and the disenfranchised, innovations such as civil service, at-large representation, and city manager and commission forms of government all benefited the urban business classes and effectively diminished the immigrant's already small voice. Even Prohibition constituted an attack on the political power of the poor. To close the tavern was to reduce the immigrant's influence by narrowing the machine's field of activity.

The tensions between city and suburb that plague America today had their origins during the late nineteenth century when the old city-country conflict became an intracity conflict over who would control the metropolis. As middle class, professional, native-born, and capitalist, the reformer tended to live on the periphery of the city. The new transportation technology enabled these people to enjoy the advantages of both rural and urban life with few of the problems of either. However, with continued mass migration to cities and with newcomers filling the former houses of the better off who were now suburbanites, the political shape of the metropolis was increasingly influenced by the great numbers who lived there, many of them newly enfranchised. These factors, combined with the organizing power of the boss in the central city districts, meant that the business classes were losing control of "their" city, and especially their business interests downtown.

Richard Hofstadter has also shown that the new conditions of city life only strengthened efforts to preserve individualism and the old values from a variety of new restraints. The general theme of progressivism, he argues, was an effort to restore a type of economic individualism and political democracy widely believed to have existed in an earlier America and destroyed by the great corporations and political machines. The influence of the well-educated, professional, and native-born American was eroded by new forces and groups; and reform reflected the progressive's efforts to hold onto the values of agrarian life, to save personal entrepreneurship, to preserve individual opportunity and the character type they engendered, and to maintain a homogeneous Yankee civilization.[52]

Reconciling entrepreneurship and interdependence was also attempted through efforts to rationalize and coordinate the system. Robert Wiebe views the period between 1880 and 1917 as a quest for a unifying system of control over the new interdependencies of an industrial, urban America which was rapidly replacing the old rural society. He says that progressives were a dynamic and optimistic new middle class deliberately attempting to substitute new values for traditional outmoded ones. The emergence of an interdependent and advanced technological society and the development of a modern national state required centralization, rationalization, bureaucracy, specialization, and regulation. Progressive reformers, recognizing this, sought to encourage these new values.[53]

This regulative approach to interdependence was supported by an ethic of "functionalism" which entered American society in the late nineteenth century. This ethic was implicit in technology itself. A *machine* ethic, it followed the logic of the machine: the parts were subordinate to the whole; they required an orderly arrangement; and they gained their meaning *only* in relationship to the whole.[54] This ethic was first applied to business management and later, by Frederick Winslow Taylor, to the organization of work itself. In its *social* application, it meant adjusting the individual ("the part") to the society ("the whole").

This functionalist ethic was one source of increased attention to "public welfare" which grew in respectability during those years. It similarly underlay the "enlightened self-interest" of a number of reformers who felt that for the "whole" to function, the "parts" must work together harmoniously. Even Jane Addams, tireless defender of human dignity, felt the entire American system to be threatened by the disaffection of a small fraction of radicals.

Much social reform during the period was motivated by a commitment to revitalize a sense of community. John Dewey was foremost among those who saw in urban life the new potential for bringing about the great democratic community. Dewey's writings represented a reversal of historic values associating democracy with the village or the country; Dewey located democracy firmly in the city.

John Dewey was clearly the philosopher of late nineteenth-century urban reform. Greatly influenced by Darwinism, he saw the future in terms of potentiality, and his thought reflected a shift in American philosophy from essence to process, from things as they are to things as they might be. His pragmatism was action-based and problem-oriented, encouraging change and experimentation. He saw truth as mutable and believed that it was preeminently *social*, benefiting both the individual and the society.

Dewey's overarching concerns were for democracy and community and how these might be joined in an urban setting.[55] Because he defined "community" as "communications," he thus directed his attention to the small "natural" unit and to face-to-face personal contact between people. Although Dewey was truly optimistic and melioristic and among the first to see the city as a positive force in American life, his efforts to achieve community nonetheless involved *taming* the city. His reform philosophy, shared by Jane Addams and to a lesser degree by Josiah Royce, reflected a fear of bigness. Emphasizing localism and the primary group, perceived to be the building blocks of democratic society, these social reformers were keenly interested in the neighborhood and family life. They were also intensely interested in education. Dewey regarded the city as the proper place for effecting the adjustment of the individual to society. The progressive school was to be a microcosm of urban social life. For other reformers like Jane Addams, the school also served as an important socializing and equalizing agent simultaneously fostering the integration of the foreign-born into mainstream American life and equipping them with the skills and tools to become upwardly mobile, economically self-reliant, and productive members of society.

Progressive reformers applied the old values of autonomy and self-reliance to the new conditions of urban life. This is what David Noble has called the contradictory character of progressivism.[56] On the one hand progressives were forward-looking in their quest for community and attempts to achieve a cooperative commonwealth. On the other hand, they retained a conservative emphasis on the libertarian values of individualism, voluntarism, and pragmatic adjustment. Noble interprets progressivism as a search for a new frontier force in industrialism which would allow for a continued expansion and social mobility. Only superficially was progressivism a rejection of nineteenth-century competitive individualism in favor of an ideal community. Most American progressives defined that ideal community as so natural and spontaneous that the individual would not have to sacrifice any autonomy and independence through group endeavor. The ideal community, he says, was so defined as to avoid the need to define the meaning of justice.

This tension between individualism and communal values that so marked the progressive age is strongly visible in the history of urban planning. The next chapter considers the origins of urban planning and the relationship between urban reform efforts and a continuing preference for "natural" values associated with physical nature.

2

Nature, Community, and the Birth of Urban Planning

The Allure of Suburban Living

Could Boston, personifying restraint, and Quincy, synonymous with freedom, be reconciled, Henry Adams, writing near the turn of the century, wondered. If Adams himself was unable to do so, other less philosophically minded Americans attempted to discover a middle ground between frontier autonomy and urban community. What had eluded Emerson as he sought both rural values and city knowledge for his children was now eagerly sought by thousands as suburban living came within their reach.

By the turn of the century, the allure of nature no longer had its basis in economics. The image was more arcadian than agrarian. Urban dwellers did not want the *economy* of nature, but they wanted contact with it. Nature was viewed as an important counterforce to cities, and contact with nature was presumed to be spiritually and psychologically renewing. With a home in the suburbs one might have the best of both urban and rural worlds: the economic opportunities of the city and the peaceful rusticity of nature.

Except for a minority of wilderness enthusiasts, the American ideal of physical nature has always been one of domesticated, bucolic landscape—a midpoint between barbarous primitivism and decadent civilization. For most of the nineteenth century, "civilization" was defined by this admixture of nature and settlement. With the new transportation technology, the suburbs came to represent this pastoral middle ground between the chaos of primitive nature and the brutal power of the industrializing city.

This perception of nature as a valuable counterforce to cities grew along with urban-industrialism. The Jacksonian belief that contact with nature was important for personal character melded with the earlier Jeffersonian one that nature was the very obverse of complexity, interdependence, and artifice represented by cities. During the late nineteenth century, another dimension was introduced: the association of nature with spiritual and psychological peace.

With the advent of modern technological civilization, a source of anxiety for many middle-class Americans, cities themselves came to reflect this conception of nature as an antidote to the raw energy of urbanism. The parks movement was well on its way by 1870, and the City Beautiful movement had begun by the early '90s. Urban—and especially suburban—architecture was increasingly inspired by the rural and the picturesque: gothic towers after the ruins of medieval Europe, renaissance mansard roofs suggestive of the country estates of French royalty, romantic balustrades and graceful peaks reminiscent of Italian villas, and cast-iron ornaments shaped into ornate and whimsical designs. In the architecture of Richard Morris Hunt, a tastemaker of the period, the home literally became a romantic castle, as in "the Breakers" or "Biltmore," mansions he designed for the nouveau riche.

For the growing numbers who moved out of the city, a piece of property and a single-family home with a bit of green grass came to represent the ideal. For those financially less able, the ideal was approximated in the double- or triple-decker. Aspirations toward upward social mobility were reflected in housing designs and ornament which were patterned after the country estates of the wealthy. A residence in the suburbs came to signify that one had proved oneself and was now a full-fledged member of American society.

It is often assumed that the great suburban migration was a post-World War II phenomenon, but the process began much earlier. With the electrification of the trolley and the extension of tracks and service into peripheral areas, late-nineteenth century Americans were moving out of the city almost as fast as they were moving into it. Warner has shown that nineteenth-century suburbanization was not greatly influenced by private developers and contractors, but was instead the cumulative result of a myriad of individual decisions. Animated by the "rural ideal," thousands and thousands of people built homes on the periphery of the city as they were able to afford it. The distance out was a function of their work hours and income, and hence their occupations.[1]

Although it was certainly facilitated by streetcars and the automobile, and by economic forces which made it more costly to build new housing in cities than on less developed land, suburbanization has not been exclusively driven by economic or technological factors. One of its major causes in this century has been *policy*. In their commitment to continued urban growth, cities have promoted expansion, using annexation as a tool for doing so. Federal urban policy has also facilitated the outward drift by encouraging population redistribution into outlying areas. Most federal highway legislation, for example, has assisted this process; and federal intervention in housing has consistently aided the outward thrust by subsidizing middle-class suburbanization through FHA guarantees and Veterans Administration loan programs (both of which favor *new* housing), and through income tax deductions for mortgage interest and real estate taxes.

Suburbanization has never been a formal, articulated federal policy, but it has been policy nonetheless at least since 1931, when President Hoover established a commission to deal with home building and ownership. Movement out became a major goal of the Roosevelt administration, which fostered it through highway construction, housing legislation, and financing. The 1933 creation of the Federal Housing Administration, for example, significantly reduced the cost of home construction. With mortgages backed by federal guarantees, lending agencies reduced their interest rates and extended home loans from five to twenty-five years. As with later administrations, the New Deal also proposed to address the housing problem through providing incentives to private enterprise. Private enterprise, however, has always found it more economical to build new housing on the periphery of the city than in the city itself. Hence most new housing has been suburban.

Early forays into low-income housing were similarly undergirded by assumptions which both valued suburban living and facilitated it. The federal government became involved in low-income housing in 1932 through the creation of the Reconstruction Finance Corporation which made loans to corporations formed to provide housing for families of low income. Again, incentives to assist private developers were fundamental to the program. Through the New Deal's public works program in 1934, the federal government first entered slum clearance, and in 1937 the U.S. Housing Authority was created to subsidize local housing efforts. This program continued until 1947 when the Public Housing Administration was created to provide loans to local public housing agencies for low-rent housing and slum clearance projects. As urban historian Zane Miller says, the basic assumption behind these programs was that "an improved physical environment within the slums would help the poor to earn their way up the socio-economic ladder and out into more pleasant [suburban] neighborhoods."[2]

From the very beginning, urban planners have strongly advocated the suburban thrust. Suburbanization, widely regarded as the savior of cities, was proposed to solve nearly all urban problems. Even when not proposed, suburbanization was nonetheless encouraged, as with zoning which facilitated the outward expansion of cities but did not direct it. Partly this was derived from urban planning's origins in the field of landscape architecture.

Origins in landscape architecture influenced much of city planning in its infancy and prefigured directions the field would take in subsequent years. Parks were among the first city planning ventures in this country. Long before urban planning was officially born with the Columbian Exposition in 1893, the planning and building of parks and park systems was an established and extensive activity. When the 1893 World's Fair opened, New Yorkers had been enjoying Frederick Law Olmsted's Central Park for nearly twenty years, Kansas City was considering plans it had commissioned George E.

Kessler to prepare for a city-wide park system, and Minneapolis had approved Horace S. W. Cleveland's 1883 ambitious plan for a system of parks and parkways in that city. As early as 1880, Chicago had 2,000 acres of parkland within the city.

The beginnings of *regional* planning in America were an outgrowth of this interest in park systems. The outer park movement, initiated in Boston in 1893, was ancestor to the regional development that characterizes planning today. Not only were the first American planners landscape architects, but the first course in city planning was housed in Harvard's Department of Landscape Architecture and the first official city planning commission, established at Hartford, Connecticut, in 1907, was created "mainly at the urging of the parks department of the state capitol."[3]

The push to plan parks reflected the commonplace perception of nature as an antidote to the commercial busyness and fast pace of urban life, and between 1865 and 1910, many supported the parks movement in the belief that open spaces and trees had therapeutic as well as aesthetic value. Noted landscape architect Charles Eliot, in pressing for a regional commission to build a metropolitan park system in Boston, was convinced that the city's rapid expansion would soon deprive her citizens of "riches of scenery such as Chicago or Denver or many another American city would give millions to create, if it were possible."[4]

Frederick Law Olmsted, the leading landscape architect of his day and seminal figure in both the parks movement and early urban planning activities, thought that parks offered city dwellers the equivalent of a day in the country. The respite they afforded was important, Olmsted felt, because scenic beauty had a favorable influence on health, vitality, and even intellect.[5] Olmsted also wanted patches of "wild forest" preserved close to metropolitan areas.[6] These provided places where one might slough off the cares and tensions of civilization. Roderic Nash, writing in *Wilderness and the American Mind*,[7] notes that:

> Olmstead felt the current surge of interest in natural landscapes was the result of many Americans perceiving that "we grow more and more artificial day by day." A "self-preserving instinct of civilization," he thought, led it to parks and preserves as a means of resisting "vital exhaustion," "nervous irritation," and "constitutional depression."[8]

The parks movement prefigured the "City Beautiful" movement by providing mitigating beauty amidst the utilitarian drabness of the industrial city. Except for the addition of fountains, statues and memorials common in European cities, the City Beautiful was essentially a continuation and broadening of the parks movement. The antidote to urban disquietude and unrest was sought through stately boulevards and malls, monumental architecture, and magnificent vistas all meant to suggest permanence and grandeur. This was accomplished by emulating the architecture of classical Greece and Rome and building on a scale sufficiently grand to "stir the blood of men," as Daniel Burnham expressed it.

Triggered by the "White City" exposition of the Chicago World's Fair in 1893, the City Beautiful movement set the standard in urban design and city planning for decades to come. Following this exhibition, Washington, D.C. in 1901 became the first city to attempt the City Beautiful on a citywide basis. There L'Enfant's 1791 plan lent itself especially well to the sweeping vistas, grand malls, axial arrangements, and formal neoclassical composition of the City Beautiful concept.

As newspapers and magazines published reports of Washington's plan, cities throughout the country followed suit, constructing tree-lined boulevards, parks, and monumental civic centers. Yet nowhere were the traditions of the City Beautiful followed on such a grand scale as in Chicago.

The civic pride behind the City Beautiful movement particularly appealed to businessmen. Urban boosterism was strong in nineteenth-century cities, and leading businessmen personally participated in beautification campaigns. Besides, the entire City Beautiful package was guaranteed to enhance the businessman's investment. Burnham's Plan of Chicago, for example, was one which recognized and favored the basic facts of urban growth in the late nineteenth century. It implicitly endorsed a perspective which assumed that continued expansion was good and that the central business district should neither be altered nor decentralized. As Scott says of the plan's assumptions,

> The city must be convenient so that its enterprises can flourish. Its residential neighborhoods must be comfortable so that workers will be efficient and content. It must be beautiful so that wealthy people will not spend their money in New York or Paris. What is good for business is, of course, good for the people, and vice versa.[9]

The World's Fair exhibition also spawned the creation of municipal art societies to beautify streets and public areas. Charles Mulford Robinson's *The Improvement of Cities and Towns*, published in 1900, provided both a rationale and a practicum for the civic art movement. Subtitled "a treatise on the practical basis of civic aesthetics," the book was a best seller, as was a 1903 sequel, *Modern Civic Art*. These books further stimulated the formation of improvement groups and civic art societies, and by 1906, there were some 2,000 such groups throughout the country.[10]

The civic awakening was astonishing. J. Horace McFarland, active in the movement, explained the beautification rage by reference to divine intervention:

> In the fullness of time God has put it into the hearts of our American citizens ... to make the habitations of men more cleanly, more sightly, and more comfortable; to act for all the people in unselfishness, to endeavor in some sense to give us here on earth in our urban habitations conditions at least approximating those of the beautiful wild into which our forefathers came a few generations ago.[11]

The civic reform movement reflected both aesthetic and utilitarian values, an irresistible combination for civic leaders, and the emphasis led the movement into transportation and hygiene issues. Robinson wrote that:

> If the end be to clothe utility with beauty, and in providing the beautiful to provide also that which will add to the convenience and comfort of the citizens, we shall best find its opportunities for usefulness by studying what has been happily called the anatomy of cities. In this there appear three groups of requirements: Those that have to do with circulation, those that have to do with hygiene, and those that have to do distinctly with beauty. No hard lines separate these classes.[12]

Robinson's statement foreshadowed the American Civic Association's interest in streets, slums, and "urban hygiene" in general. Formed in 1904 through the merger of a number of civic leagues, the American Civic Association sponsored the celebrated "Model Street" built in St. Louis in conjunction with the centennial of the Louisiana Purchase. Its buildings, it architecture, its playground, street lights—and even the paving materials of the street itself—all testified to the harmonious merger of beauty, utility, and hygiene.

Through the work of the American Civic Association and others like them, apologists for the City Beautiful used the movement as an instrument of social planning and joined forces with those seeking slum reform. The St. Louis Committee, for example, declared that:

> the indiscriminate herding together of large masses of human beings ignorant of the simplest laws of sanitation, the evils of child labor, the corruption in political life, and above all, the weakening of the ties which bind together the home—these are dangers which strike at the very roots of society. To combat them the government must employ every resource in its power.[13]

The principal means proposed for combatting these evils was the civic center. As the St. Louis Committee reasoned, the neighborhood center had *functional* value, since "it would center the interests of the people in the neighborhood and would enable the different interests to supplement one another." It had *aesthetic* value, in that "it would give a splendid opportunity for an harmonious architecture and landscape treatment of the various buildings, thus adding to the intrinsic beauty of each." It would be of *inspirational* value, in that "it would foster civic pride in the neighborhood and would form a model for improvement work." It had *educational* merit since "it would give the immigrant—ignorant of our customs and institutions—a personal contact with the higher functions which the government exercises towards him" and convince him that "the government is, after all, maintained for his individual well being as well as for that of the native-born." Finally, it would *strengthen democracy* and political involvement by "develop[ing] a neighborhood feeling, which in these days of specialization has grown weak, with a resulting lack of interest in local politics and the consequent corruption and disregard of the best interests of the people by their representatives."[14]

The assumption of the St. Louis Committee that the neighborhood civic center would solve most pressing social ills reflected a general turn-of-the-century tendency to look to technical solutions for social problems. Most proposals put forth by the early urban planners were premised on physical remedies to social problems. Bigger tenements, more space, cheaper transit, dispersion, and zoning all reflected the prevailing view that problems materially manifested could be solved through physical means.

Public Health and the Impetus for Slum Reform

Concern for the public health has been responsible for much of what subsequently has been regarded as "true social reform," and protecting the public health also has motivated much urban planning. The first metropolitan authority in this country, established in Boston in the 1840s, was created in direct response to the severe pollution of the Charles River. Efforts at housing reform were similarly triggered by fear that hygienic conditions in the slums might spread.

The broadening of support for tenement and slum reform, as Clinard has said, was inspired "more by emotional and aesthetic revolt against [the] physical ugliness [of the slums] and their danger to society than by full appreciation of the plight of the slum dweller himself."[15] Clinard notes how copies of Jacob Riis's book, *How the Other Half Lives*, were found in the most fashionable homes and motivated society ladies to hold benefit luncheons and dances to raise money for the poor. Riis' book, he says, "was no cry for social justice but a call to the propertied classes to bestir themselves lest the crime engendered in the slums and diseases bred there invade the comfortable quarters where ladies and gentlemen resided."[16]

The tenement was the first focus of housing reformers. To the press, settlement house workers, public health officials, and many of the early planners, it represented the prime social evil. Years before Hull House workers and social statisticians mapped its coincidence with crime and disease, the tenement was equated with poverty, vice, and filth. It took no statistical data to appeal to the public's fear that disease, crime, even pauperism, might spread, and the first regulations were in response to this fear. In prezoning days, the tenement and slum lay close to busy commercial districts and bordered some of the better residential neighborhoods. Thus the first regulations were those which demanded an upgrading of hygienic conditions or sought protection against the danger of fire. The Massachusetts Bureau of Statistics of Labor, for example, investigated tenement house conditions in 1891 and recommended legislation, which was quickly passed, prohibiting nonfireproof tenements.[17]

Slums were an immigrant problem, and the development of the American slum was closely related to successive waves of immigration.[18] The slum developed in response to insufficient housing units and to a market economy so glutted with labor that wages were too low for thousands to afford what decent housing was available. Had the slum not existed before they arrived, the immigrants would necessarily have created it. In the first place, the period of massive migration from European to American urban centers coincided with rapid urbanization *within* American society. There simply was not enough housing to meet the new demand, thereby ensuring that thousands would be forced to double up in small rooms or to live in cellars, stables, and makeshift shacks. Second, given the exploitation of the immigrant in the industrial workforce (made possible by an abundance of cheap labor), the immigrant's scant income and irregular work guaranteed that no adequate housing could be afforded. A 1910 New York commission, hoping to compare native and immigrant tenement conditions, was unable to find a single tenement in one area occupied by a native-born American.[19]

The worst slums were in cities with limited room to expand, as in New York, where countless immigrants were crowded together on Manhattan Island. A tenement house commission in 1894 noted that slum areas in Manhattan had the highest densities in the world.[20] In cities with more room to expand, such as Philadelphia or Chicago, slum conditions were appalling, but less severely so than in New York or Boston. Not surprisingly, the earliest efforts at slum reform originated in these two cities.

New York's problem was especially acute given its inherited land plan platting the city into long rectangular lots. The Commissioner's Land Plan of 1811, which divided the city into lots 25 x 100 feet, made it nearly impossible to design multifamily high-rise buildings without sacrificing light and air[21] and assured that ventilation would be inadequate when existing buildings were subdivided into apartments.

The earliest tenements were "railroad flats," first built in the 1840s by entrepreneurs recognizing the profit to be made in high-density housing. Given the lot size and the division of the building into several units, 75 percent of all rooms in the railroad flat were unlit and unventilated except by doors opening onto rooms in the front or back of the building.[22] The railroad flat became prevalent after midcentury, and its gross defects conditioned the early housing reformers' concern with light, air, and sanitation.

The movement resulting in tenement house reform originated in New York in the 1860s where the first regulations outlawing public privies and prohibiting basement occupancy were enacted. As with subsequent regulations favoring stronger laws and stricter enforcement, these restrictions were not successful. No one seemed to recognize that higher standards for tenements, which nearly all reformers preached, meant higher, and prohibitive, costs for the immigrant. Better construction, better sanitation, more windows, and more space all meant higher rents; yet the immigrant's *inability* to pay rents for adequate housing was the root problem in the first place.

The failure of the 1867 legislation to solve the tenement problem only served to fan interest in doing something about the horrendous living conditions found there. One solution was the "dumbbell tenement," an obvious improvement over the railroad flat that it was widely adopted.

So called because of its shape, the dumbbell was the result of an 1878 competition for a model tenement sponsored by *The Plumber and Sanitary Engineer*. Criteria for design submissions were that the building fit the New York lot size 25 x 100 feet, that it be designed for maximum profit yet still allow every apartment an outside window, and that it constitute an improvement over the railroad flat. One year after the competition, the dumbbell was made mandatory in New York City. Although it was widely built, it neither eradicated nor slowed the tenement problem.

Redefining the Problem: From "Housing" to "Slum" to "Congestion"

Whereas earlier generations had perceived "the housing problem" as a *tenement* problem, by the 1890s it was coming to be perceived as a *slum* problem. This distinction, although subtle, was important. "Slum" connoted not merely house, but house, street, and neighborhood. This shift in perception reflected two things: first, the Progressive's concern with the primary group, the family, and a belief that the street and slum neighborhood were bad for children; and second, a growing suspicion that the answer to the slum problem was not to be found solely in the physical structure of a building.

The new social statistics movement greatly influenced this change in perception. Some three to four thousand surveys were produced around 1900, many of them by private organizations. Even the federal government became interested in data collection. In 1892 Congress authorized an investigation of slums in cities with populations of 200,000 or more, but the study was grossly underfunded, thereby limiting the survey to Baltimore, New York, Chicago, and Philadelphia, and only to certain sections of these cities.[23]

One solution to the "slum problem" was to tear down tenements and replace them with parks and playgrounds. Where this was not possible, parks could be built nearby. The New York legislature in 1894 appropriated five million dollars to build small parks in crowded sections of slums. Boston in 1889 built a ten-acre park near one of its densest areas. Chicago in 1903 built its first playground, the land a gift from William Kent to Jane Addams for that purpose.[24]

Another approach to the "slum problem" was philanthropic housing, a major development of the 1894 period. This concept was itself tied to yet another "solution," that of dispersion. The interest in philanthropic housing was related to a further redefinition of "the housing problem": it was not merely a *house* problem, but a *neighborhood* one, not solely a problem of *light*, but of *congestion*. Behind this reformulation of the problem as one of *congestion* was the emergence of a solution, the new transportation technology, making decentralization possible.

Elgin Gould, a major exponent of this concept, believed that philanthropic capitalists should finance housing built on the periphery of the city. Newly available transportation would then enable the better-paid workers to move out, and the older dwellings could thus be made available to the lowest paid. A year following the publication of his book, *The Housing of the Working People*, Gould formed the City and Suburban Homes Company to advance his ideas, and the company built several apartments in Manhattan. Yet philanthropic housing, like the dumbbell tenement, did not solve the housing problem. The problem was not caused, as Gould assumed, by exploitative landlords; it was related to the cost of land compared to workers' salaries. Neither Gould nor many of his contemporaries fully grasped the intractable nature of the housing problem in a free market economy.

Gould's proposal was tied to relieving congestion, as were the majority of recommendations advanced around the turn of the century. Several studies attributed moral degradation and physical suffering to overcrowding, and some found congestion to be *the* cause of poverty, misery, and disease. Clinard relates that a Chicago study in 1901 reported overcrowding to be *the* major problem in the tenement districts; "there was no more important test of tenement house conditions than the amount of space covered by buildings."[25]

Concern over congestion similarly stimulated the first national urban planning conference. At the "First National Conference on City Planning and the Problems of Congestion," held in Washington in 1909, financier Henry Morgenthau expressed the dominant feeling that "there is an evil [congestion] which is gnawing at the vitals of the country, to remedy which we have come together—an evil that breeds physical disease, moral depravity, discontent, and socialism—and all these must be cured and eradicated or else our great body politic will be weakened."[26]

The "cure" for most conference participants lay in redistributing population to outlying urban areas. Most subscribed to "the trickle down effect," believing that the poor could obtain better housing if the middle class were removed from competition for older homes in the central city. Inherent in this concept was the idea that older housing should serve as a staging ground for upward social mobility, and that home ownership in new areas was the geographical counterpart of social and economic stability. This trickle down theory has a long history in urban planning, yet its fallacy was pointed out as early as 1919 by housing expert Edith Elmer Wood who estimated that "a third of the people in the United States were living under substandard housing conditions," and that "only the wealthiest third of the population constituted the effective market for new private housing."[27]

Absorption in the problem of "congestion" accounts for many proposals advocating planned dispersion as well as for urban planning's longstanding interest in transit. Along with parks, roads were among the first planning ventures in America, but in the early years of this century, transportation took on new meaning as a solution for social problems. Adna F. Weber, for instance, author of the 1901 book, *The Growth of Cities in the United States: 1890-1900,* hailed plans for rapid transit from the business center to the residential outskirts as the only effective solution for the problem of congestion. "Adequate space for the housing of the people lies at the basis of all reform," he insisted. Any other remedy was merely palliative.[28]

Many believed that by encouraging factories to locate on the fringe (an early form of zoning) one could prevent further densities in older areas of the city. Most proposed to accomplish this through foresight in street location. Robert Anderson Pope, a participant in the 1909 conference, proposed that the German *Ringstrasse* be applied to American cities to lower densities. A circumferential route would yield a more equitable distribution of land values because traffic could go from point to point without going into the city. "The same principle can be applied to beltline railroads," he said, "and by means of this provision, factories of all kinds can be attracted to the outskirts, and will eventually bring with them their employees from the city centers."[29]

Benjamin C. Marsh, secretary of the 1906 Committee on Congestion of Population in New York City, also wanted to locate factories on the suburban fringe. A strong social reformer, Marsh took the City Beautiful to task for emphasizing things which were tangential to the countless thousands who needed decent housing. In his view, housing was *the basic* problem and it could be solved *only* by redistributing population into outlying areas. Marsh believed that regulating factory location was mandatory, and he argued the right of the community to do so. "The city should," he said, "have the right to say to the prospective employer of labor: 'Before you locate your factory we must be assured that due regard is had to the welfare of those whom you will employ, and we stand ready to help you in securing the proper transport facilities for your freight...'."[30]

Marsh's ideas on zoning were picked up by other planners, but the spirit behind them was not. Influenced by Henry George and the Fabian socialists, Marsh was especially impressed with German town planning and zoning concepts where the rights of the community usually took precedence over the rights of the individual. When the first City Planning Institute was formed in 1917, and most reformers had come to regard zoning as the most practical means of improving housing conditions, Benjamin Marsh had become isolated from the mainstream of city planning and was no longer active in its causes.[31]

The City Scientific and Functional Urban Interdependence

A 1917 publication of the American Institute of Architects, *City Planning Progress*, revealed that the City Beautiful was still strong and prominent. Of the 227 illustrations the book included, the majority pictured civic centers and grand monuments, and less than five percent depicted residential and low-cost housing.[32] In their preface to the book, the editors stated their firm conviction that:

> City planning in America has been retarded because the first emphasis has been given to the "City Beautiful" instead of the "City Practical." [We] insist with vigor that all city planning should start on a foundation of economic practicableness and good business; that it must be something which will appeal to the businessman, and to the manufacturer, as sane and reasonable.[33]

Of course the City Beautiful had appealed to the merchant princes from the beginning, and during the late nineteenth century, business interests were generally quite disposed to favor municipal reform. (A prevalent idea during the period was that graft and corruption victimized legitimate businesses by sapping their profits.) But the City Practical had even greater appeal. When presented as a systematic method of urban reform, city planning captured the alert businessman's interest in efficiency and dovetailed nicely with scientific management principles then being applied profitably to the conduct of business.

George B. Ford, one of the editors of *City Planning Progress*, was instrumental in converting planning from the City Beautiful to the City Scientific. Ford was convinced that determining the best plan for a city was solely a matter of proceeding logically from the known to the unknown—of gathering factual information, analyzing it, and discovering that in almost every case there was "one, and only one, logical and convincing solution of the problems involved."[34]

The City Scientific emphasized the city as a functional unit of parts harmoniously working together for the good of the unit. For planning, the practical ends of the City Scientific thus became efficiency and convenience, orderly and rational growth, and utility. City planning, as the Pittsburgh Civic Commission put it in 1910, was "municipal conservation."[35]

A purely functional definition of interdependence, and a largely physical definition of planning, were reinforced by the new scientific, utilitarian ethic. Planning's new thrust meant a renewed interest in rational street planning and circulation systems. Rationality and utility also gave strong justification to the comprehensive plan, which emerged during the period as an efficient and logical means to solve urban problems. Rationality also inspired planning's interest in zoning. "Incompatible" land uses were viewed as inefficient and disorderly, impeding the rational development of cities. As George Kessler, invited to Dallas in 1910 to prepare a plan for that city, said:

> Regard for the interests of the people at large means that a city should be divided into areas and zones, each devoted to its own particular purpose. The greatest possible accessibility for all should be provided in ample and direct connecting thoroughfares and all barriers, such as railroad grade crossings, narrow congested streets and excessively long blocks, should be removed and corrected.[36]

Zoning appealed to an array of interests. *Business and commercial groups* favored the concept because functional separation of land uses ensured that the central business district would remain as it was, and one's investment would thereby be protected. *City officials* approved it because they believed mixed land uses gave rise to serious congestion and traffic problems. *Housing reformers* endorsed the concept because zoning restrictions could prevent tenement houses from growing and blighting new areas; and by regulating height and the spaces between buildings, new tenements might at least have a modicum of light and air. *Individual homeowners*, well aware that formerly fashionable areas had developed into slums, saw in zoning a means to prevent the construction of tenement houses in suburban areas. And given the ethic of efficiency prevalent at the time, it was *generally accepted* that an orderly city required that residential, commercial, and industrial areas be protected from incompatible uses.

The original legal vehicle for zoning was not eminent domain but nuisance litigation derived from the common law notion that one could harm one's neighbor. Originally, nuisance litigation was initiated by one's immediate neighbor for harm presumably done to that neighbor. It was not justified in terms of the general welfare until after 1890 when nuisance litigation evolved into more prescriptive laws invoked in terms of public well-being. The first instance of this related to public health concerns.

Zoning did not begin with the celebrated 1916 New York resolution in which the Board of Estimate adopted Edward M. Bassett's scheme for dividing the city into various districts. In some ways, the New York resolution was the culmination of practices which had been going on for several years. The first zoning restrictions were related to preserving single-family residential areas from invasion by factories, stores, and apartments. Mel Scott reports that the legislatures of Minnesota, Wisconsin, and Illinois as early as 1913 empowered cities of certain classes to establish residential districts from which commercial and manufacturing establishments would be banned. In Minnesota and Wisconsin, these zones were established by petition of homeowners.[37]

Broader application of the principle of comprehensive zoning first occurred in New York City, initially in response to building heights. The report of the 1911 Commission on Congestion of Population, for example, cited skyscrapers as breeders of congestion and traffic, and recommended limits on building heights. New York's citywide zoning ordinance was an outgrowth of this commission. The group pressed the Board of Estimate to create a Committee on Height, Size, and Arrangement of Buildings, which it did, and in 1913 a new body was formed: the Commission on Building Districts and Restrictions. At the instruction of this committee, Edward M. Bassett and his staff spent two years working on a zoning ordinance.

The Commission's desire to use zoning as a tool to relieve congestion was strongly supported by New York's business interests. The prestigious Fifth Avenue Association, comprised of merchants in that area, was greatly alarmed by the invasion of manufacturing lofts which threatened the economic stability and commercial character of the avenue. In a full-page newspaper ad, the association threatened to boycott all manufacturers who did not remove their plants by a specified date, and successfully sought the cooperation of property owners, and especially "every financial interest," in banning lofts from the area. Scott notes that

> the large corporations and financial interests, Bassett said, urged "that we use the greatest speed to put these restrictions into force, so that localities shall not be invaded with unsuitable uses before the law can go into effect."[38]

Scott also notes that "long before this combined ultimatum and request for cooperation appeared, the major real estate concerns, life insurance, title and trust companies, savings banks, and commercial and civic associations were...already allied with the...mercantile establishments."[39] In fact, housing reformer Lawrence Veiller, a member of the Commission on Building Districts and Restrictions, refused to sign the final report because he considered its recommendations too favorable to those interests.

Following New York's adoption of its zoning resolution, Berkeley, California approved much more stringent regulations. Whereas New York's ordinance had provided for three categories of land use—residential, commercial, and unrestricted—Charles H. Cheney's resolution for Berkeley rigidly segregated the use of land into twenty-seven classes of districts. Berkeley's ordinance had separate zones for industrial and commercial uses, but it also authorized one type of district for single-family homes, another for two-family homes, and still another for apartment houses.[40] The idea behind the Berkeley ordinance was that such rigid segregation was best for everyone concerned. Not only did residential areas benefit from such protection, but industrial areas gained too. At the National City Planning Conference in 1917, Cheney reported that:

> Some manufacturers said to us... "Why, if the city keeps factories out of residence districts, should not residences be kept out of factory districts?" We find in most cities the most abject poverty and the worst tenements and bad housing conditions in the factory neighborhoods. When we want heavy traffic pavement for heavy hauling with spur tracks in the sidewalk areas, these...homeowners appear before the City Council and holler so loud that the improvements are held up. So we have dejected housing and hampered industry.[41]

The emphasis on order, rationality, and efficiency which underlay zoning was absolutely consistent with progressive reform. Between 1907 and 1917, over one hundred American cities adopted zoning ordinances. With the 1924 Standard State Enabling Act, which provided state-imposed restrictions, zoning plans spread across the country to municipalities which otherwise lacked the power to enact them. Most of these cities adopted zoning without reference to a citywide plan. Like the New York ordinance, zoning was not invoked as a planning tool; it was rather a vehicle to restrict land use to present patterns. The enormous popularity of zoning followed from this. By segregating uses of land, zoning segregated the users of land, and it thus enabled continued economic growth and urban expansion without having to contend with the social problems of prezoning days.

It was this expedient solution that prompted Frederick L. Ackerman in 1919 to chastise the city planning movement for ignoring "the causes which give rise to existing maladjustments." In their preoccupation with zoning ordinances, he said, planners had become unduly concerned with so-called "normal" tendencies of city growth. In Ackerman's view, these "normal tendencies," as planners interpreted them, represented "the right of the individual to use the community as a machine for procuring individual profits and benefits, without regard to what happens to the community." America would have maladjusted communities, he continued, "so long as the spokesmen of city planning continue to proclaim that adjustment can be had without touching the sacred causes of maladjustment."[42]

Critics like Ackerman and John Nolen, who believed "we have heretofore given too much attention to caring for the mere wreckage of society, and too little toward establishing a better social order that would permanently reduce the amount of wreckage,"[43] were rare. But they were not alone. The 1920s saw the emergence and growing influence of a new group of thinkers, America's first generation of professional urbanologists, whose ideas would profoundly affect planning practice in the coming years. As earlier reformers had identified "the problem" as one of "house," then "street," and then "neighborhood," this group redefined it in terms of the entire city. Its remedy, therefore, required comprehensive and coordinated planning of the total urban environment. These urbanists were also the first self-consciously *social* planning theorists who offered a critique not only of urban *form* but of urban *life*. They were keenly interested in the garden city idea with its unique blending of social and physical elements which was then under discussion in England. They followed its development closely and brought it to America in the 1920s where it took a peculiarly American interpretation consistent with cultural attitudes toward nature, culture, freedom, and disorder.

3

Ebenezer Howard and the Garden City Idea

Any discussion of the garden city in America must begin with Ebenezer Howard's book, *Garden Cities of Tomorrow: A Peaceful Path to Real Reform*,[1] published in 1898. This slim volume has garnered worldwide influence. The book has given all modern languages a new term, is considered a classic in urban planning literature, and continues to shape the designs of numerous suburban developments. Its most important effect, however, was that it gave impetus to the major program of new town building undertaken in England following World War II. This effort in turn led to further "garden city" building in many countries, including the new town renaissance in America. The concept must be counted among the more far-reaching reform proposals of this century.

Given its impact, one might assume that Garden City's originator was a scholar or political theorist. Ebenezer Howard was neither. An unassuming man without much formal education, he spent the better part of his adult years as a court reporter. Throughout his life Howard worked on various inventions which, as Osborn recalls, probably brought him less money than their development cost,[2] but this aspect of his character was important in shaping the practical details of his famous proposal. After publishing *Garden Cities of Tomorrow* he founded the Garden City Association in 1899 (later to become the Town and Country Planning Association) to advance his ideas and garner the support to test them in practice. This was done with two garden cities. The first was built at Letchworth, 35 miles north of London, in 1903. Howard lived there until 1921 when he relocated to Welwyn, the second garden city, which was begun in 1919 to test his theory of clustered cities functionally related one to another. Howard was knighted in 1927 and lived at Welwyn until his death in 1928.

Despite its inherently bold character, the garden city concept over the years has come to be identified with a theory of small towns, with suburban development, with intensive family and neighborhood life, leisure activity, felicitous site design and fixed densities. This is highly ironic, for nowhere in *Garden Cities of Tomorrow* did Howard discuss these presumed "characteristics," much less identify them with the garden city. As Lewis Mumford has observed, Howard was little concerned with the outward form of the new city but greatly concerned with the *processes* that would produce it.[3] His primary concerns were social and economic, not aesthetic and formal.

The mistaken emphasis on "garden" attributed to Howard has been costly for his conception of the city. Certainly Howard wanted Garden City's citizens to enjoy "the free gifts of nature,"[4] but to regard Garden City as the embodiment of a nostalgic longing for the presumed rural simplicity of a bygone age misrepresents the man. Much influenced by Bellamy's *Looking Backward* (and instrumental in its publication in England), Howard was a technological progressive who celebrated modernization. He was quick to promote emerging possibilities, and only the most advanced techniques and machinery were used in Garden City. He also saw (and employed as a planning principle) the communications potential of rapid transportation. Like many of his contemporaries, he firmly believed that science and technology could assist the social progress of the age. He saw industrialization as a positive social force, creating more wealth and providing means other than resource redistribution for effecting the elimination of poverty—a subject that concerned him greatly and which Garden City was proposed to address.

As a practical man, Howard was more enthralled with efficiency and economy than with beauty. Influenced by theories of scientific management, he was an apologist for city planning because planned cities were less wasteful than conventional ones, and Garden City was economical and profitable, as well as moral, in his view. Underlying *Garden Cities of Tomorrow* was a functional ethic where individual parts gained their meaning in relation to the whole and where beauty was to be found in the interdependent working of the system. As Howard proposed it, the garden city was no pristine untouched state of nature; it was itself a technology, created to accomplish a specific purpose, quite contrary to the forces of the "natural" world and specifically designed to correct its deficiencies.

Despite his strong interest in technology, Howard nevertheless viewed the garden city not as an end in itself but as a *means* to an end, the larger purpose being "a higher and better form of industrial life generally throughout the country."[5] He wished to demonstrate "a better and more commonsense view of how towns should be built,"[6] but his overriding purpose with Garden City was "to lead the nation into a juster and better system of land tenure."[7] As one who travelled in mild reformist circles, Howard followed many of the political and economic issues of his day. Certainly the one which most interested him was the "land question," particularly as it bore on the creation and distribution of wealth through population migration. In Howard's time, industrialization and urbanization had led to the steady impoverishment of rural areas while in the cities great individual wealth and mass poverty appeared side by side. As the urban population and its economic activities grew, urban land values rose with the "unearned increment" accruing to landowners while the increased rents, prices and the cost of urban services were borne by those least able to afford them. In proposing Garden City as a means of regulating urban economic forces, Howard was responding to deep structural problems in the industrial economy.

Many nineteenth-century theorists had related land reform to other needed changes. Marx, Henry George, J. S. Mill, and Herbert Spence, all of whom influenced Howard,[8] had made that connection, but Howard differed in the importance he attached to land reform. While the socialists held that land reform was a necessary but insufficient condition for the reform of society, Howard was convinced that it alone was adequate and would by itself lead to other reforms. Conversely, he was convinced that with no land equality there could be no true equality. He believed that land was the only permanent form of wealth. Since all other wealth was ephemeral, its redistribution would make for but a transitory justice. Enduring reform had to begin with the land. "The special importance of the land question," he insisted, was "the true path of reform."[9]

Elements of Garden City

No precise definition of the garden city was given in Howard's book, but some years later a definition was formalized by the Garden Cities and Town Planning Association (so renamed in 1909) in consultation with the author:

> A garden city is a town designed for healthy living and industry; of a size that makes possible a full measure of social life, but not larger; surrounded by a rural belt; the whole of the land being in the public ownership or held in trust for the community.[10]

None of these elements were original with Howard; it was in their synthesis that the brilliance of his concept lay. The key elements and their interrelationship were highlighted by Lewis Mumford, an early supporter of Howard's ideas:

> The provision of a permanent belt of open land, to be used for agriculture as an integral part of the city; the use of this land to limit the physical spread of the city from within, or encroachments from urban development not under control at the perimeter; the permanent ownership and control of the entire urban tract by the municipality itself and its disposition by means of leases into private hands; the limitation of population of the number originally planned for the area; the reservation for the community of the unearned increment from the

growth and prosperity of the city, up to the limits of growth fixed; and moving into the new urban area of industries capable of supporting the greater part of its population; the provision for founding new communities as soon as the existing land and social facilities are occupied.[11]

As Howard conceived it, Garden City was first and foremost a town with the economic and political characteristics of towns. It was not a suburb. It was designed as a center for industry, employment, commerce, culture, education, social life, and even agriculture—and it was to supply a range of services to a diverse population consisting of all classes. The *economy* of Garden City was a central feature of the proposal; the major needs of the city's residents were to be met within the community, and there was to be sufficient population to support a variety of industries and commercial activities.

These activities were zoned, according to the wisdom of the day, for convenience and efficiency. The particular spatial scheme in *Garden Cities of Tomorrow* was meant to be suggestive only and is a minor feature of the scheme.

Garden City was also conceived as a *political unit* with a governmental structure and substantial legal powers and responsibilities, including the right of taxation. Garden City was administered by a Board of Management consisting of an elected Central Council and Departments of Public Control, Engineering and Social Purposes. This agency exercised traditional municipal powers as well as the authority normally held by landlords under the common law. Modeled after a successful business organization, Howard's administrative structure was a precursor to the city manager form of government. Consistent with his belief in the efficacy of science and technology to bring about the great community, Howard perceived the governance of Garden City as primarily a managerial problem, and not one of adjudicating conflicting value hierarchies. Even so, Howard carefully attended to governmental structure and responsibility, an area which has unfortunately been neglected in much new town conceptualization. Garden City's governance was highly democratic and decentralized. Howard was committed to community self-determination and he envisioned a great deal of local control over the town's institutions—including the regulation of commerce through controlled competition, and the nature and extent of municipal enterprise (which he hoped would include, but did not compel, the provision of medical care and pensions).

As he outlined the concept, Garden City was of *a size that makes possible a full measure of social life, but no larger*. The city was limited in area and in population, its optimum size determined by the numbers necessary to support the economic and social needs of its residents as well as the essential municipal services the population required. For Howard this population was 30,000 people on a Garden City estate of 6,000 acres. The city's growth was resolutely limited to this number, with further population directed into other new towns. This was "growth through colonization." Acting as a physical limit on the areal expansion of the city was the *encircling greenbelt*. Permanently zoned agricultural, and consisting of five-sixths of the entire land area, the greenbelt limited growth from within and from without. It also served the important economic purpose of integrating agriculture into the urban system and thereby revitalizing the rural economy. The steady depression of rural regions was a constant concern of Parliament in Howard's day. Fluctuations in business cycles and world economic conditions had made agriculture vulnerable, resulting in unstable markets and prices. The mechanization of agriculture itself contributed to the depression of rural regions and accelerated the conversion of the rural poor to the urban poor as vast numbers sought employment opportunities in the industrial cities. Howard was convinced that the problems of both country and city were addressed by the land reform that underlay the garden city concept.

In Garden City, the entire estate, both town and agricultural, was to be held in common ownership. Howard's insistence on this as an irreducible principle of Garden City—the "master key" of reform—places the garden city concept squarely in the tradition of socio-economic reform addressing *distributional* issues in society. It is this feature, however, that is most frequently absent in the new towns that followed Howard. He believed absolutely that "the path of land reform" was "the foundation on which all other reforms must be built."[12] Therefore all land—and structures—in Garden City were collectively owned and leased to individuals. Each lessee paid a single "rate rent" which was then applied toward amortizing the loan and financing a wide range of potential city services. This rate was a rent on *the land*, and not on its productive yield. The *community* therefore benefited from the increased land values attributable to their aggregation, while *individuals* profited from their own productivity. Not only was common ownership of land morally correct, but it was economically advantageous by making Garden City a profitable enterprise. With the increment accruing to the community, Howard reasoned, more revenue would be available and prices would be generally lower.

Howard specified that ownership of land in Garden City was to be *municipal*, not national. He believed strongly in local self-government[13] and objected to state ownership wherein those who held control were far removed from those directly affected by that control. Land reform therefore meant *municipal* (and not merely public) ownership of land, a point of difference between Howard and many of his followers. This distinction is not included, for instance, in the "formal" definition of the garden city given earlier.

Howard's vision of the future was of an entire nation of garden cities, each limited in size, each with decentralized political control and each therefore different, but all arranged in careful relationship to one another. Howard imagined perhaps ten such garden cities functionally grouped together and connected through rapid transportation. He believed such an arrangement would permit the advantages of the large city without the liabilities of the metropolis, for several cities clustered together could mutually support truly urban institutions (like the university, museums, or a symphony) which would be too costly for a single city to finance. A nation of clustered garden cities, Howard believed, would have the effect of restructuring the large dense metropolitan areas. As industry and the workforce moved to the new satellite towns, he assumed land values in the historic centers would fall. Howard welcomed this, believing that decongestion would hasten the regeneration of London into a more humane city with only one-fifth its population size.[14] London might then become, along with the new satellite towns, a truly "social city."

Through the creation of new towns linked together, and the reconstruction of the old cities, Howard believed his proposal would serve as a "steppingstone to a higher and better form of industrial life generally throughout the country."[15] This was his conception of the inherent value of the garden city.

Certain aspects of the garden city outlined in Howard's book were not included in the definition framed by the Garden Cities and Town Planning Association. Howard envisioned the emergence of a deep cooperative spirit within Garden City and presumed that municipal enterprise would extend beyond the provision of ordinary public services to social welfare. Although much was left to private enterprise in Garden City, Howard hoped that "promunicipal" activity, undertaken on behalf of the community but not by the municipality per se, would become a vital part of the city's economy. He suggested the formation of building societies and banks on this model, but he left this to "local option," which is itself another important theme in the proposal. He fervently believed that Garden City fostered the true social spirit and that cooperative institutions would flourish there.

Garden City was to be built on agricultural land purchased and developed by a limited dividend corporation. The financing of the city through private capital was an important dimension of his plan. For Garden City to be a practical alternative to "unhealthy" urban growth, the concept had to be replicable within the social and economic limitations of contemporary society. Howard believed this approach (which was subsequently used to build Letchworth and Welwyn) caused "no ill will, strife or bitterness; is constitutional; requires no revolutionary legislation; and involves no direct attack upon vested interest."[16] Only in its later stages, as the garden city movement gathered force, would Parliament need to intervene to assure the acquisition of large tracts of land at equitable prices.

Finally, the garden city as Howard envisioned it was a unique amalgam of public and private, individualism and communtarianism, capitalism and socialism. Howard was adamant in preserving for the community its due, but he was equally concerned to safeguard private enterprise. The institutions of Garden City—economic, political, and social—were carefully crafted to maintain this balance. And "balance," too, is a vital concept within Garden City, just as it was characteristic of Ebenezer Howard, a thoroughgoing moderate.

Above all, Howard saw Garden City as a demonstration which would show by force of example a better way, and he trusted to "the inherent advantages of the system leading to its gradual adoption."[17] "Granted the success of the initial experiment," he wrote, "there must inevitably arise a widespread demand for an extension of methods so healthy and so advantageous."[18]

This experimental approach led Howard and others persuaded by his ideas to pioneer an initial garden city and then a second at some remove from the first. Despite the opportunity to influence Parliament towards adopting some of his concepts in its postwar housing program, Howard wanted to test his theory of social cities functionally yoked together and would not abandon this vital aspect of his scheme. For this he was criticized by Lewis Mumford who felt that Howard had subordinated truly important work "to a muddled and wasteful effort at town extension and estate building within the existing municipal areas."[19] Mumford regarded Howard's initiative at Welwyn as reflecting the "impatience of an old man" who "sought to duplicate his original success instead of widening it into broader channels."[20] The wider channels Mumford preferred were those advocated by F. J. Osborn, an early associate of Howard and chief architect of the governmental new town program that later emerged. After the first World War, Osborn viewed the new towns concept as addressing in a unified way national needs for housing, industrial rehabilitation, and urban improvement. This was the direction subsequent new towns in Britain have taken.

The New Towns Program in Britain

Some 28 new towns, differing in density, character, location, and economic potential, have been built in Britain since 1946 when Parliament adopted a new towns policy whose origins can be traced to Howard's ideas and experimental garden cities. Less a vehicle for civilizational reconstruction than he had envisioned, the British policy has instead concentrated on accommodating metropolitan growth and meeting housing needs.[21] The government entered the new towns picture in an effort to relieve congestion in the major industrial cities, particularly London, and this orientation inevitably meant that the new towns would differ importantly from Howard's design.

Between 1946 and 1949 eleven new towns were designated, eight of them around London. Two were built in the 1950s and a dozen in the 1960s, most in England but a handful in Scotland and Wales. After 1970 no new towns were designated. Under the conservative Thatcher government, the publicly held assets of the new towns are currently being sold to private interests and the new town program will be phased out by the end of this decade.[22] During the 1960s and early 1970s, however, much national attention was directed toward new town building, resulting in a program which both embraced and altered features of the Garden City as Howard had outlined it. Several important differences should be noted.

The New Towns Act of 1946, which set initial guidelines for the program, specified that members of the development corporation were to be appointed by, and responsible to, the central government, and not the local populace. Howard had advocated the formation of a limited dividend corporation to finance the town, but the New Towns Act specified that development corporations could borrow money *only* from the central government with all profits returned to the government.[23] Hence the program has been beneficial for the central government as landlord, but not for the communities themselves. The towns have not profited from the increment in land values that they have generated. This method of financing has further meant that community self-determination is radically decreased and that the general redistribution of income Howard hoped to effect through Garden City has not been realized in the British new towns.

Second, the rental of land and structures as Howard had stipulated was not followed strictly in the government-sponsored new cities. This policy has changed over the years. Under the 1946 act, the development corporations were empowered to rent or sell sites and structures. Most industrial and commercial property was leased, while residential property was consciously mixed to include both rental and home ownership. Current policy under the Thatcher government encourages home ownership and the sale of commercial and industrial assets to private interests.[24]

Third, and contrary to Howard's intentions, the British new towns policy has made no provision for associating the new towns with their surrounding agricultural areas. Howard considered the agricultural estate an inherent part of Garden City's economy, and he saw in the location of town and country great opportunities for contending with urban environmental problems. In the British new towns, however, the greenbelt has been used almost exclusively to contain development.

Finally, no effort has been made in England to pursue the creation of smaller, clustered cities. Instead the optimum population of towns was revised upward from the twenty to sixty thousand range set in the New Towns Act of 1946 to population goals from 100,000 to 250,000.[25]

Despite these differences, the British experience with garden cities has conformed more closely to Howard's vision than has the American. In England a large proportion of the property (until recently) has been owned by a nonprofit public body, whereas in the United States virtually all land in the new towns has been privately owned.

The land acquisition process has been entirely different in the two countries. The New Towns Act empowered development corporations to purchase whatever land was required for the city at purchase prices which would have obtained had no new town been built on the site.[26] Consequently real estate speculation has been curtailed, unlike in the United States where it invariably accompanies rumors of a new development.

Through the development corporation's regulatory powers, British new towns have been much more successful than their American counterparts in preventing the growth of mere dormitory suburbs. Howard's idea that the garden city should be a place for living and working has generally been realized. For some years the use of an "Industrial Selection Scheme" permitted job applicants to be matched with job opportunities in the new towns.[27] Housing has generally been available only to those who work there, and housing shortages have ensured that few job openings are passed up. By contrast most new town residents in America do not work within the city.

More than in any other country, British new town strategists have seriously attempted to realize Howard's goal of social balance. "Balance" has been generally accepted to mean a class composition which conforms to the class characteristics of England and Wales as a whole. New town planners have further accepted the idea that each neighborhood should be socially balanced—an enormous challenge given the tendency of people to sort themselves out by social class.[28] Efforts to redress the class and income segregation characteristic of American cities have been attempted in a few new towns but with limited success. Private enterprise has built housing whose cost generally has made it difficult for the less affluent to live there, and industries that have located in the new towns have favored high-skill occupations. These factors have largely excluded lower-skilled, lower-income groups from settling in the American new towns. Britain has faced similar problems, but governmental rent subsidies have enabled more lower-income families to afford housing in the new towns than have been able to do so in the United States. Through controlling rents, the development corporation has also been able to subsidize low-income housing to a certain extent and this has been done in several of the towns.

As the British modified Howard's ideas to suit contemporary needs, so too did the Americans. New town planners and theorists in this country have reinterpreted the garden city in accord with cultural practices and beliefs that are distinctly American. We turn to this reinterpretation now.

4

Radburn, New Jersey: "A Town for the Motor Age"

The garden city was brought to this country by the Regional Planning Association of America (RPAA) and their beliefs and interests largely determined the expression it has taken. Representing a new generation of socially responsible writers and professionals interested in the city, the RPAA was a small and highly active group who met regularly—sometimes two and three times a week—for a decade between 1923 and 1933. Membership included many of the giants of urban planning history: social critic Lewis Mumford; Clarence Stein and Henry Wright, architects and planners; naturalist Benton MacKaye, the originator of the Appalachian Trail and the "townless highway" that prefigured the modern freeway; housing experts Catherine Bauer Wurster and Edith Elmer Wood; economist Stuart Chase; Alexander Bing, real estate entrepreneur and developer; Frederick Bigger, who figured prominently in the greenbelt program; Frederick Ackerman and Tracy Augur, who served as consultants to the greenbelt program; Clarence Perry, originator of the "neighborhood concept"; and Charles Harris Whitaker, editor of the *Journal of the American Institute of Architects*.[1]

Directly or indirectly, the ideas of this small group of friends influenced Radburn and the greenbelt program, of course, but also the Tennessee Valley Authority, the Appalachian Trail, the Civilian Conservation Corps, and the Rural Electrification Administration. They were influential in directing attention to the relationship between capital and housing, both in quantity and quality, and they were early advocates of public housing. Government involvement in housing beyond minimal standards legislation is largely owing to their efforts. And through "The Radburn Idea" they influenced scores of new cities including Vallingby (Sweden), Kitimat (British Columbia), Chandigarh (India), and the entire new towns renaissance of the 1960s in Britain and America. They also influenced several generations of planners. "The Radburn Idea" remains one of the strongest and most enduring intellectual streams in urban planning.[2]

Never numbering more than twenty people, the RPAA was what in today's terms would be called a "network," a group formed more for self-education than for advocacy of a single perspective. Such an informal approach permitted a lively diversity of opinion, as was the case, and yet there was broad agreement on the concept of regionalism.[3] This theme provided the organizing force for most of their discussions and such projects as were jointly undertaken. Lewis Mumford, clearly the group's intellectual leader and its prime spokesman, developed and communicated this regional philosophy most fully.

Mumford saw American history in terms of a series of population migrations. The first was that of the land pioneers who settled along the seaboard and up the river valleys, opening the continent west of the Alleghenies. The second migration was from the countryside and Europe to the factory towns created by steam power and the railroads. The third was the movement of people and materiel into the large industrial cities. The first migration had "denuded the country of its natural resources," Mumford wrote, while the second had "ruthlessly cut down and ignored its human resources."[4] The third had resulted in a steady drain of people and capital from the industrial towns and villages and a concentration of these as well as culture in the large urban centers. "The first migration sought land; the second industrial production; the third, financial direction and culture."[5] To effect the union of these three was the task of the "fourth migration" which existed as a present possibility. Mumford argued that the technology of the automobile, coupled with telephone, radio, and rural electrification, could foster a new settlement pattern of planned regional dispersion which would "give to the whole continent that stable, well-balanced, settled, cultivated life which grew out of its provincial settlements."[6]

"The fourth migration" became something of a metaphor for RPAA members' concerns, but certainly none shared Mumford's finely developed and encompassing philosophy of organic regionalism, shaped as it was by the socio-biology of Patrick Geddes, Mumford's wide knowledge of human cultures, and his extraordinary gift for synthesis. The regionalism that other RPAA members clearly shared was a commitment to the decentralization of what Stein had labeled "dinosaur cities."[7]

For all practical purposes, Radburn was an RPAA project. Not only were its planners, architects, and chief financier charter members, but the town itself was built to test many theories and views held by the membership at large. These included the ideas of Ebenezer Howard, but they went far beyond what Howard had outlined. The RPAA accepted many garden city principles, but they considered the concept a starting point and not an end in itself. It was, as Mumford said, "just a single thread in the new warp and woof"[8] of their conception of regional planning. Other threads in the skein included the ideas of Patrick Geddes, Thorstein Veblen, John Dewey, and Charles H. Cooley. The social-psychological theories of Cooley were particularly influential and yoked planning in Radburn with many of the concerns of the older progressives, particularly their desire to reduce urban disorder. Radburn's major purpose was interpreted as demonstrating how good planning was that which met the requirements of "contemporary good living."[9] As Geddes Smith hailed the city's major accomplishment, Radburn was "A town built to *live* in—today and tomorrow. . . . A *new* town—newer than the garden cities, and the first major innovation in town planning since they were built."[10]

The group first began with Sunnyside Gardens, a housing development conceived as a trial run before addressing the "ultimate purpose of building an American garden city."[11] The RPAA's brand of regionalism rejected both the metropolis and the suburb, but the group felt that prior experience was needed before attempting the more ambitious project. A limited dividend company was formed through the initiative of Alexander M. Bing, and a site in the Borough of Queens near Manhattan's business center was chosen. There the City Housing Corporation (CHC) purchased 77 acres, 55 of which were used to create the Sunnyside Gardens community of 1,201 family units.[12] The development was built between 1924 and 1928, with RPAA members Clarence Stein and Henry Wright serving as chief planners and architects.

The immediate objectives at Sunnyside reflected the group's concern over the scarcity of private capital available to finance adequate housing for families typically excluded by mortgage and real estate interests. Stein had served as Chairman of the New York State Commission on Housing and Regional Planning under Governor Al Smith and had become the RPAA's leading spokesman on this subject. In fact, during these years Stein viewed his central challenge as enlarging access to decent housing by reducing its cost.[13] This accounted for his strong commitment to population dispersion to outlying land where housing and community services could be provided at substantially greater savings.

At Sunnyside, the City Housing Corporation hoped "to produce good homes at as low a price as possible, to make the company's investment safe . . . [and] to use the work of building and selling houses as a laboratory in which to work out better house and block plans and better methods of construction and financing."[14] The larger goal of the CHC was "to create a setting in which a democratic community might grow."[15]

Planners were forced to work within the established gridiron street layout, but they were still able to group apartment buildings and single- and two-family houses given the primarily industrial zoning of the area.[16] The structures were almost entirely row houses situated to create parks on the inner part of the blocks. Houses fronted the common courtyards, but each had its private garden on the rear side. There were six acres of interior green commons. While Sunnyside was essentially a housing project, the Corporation nonetheless set aside three and one half acres and equipped this area as a recreational park. A house was converted into a community building. At one point the Corporation also employed playground directors.

With Sunnyside prospering, the Corporation proceeded with its original goal of building a garden city. "In our minds' eye," Stein recalled, "we still had the theme that Ebenezer Howard had created so vividly in his book *Garden Cities of Tomorrow*. We believed thoroughly in greenbelts and towns of a limited size planned for work as well as for living."[17] Thus conceived, Radburn was begun in 1928. Stein and Wright again served as chief planners. They were joined by Frederick Ackerman, a fellow RPAA member.

The site for Radburn was chosen 16 miles from New York City in the Borough of Fairlawn, New Jersey. Given their interest in relocating urban population into new regional cities of different sizes, RPAA members rejected both suburbanism and metropolitanism. But they did embrace a concept of urbanism with cities in relationship to one another much like Howard's "clustered cities" concept. Hence the suburban location of Radburn. On this site the CHC planned to build a new town with an ultimate population of 25,000 complete with commercial and industrial offerings. Fairlawn was poor and rural, with no zoning ordinance or official road plan, and this meant that difficulties earlier encountered at Sunnyside could be avoided. Wright's studies had demonstrated that parks and other amenities could be provided at no additional cost if the gridiron was abolished and a more efficient layout were used.[18]

Radburn was planned as a series of three neighborhoods of 7,500–10,000 people, each with its own elementary school and shopping center. A larger commercial center was planned as a regional market, and along with industry, this was to be located on the periphery. When the first residents moved into Radburn in the spring of 1929, two of the proposed three neighborhoods were underway. Some 400 families lived there in the early years, but the Depression prevented the completion of either of the two neighborhoods and the third was never begun. The City Housing Corporation was forced into bankruptcy and lost most of the land outside the two developed superblocks.

Although originally begun as a garden city, few of the critical elements of Howard's plan were included. The developers liked the idea of essential protection the greenbelt provided against outside encroachment, but there was not enough land to have both the greenbelt and the three proposed neighborhoods, so the greenbelt was excluded from the start.

As a part of a larger vision of regional population dispersion, the developers also planned for industry. With the Depression, however, none came; and with no greenbelt and no industry, Radburn was forced, as Stein admitted, "to accept the role of a suburb."[19] Ironically, the town's residents would deem its suburban character an asset. A major study conducted between October 1931 and April 1933 by Robert Hudson, a member of the corporation's staff, remarked that "the livelihood of the community is not dependent upon the fortunes or misfortunes of one industry or institution."[20] From the very beginning most Radburn residents were commuters. Hudson noted that 70 percent of the men were employed in New York and 17 percent in New Jersey. They had moved to Radburn because "they had business connections in the metropolitan area and need[ed] a desirable, economical place to live, where they and their families [could] enjoy the amenities of life that are not found in all suburban communities."[21]

Ostensibly built for families of "moderate income," another concern of RPAA members, Radburn nonetheless attracted a more affluent and economically homogenous group than developers had hoped. Most residents of the community, including women, were college-educated. The average age for men during the period of Hudson's study was 35 years; for women it was 33.[22] Insofar as these were "moderate income" families, the term applied more to an age-relative stage in the income cycle than to a general economic condition.

Radburn's developers never intended their town to be a garden city where all land was held in common ownership. Bing and fellow board members of the City Housing Corporation considered this "impractical" in the New York area given "the difficulty of mortgaging leaseholds, and of selling property when the ownership of the land did not go with the house."[23] They believed that similar purposes could be served through private covenants and protective restrictions, which were employed at Radburn. RPAA members saw advantages in common ownership of land but were not committed to this tenet of the garden city. In fact Charles Whitacre, who had been a strong advocate of land reform, became detached from the group after its members failed to support the single tax movement.[24] In Radburn, only the inner block parks were held in trust for the community.

The Depression contributed to Radburn's failure to materialize as a garden city, but it was not the sole cause. *The developers themselves changed the city's goals.* "In spite of the avowed intention of the Corporation to create a Garden City," Stein wrote, "eventually the pressing need of demonstrating The Radburn Idea overshadowed the Garden City idea. In large part it superceded it."[25]

"The Radburn Idea" assumed such importance because it uniquely addressed physical and social problems of interest to the RPAA. It offered great economic savings, and so created a superior environment at less cost, theoretically enlarging the housing stock for the moderate income; it presented a technical solution to problems associated with the automobile (and the auto was central to realizing the regional development to which the group was committed); and it provided a prototype for the new town's *raison d'être* as meeting requirements for "contemporary good living."

"The Radburn Idea" had five interrelated elements. Technically it meant: (1) the superblock; (2) specialized roads; (3) separation of pedestrian and automobile traffic; (4) houses turned to front the park; and (5) the park as backbone of the neighborhood.[26]

Spatially it meant the organization of the city into a series of integrated superblocks, each a mile or greater in circumference and 30 to 50 acres in size, and each centered around a spacious green park. Around this open space, houses were grouped informally through cul-de-sacs, an arrangement popularly thought to encourage social interaction. Whether single-family home or apartment building, all residential structures had two sides, each with different functions. The living and bedrooms fronted the park, while the kitchen and utility areas opened on the rear courtyard. Through streets surrounded the superblock but did not penetrate its interior. Only access lanes opened into the cul-de-sacs. A system of overpasses and underpasses was used for safety. Pedestrian traffic was directed along the parkway where the only sidewalks were located. Separating "incompatible" uses was considered safer, more rational, more economical, and more aesthetically harmonious. Unlike conventional cities, where "porches faced bedlams of modern thoroughfares with blocked traffic, honking horns, noxious gases... parked cars, hard grey roads and garages,"[27] Radburn had resolved the problem of the automobile so vital to the city's very existence. This feature alone earned Stein and fellow planners enthusiastic praise. One writer hailed the city as "a town 'for the motor age.' A town turned outside in—without any backdoors. A town where roads and parks fit together like the fingers of your right and left hands. A town in which children need never dodge motor trucks on their way to school."[28]

While not accepting many of Howard's tenets, planners did embrace the economizing ethic so fundamental to his thinking. Stein shared with Howard a highly detailed critique of the spiralling costs of congested metropolitan areas where urban services and housing were exorbitantly expensive, and both embraced comprehensive planning for a targeted population within a defined area in order to control the "overhead" factor associated with "dinosaur cities."[29] By employing "The Radburn Idea," Stein showed how the town needed 25 percent less area for streets and utilities.[30] Similar economies were effected through continuous large-scale development on unimproved virgin land. This ethic of "the-good-city-achieved-through-economic-efficiency" has been prominent throughout the new towns movement. In Columbia, Maryland, for instance, the substantial open space (perhaps the city's most celebrated feature) was made possible by spreading its purchase price over the city's entire 14,000 acres, making for a nominal $100 per acre additional cost.[31]

As seen through the eyes of Clarence Stein, historian of the new towns movement during the interwar years as well as Radburn's chief proponent, the city's most enduring achievement lay in its responsiveness to the times. Older cities were "obsolete," "unworkable," and "dangerous." Among their basic "evils" were their "dangers to life and health"; "congestion"; "loneliness"; "lack of nature"; "waste of time, money, and energy"; and "ugliness." New towns were needed to counter this urban obsolescence by offering "nature," "safety," "beauty," "economy," and "spaciousness."[32] In these contrasts Stein virtually echoed Ebenezer Howard; yet in redefining the new town's purpose he departed widely from Howard's ends. Whereas Howard sought to lead the nation to a more just system of land tenure, Stein sought to eliminate "obsolete cities" and build instead "contemporary" ones which took into account the new "requirements of the period": the automobile, specialization, mechanization, increasing leisure, greater equality of opportunity, a higher material standard of living, and growth and change.[33]

In "Indications of the Form of the Future," reflections on his extensive experience with new community building, Stein distinguished between "new towns" and "newly created" towns on the basis of their "harmony with present-day culture."[34] A newly created town may be newly built, but it was nonetheless "fitted to an age long past";[35] a truly *new* town, such as Radburn, always presented "the possibility of revising the setting to keep in harmony with the changing show."[36]

In redefining the goal of new towns, Stein both shaped and foreshadowed the direction the new towns movement would take in this country. Like Stein, new town planners who followed him would contrast the "contemporary" with the "obsolete past" even as they used the modern to recapture an earlier America. In American new towns, "contemporary" would be expressed in an idealized conception of a preindustrial village where close-knit families were presumed to exist and democratic cooperation was considered spontaneous and natural. Such premises took Radburn's planners directly into the realm of social planning where "The Radburn Idea" also figured prominently. Like many progressive reformers, they believed the primary group to be threatened by urban life and so emphasized the "family neighborhood" in their plan. In Radburn we first see "the city" itself defined as a completely integrated set of family neighborhoods.

The notion that the family should serve as a model for society is a very old one, derived from the religious conception of God as father protecting and nurturing His children who, in filial love and duty, protect and nurture one another. For many nineteenth-century communitarian groups, the family was consciously employed as a model for the organization of the community. Either the community was perceived as an extension of the nuclear family, or the community was itself to be the family.[37] The family-centered basis of the new towns is quite different from this. These are not familistic cities, but cities of nuclear families. The image does not convey the same diversity of membership nor the same communal responsibility for all its members that is implied in a familistic city. In Radburn and other new towns that followed, the city was not ordered on the model of the family as a system of expanding relationships and responsibilities. Instead, what was emphasized was life *within* a collection of nuclear families.

The Family Neighborhood

"Man is submerged in the colossal human swarm," Stein wrote, "his individuality overwhelmed, his personality negated, his essential dignity is lost in crowds without a sense of community."[38] In this statement, so representative of RPAA thinking, is revealed the extent to which RPAA members were pursuing social goals when they undertook the building of Radburn. The ideas of Charles H. Cooley particularly influenced their emphasis on the family neighborhood. A pioneering social psychologist, Cooley stressed the social (as opposed to the biological) origins of the human personality, and held that the healthy personality developed its attributes only through interaction. He thus regarded the primary group and neighborhood as the main nurturers of both the individual and the society. He also believed that "the organization of society may not only fail to give human nature the moral support it needs, but may be of such a kind as...to promote degeneration."[39]

Among RPAA members there was marked concern for cities' effect on family life and upon procreation. Stein identified the declining birthrate as one of the "evils" of the modern city,[40] and Mumford contended that the garden city would have a salutary effect on fertility. He wrote:

> the task of our age is to work out an urban environment that will be just as favorable to fertility, just as encouraging to marriage and parenthood, as rural areas still are... the sort of city [Howard] projected was precisely the kind whose population will be biologically capable of reproducing itself and psychologically disposed to do so. With the prospects of a dwindling population if the past tendencies toward urban concentration continue, the question now becomes not whether Britain and the United States can afford to build Garden Cities, but whether they can afford to build anything else.[41]

Seeking to encourage marriage and family life, Radburn's planners were conscious of the effect the physical design had on the primary unit. Stein observed:

> Doing things together is an everyday indication of happy family life. This grows out of the physical plan and the plan for living. Mother and children can spend the afternoon together at a swimming pool by strolling across their park; father and daughter can play tennis on Sunday morning—within easy call of the dinner bell.[42]

Hudson pointed out that most of Radburn's community activities were deliberately arranged "so that men and women [could] participate in them together, making for the creation of 'family' interests."[43]

Concern for the nurturance of the individual personality as outlined by Cooley led Radburn's planners to special concern for children. Stein was absolutely correct when he said that "Radburn was above all else planned for children,"[44] and it is indeed striking how young children dominate the plan and define the institutions of the city. Other cities have been given form by economics, technology, or socio-cultural groupings, but the organization of Radburn and nearly all subsequent American new towns has been predicated upon children from toddlerhood to puberty. Substantial recreational facilities and programs were geared to this age group. Moreover, the interior parks of the superblocks, the very heart of the city, were intended for children. From the central park or the front lawn, the world of Radburn's children was circumscribed by house and green.[45] The houses encircling the park provided a cocoon insulating children from the disorder, stimulation and melange of humanity so characteristic of urban life. Certainly RPAA members were influenced in this protective approach by child welfare and settlement house workers who labored to remove children from the streets, which were considered physically and morally harmful. In Radburn the streets were removed from the children.

Also revealing the central importance of children to Radburn's conceptual scheme was the organization of the community around the elementary school. The young child therefore determined the *social* limits of the city. The elementary school also defined the *political* unit in Radburn. Membership in the First Radburn Citizens Association, the sole political voice of the residents, was defined by the geographical boundaries of the area served by the elementary school. In restricting membership on this basis, the residents of the first developed superblock embraced the concept of decentralized neighborhoods and assumed that later residents would form similar associations as determined by their elementary schools.[46]

Given its physical design and social and political referents, the superblock was naturally appealing to those in their childbearing years. The first forty families were couples in their thirties with children of early- or preschool age.[47] They too contributed to Radburn's character as a city for children. One of the subcommittees of the Citizens Association was devoted to "child environment," and nearly one quarter of all adults in the community belonged to the PTA.[48]

Many of the activities sponsored by the Radburn Association were ones which appealed to young children or to adults with children of elementary-school age. The extensive children's recreational program was designed with the "further development of the child" in mind,[49] and by far the most popular of several courses offered by the Citizens Association was a series on child development. Nearly a third of all women in the community participated in one of these courses which were subsidized by the Radburn Association on the grounds they were valuable to the community.[50] Courses in French and German were purely personal, however, and did not merit subsidy. The Radburn Association also helped defray expenses for the nursery school.

Combined with Cooley's views on the primary group, the theories of sociologist Robert Park helped orient Radburn along neighborhood lines. One of Stein's continuing criticisms of "normal" cities was the constant mobility within them. Stein felt that people were always "going somewhere" rather than engaged in "productive, worthwhile, and enjoyable occupations."[51] Park's ideas supported Stein's desire to firmly relate people to a *place*. Park believed that circles of relationships formed moral communities which tied people down; in the absence of these, moral deviance was inevitable.[52] Later Louis Wirth would further refine these concepts and contend that urban life was based on "secondary" relationships which were anonymous, segmented, and transitory, whereas personal, holistic, and permanent relationships were "primary," and found in nonurban settings.[53] As Albert Guttenberg says:

> With learned treatises such as [these] to support them, urban reformers regarded the ordinary family neighborhood as the seed of social regeneration. Structurally, the family neighborhood was part of the city. Morally, it was the very antithesis of the city. The task was to rescue this good seed from the surrounding city and use it to rear up a new and healthy social order.[54]

This idea was institutionalized in Clarence Perry's "neighborhood unit" concept, in which the elementary school centered neighborhood became the organizational building block of the community. This concept had its first full expression in Radburn, and Perry helped define it at an RPAA conference. Perry called his idea "the physical basis for that kind of face-to-face association which characterized the old village community."[55] It was wholeheartedly embraced by Stein who felt that a central meeting place like the school provided "a setting for neighborly friendship and cooperative participation in common activities."[56] Coupled with "The Radburn Idea," the neighborhood design removed "artificial barriers" to the "free and unrestricted development of common mind, common interest, and common support."[57] Hudson wrote:

> Acquaintanceship grows slowly in the "checkerboard" city where contacts are usually one at a time, constantly delayed and often stopped by a single misanthrope or by the barrier of an intersecting street.[58]

In Radburn, however, it was "indeed an unusual person or family that [did] not grow and expand in community mindedness."[59] Stein observed that:

> The informal relationship of houses, the ease with which one can cross a couple of lawns and call out "Who's Home?" has affected the social and civic expression of the people. Neighbors can see each other frequently and with little effort. Pooling of interest and effort follows.[60]

"Just below the surface," Stein wrote, "one finds all about the town an awareness of neighbors and their interests, of their abilities, their ambitions and their needs."[61] Just as the family was regarded as the building block of society, so was the neighborhood seen as the building block of the nation. Civic responsibility thus interpreted was closely related to the concept of neighborhood decentralization. Writing of Greendale, Stein firmly asserted that small neighborhoods were "essential for eye-to-eye democracy—and this is basic, not only for local government, but for national freedom and worldwide security."[62]

The presumption was that simple democratic face-to-face interaction would prevent any dispute or conflict from materializing which could not be handled peacefully and amicably among friends and neighbors.

The "democratic" neighborhood so conceived, however, was not *the diverse urban* neighborhood—not the heterogeneous neighborhood of different ethnicity, age, family types and sizes, child-rearing practices, religion, race, lifestyles, and values. Nor was it the decentralized urban neighborhood of the boss and the political machine. Given its very diversity, the *urban* neighborhood was fraught with potential discord and irreducible differences. Radburn planners, on the other hand, based their neighborhoods on an *assimilative* model where "community" was sustained by commonality and sameness. It was a model designed to avoid pain and acceptance of "otherness" which perforce must be encountered in cities. Richard Sennett[63] argues that one cannot separate intense family life in suburban homogeneous settings from a decrease in the complexity of social forms urged by planners. He interprets both as a seeking after solidarity and a desire to escape experiences that might create complexity or disorder. The simplification of the social environment as epitomized in the suburbs is an attempt to minimize "all extraneous elements, all unknowns [and] unforeseen social conditions of surprise."[64] He contends that planners have supported this view of conflict as "evil" rather than as endemic to human society and vital for human maturation, and have thus defined good relations as "conflict free, understandable in advance by defined rules, and stable over a long period of time."[65] This certainly was a part of the neighborhood concept at Radburn.

This assumption of effortless, harmonious, democratic cooperation must be considered in explaining the near absence of political institutions in Radburn and in most other American new towns. Since harmony and cooperation were presumed to be the "natural" state, it appears that no formal mechanisms or institutions to mediate conflict were required. Certainly none was created. Planners apparently assumed that conflict and discord would not exist if "artificial" barriers were removed. In fact, the community of Radburn was conceived in such apolitical terms that the "city" was not even a city in the legal sense. Like so many other new towns, Radburn was not incorporated as a separate political entity. And with the city so defined, the "political" was largely perceived as "administrative."

The town was governed by the Radburn Association, a nonprofit corporation created by the City Housing Corporation "to fix, collect, and disburse the annual charges, to maintain the necessary community services, parks, and recreation facilities, and to interpret and apply the protective restrictions."[66] The Association was empowered to impose a tax, limited to half again the prevailing rate of the Borough of Fairlawn, to finance services which the Borough did not provide. These included some of the usual municipal services, like street maintenance, but the tax also covered trash collection and spraying trees on private property. The additional tax supported the social program, including the extensive recreational activities and the adult education discussion courses.

The Association's nine-member Board of Trustees was comprised of civic leaders from New Jersey and officers of the City Housing Corporation. The Board fixed policy, but the day-to-day administration of the city was handled by a manager. The residents had no representation on the Board during the early years, yet the Association had the powers and functions of a municipal government, including taxation.

Citizen representation, on the other hand, was through the Radburn Citizens Association, a voluntary organization formed "to discuss questions of community interest, to formulate and express community opinion, and to cooperate in creating a community life."[67] Organized into seventeen subcommittees, the group was active in community affairs. It sponsored the library and the nursery school and also the adult discussion courses for "personal enrichment" which the Radburn Association then subsidized. These courses were virtually the only exclusively "adult" activity in Radburn's official social program, and reflected the influence of social philosopher John Dewey on RPAA planners.

The Radburn Association was "charged with the happiness of community living." This was defined in *social* as opposed to *political* or *economic* terms. And "social" became virtually synonymous with "recreational." A major goal of the Association was to provide "ample opportunity for participation in healthful and pleasurable recreational hobbies,"[68] and, in fact, many residents came to Radburn because of this.[69] Through taxes levied by the Association, the residents financed two swimming pools, tennis courts, handball courts, a gymnasium, classes, and facilities for basketball, volleyball, ping pong and shuffleboard. They subsidized dancing classes and community dances and paid for two athletic fields and two playgrounds fully equipped for children's games.[70] They supported a daily program during the summer for all children from eighteen months old to eighteen years old,[71] and an afterschool program several days a week during the school year. In addition to bearing the costs of the facilities, the residents also paid for recreational leadership.

There was only one religious institution in the town: The Church in Radburn. It was supported by five Protestant denominations and "all faiths and creeds were invited to its assemblies."[72] The church's offices were supplied by the Radburn Association and religious classes were held in the community center. Hudson noted that "the community is so thoroughly planned in all its social and other functions that there is scarcely any work left for the church except in the field of spiritual welfare."[73]

If conflict was unlikely in such a harmonious setting, conflict might yet originate from the outside. In Radburn it came from Fairlawn. Fairlawn votes defeated the projected high school in 1935, capping a long history of tension between Fairlawners and Radburners. Stein observed that:

> The inability of Radburn to expand in an orderly fashion, as planned, created a very small town with exceptional facilities, in the midst of people for whom the Borough could not afford similar advantages.[74]

A lesson Stein learned from this (and one of his recommendations years after Radburn was built) was that "a separate political entity is required by a New Town with a new form and advanced objectives, so that it may freely and clearly carry out its purposes."[75] He acknowledged that:

> If a town cannot be large enough to include a normal cross-section of American people or to serve with its facilities the entire population of a political unit, the bad social effects might easily outweigh the benefits.[76]

Political mechanisms were necessary as planning *tools* so that the city would not be hindered by *outside* forces; they apparently were not necessary to govern, restrain, or mediate differing values and interests from *within*. Was this because no abiding differences were presumed to exist? Stein could not understand why residents of the "community" he had earnestly labored to create in Sunnyside Gardens could turn against the City Housing Corporation and ultimately strike them in an effort to retain their homes when the

Depression hit and they were no longer able to meet their mortgage payments. In this they were "wrong," he said, "no matter how just their resentment." He mourned the resulting "disunion" which "ended the most constructive development of community life" and lamented that Sunnyside had "never regained its sense of unity as a neighborhood."[77] He could only attribute the dissension to vast and impersonal economic forces; disharmony was not the result of competing interests endemic to human culture. There could be no fundamental discord in such a well-planned city.

In any plan, what is omitted speaks as profoundly as what is included. Both reveal fundamental values and conceptions of reality. So it is with Radburn. In the virtual absence of political institutions, coupled with the prominence given physical nature, we see the arcadian premises underlying "The Radburn Idea." The city's center has always spoken to what a civilization has most valued. The temple, the palace, the court, the market, the bank, and the skyscraper are symbols of the cultures in which they appeared. In Radburn, this sacred space is held by no human artifact, but by physical nature. The vast open space in the heart of Radburn is a reversal of all historic values associated with a city's center. Stein felt that "creative and re-creative leisure" in contact with nature was essential for spiritual renewal.[78] "In the canyons of the city, nature is obliterated by the hard masonry. Man is lost in the stony urban desert, with increasing distances between him and his natural abode of fields and woods,"[79] he wrote. Like other RPAA members, Stein feared that the "machinery of the modern industrial city" was crushing the "spirit of fellowship and cooperation,"[80] and the necessary antidote to this oppressive force could be found solely through beneficial contact with nature. "The Garden City would preserve something of the outdoors within reach of the urban districts," he wrote. "But this is tame. We need the big sweep of hills or seas as tonic for our jaded nerves."[81]

In so many ways, the living green open space was more than the backbone of the neighborhood; it was the very foundation of the community. It provided spiritual renewal; it supported wholesome recreation; it offered a common meeting ground; it symbolized the essence of simple natural democratic cooperation. And, Stein said, "it is so spaciously open that one thinks of a lordly estate, but it is filled with democratic life."[82] One did not have to have great wealth or enjoy aristocratic descent to benefit from the rich verdure and repose nature offered in Radburn.[83]

The central park and its gardens became Radburn's substitute for the greenbelt it did not have. This too would come to be interpreted positively. "Our thoughts as planners," Stein wrote, "were concentrated on the value of the living green close to homes in the midst of superblocks; it seemed more essential than greenbelts."[84] The green, severed from any economic or structural function, became purely a source of beauty and repose. It was no wonder that the Garden Club in Radburn should list as its goals such mixed objectives as "the improvement of gardens in the community" and "the promotion of plans to further the development of Radburn as a garden city."[85] Radburn's design was influenced at least as much by Frederic Law Olmsted as by Ebenezer Howard.[86]

The peaceful green throughout Radburn was evocative of all that Stein saw of value in the new towns experiment. Taking the reader on a spring tour of the city, he describes the little girls happily playing tag, the little boys playing baseball. A family in dripping bathing suits approaches; children gaily ride by on bicycles. Homeowners are trimming hedges or applying a new coat of paint. And "above all, it is the natural green that dominates and controls the picture,"[87] bringing repose to the fortunate citizens of Radburn. It is an idyllic image, one that conveys lush greenery, happy laughter, and serene contentment. The image is clearly contrasted with the "outside world":

> We go through an underpass to the next superblock.... If we look up we may see an automobile against the sky. We had forgotten that our civilization is dominated by motors. Nowhere within the peaceful superblocks are you reminded of their existence. In early June the rosebushes dominate the landscape in the passage between the two superblocks.[88]

Radburn was a leisure city from which the very basis of leisure—productivity through technology—was absent. Hudson likened the town to a "college campus" in its lush and peaceful appearance and the influence its citizens had upon it.[89] Yet college life, like leisure, is dependent upon a materially advanced civilization wealthy enough to release a portion of the populace from the tasks of production. The productivity to which "the town for the motor age" owed its existence was to be found in the great metropolitan centers without which, ironically, there could be no leisure cities such as Radburn.

On redefining the garden city as he did with Radburn, Stein foretold the direction American new towns would take over the next decades.

> From the days of Sunnyside to those of Baldwin Hills Village we have been in search of new or revised solutions of the setting for communities as well as for family and individual living. We have sought ways of bringing peaceful life in spacious green surroundings to ordinary people in this mechanical age. We have tried to simplify the complexity of needs and desire as contrasted with means, and thus to make changes, from the obsolete methods of the dead past, economically feasible.[90]

And these are the very strains which have endured in urban social planning.

5

Greendale and the Greenbelt Program

The Greenbelt Program

The three greenbelt towns built during the Depression years were the most significant American experiment with garden city building the nation has yet seen. Built by the Roosevelt administration between 1935 and 1938, and administered by various federal agencies until they were sold in the early 1950s, the greentowns brought government into housing on an unprecedented scale and into city building for the first time.

Although remembered and admired primarily for their physical planning, the greenbelt cities were far more noteworthy as experiments in social and economic reform, and they still remain close to the urban frontier in this respect. The greentowns were designed for low-income families, and for this reason alone they remain singular in the history of American new towns. They were not mere housing projects, either, although they were built partly in response to housing needs. The decision to build *cities* for the low income was of profound importance since it signified an understanding that housing was only one dimension of "the problem." More fundamental was the general disenfranchisement of the poor who lacked voice and influence. Urban slum dwellers relocated in the greentowns were not simply trading one landlord for another; their residency carried with it the legal and political rights of citizenship.

All the greentowns bore a remarkable resemblance, in detail as well as philosophy, to the garden city of Ebenezer Howard's creation. The greentown program was premised on the single ownership of land, controlled land values, rental of both land and structures, and the conception of the city as a legal and political entity with a municipal government and formal relations with other governmental entities. It was based on the provision of necessary public services by and for the community and financed by them, the symbiotic relationship between rural and urban economies, the functional greenbelt, and the presence of cooperative institutions. The reformist impetus for both Garden City and the greentowns was the same: the impact of urbanization on the new industrial poor—the low-income worker driven from farm to city by economic forces beyond the individual's control.

At the same time, the greentown program represented the continuation of a much longer and contradictory tradition in America. Broadly, this tradition involves a pessimistic analysis of urban life, a rejection of complexity, and a suspicion of human artifice. In American planning history this is related to the arcadian tradition and assumes that social goals are best served through an economizing ethic, spatial arrangements, and contact with physical nature. The social state is presumed to be one of spontaneous harmony; therefore, "social planning" consists of removing barriers to this natural democratic state. Planning itself becomes a tool for restraining change and not for directing it. While the intellectual roots of this tradition are old indeed, they were first combined systematically and applied to the creation of a new city in Radburn. The greentowns represent a continuation of this aspect of American thought so well expressed in "The Radburn Idea."

The story of the greentowns is a fascinating one, told in great detail by Joseph L. Arnold in *The New Deal in the Suburbs*.[1] When the federal government undertook the building of these towns, it did so not to develop garden cities or to demonstrate superior urban design, but to create jobs. The greentowns were a relief effort tied to economic recovery. The Emergency Relief Appropriation Act (ERAA) of 1935 allocated \$4,888,000,000[2] to finance government projects which would provide work for those on relief rolls. Within general guidelines directed towards relieving unemployment, FDR was given wide discretionary power in spending this money. The President was undeniably sympathetic to the housing problem, firmly committed to planning, and genuinely interested in *urban* planning, but his overriding interest in the new towns was indisputably related to their relief function. When funds were finally allocated for the greentown program, the Works Progress Administration had a firm hand in how they were spent. Altogether the towns provided jobs for twenty to thirty thousand men. Arnold reports that more than thirteen thousand men worked on Greenbelt, Maryland, making it one of the largest single projects built during the New Deal.[3]

The greentown program was the brainchild of Rexford Guy Tugwell, Undersecretary of Agriculture, close advisor to the President, and head of the Resettlement Administration (RA) which built the towns. An agricultural economist and faculty member at Columbia University, Tugwell was well aware of the interconnections between urban and rural issues. As he envisioned the project in the early days, the towns would address the needs of both urban and rural poor.

The Resettlement Administration was created by Executive Order on April 30, 1935. A consolidation of a number of existing agencies, the RA had only one new division. This was the Suburban Division, charged with creating the greentowns. Under section (a) of Executive Order 7027, the RA was empowered "to administer approved projects involving resettlement of destitute or low-income families from rural and urban areas, including the establishment, maintenance, and operation, in such connection, of communities in urban and suburban areas."[4]

Broadly speaking, the RA had three purposes: (1) to provide aid (through loans, technology, and educational programs) to those on economically marginal farms which might yet be made productive; (2) to relocate those on submarginal farms to more productive land; and (3) to resettle those who could not be relocated on farm land. This included both urban and rural populations.

Neither Tugwell nor Roosevelt believed it was feasible to relocate slum dwellers in semiagricultural communities nor resettle all displaced farmers on agricultural land.[5] They believed that increasing technological productivity in agriculture would accelerate migration to urban areas which would further exacerbate basic social problems. The economics of urban land meant that rural families, pushed from the farms and seeking jobs in cities, would pay proportionately higher rents to be near employment. Hence the RA based its program on the assumption that the *suburban* community, connected by rapid transit with the city, was the best way to proceed.[6] Land on the fringe of the city was much cheaper, making it possible to provide adequate and affordable low-income housing. The greentown program, Tugwell said "accepted a trend instead of trying to reverse it."[7] He believed that the suburban migration had been temporarily abated by the Depression but that it would resume as the economy improved.

Under Tugwell and John Lansill, director of the Suburban Division, the RA initially planned to build nineteen satellite towns close to major cities, but the number was soon narrowed to nine. These nine towns were the basis for Tugwell's first request for $68 million from Roosevelt.[8] Because ERAA guidelines specified that funds be used for creating jobs, Tugwell competed for money with the Works Progress Administration and the Housing Division of the PWA. Arnold reports that at the September 12, 1935 meeting in which the funds were distributed among the various agencies, Roosevelt approved Tugwell's $68 million request, but allocated only $31 million. Roosevelt further stipulated that all land for the towns be purchased and construction begun by December 15, 1935. Since there was no assurance that Congress would appropriate additional relief money, or that he would commit additional funds to the project, the President stipulated that all the towns had to be *completed* by June 30, 1936. Moreover, he required that the Suburban Division of WPA was to determine if the supply of relief labor justified the expenditure, and, if so, that each laborer was certified as on relief and unemployed.[9]

The conditions attached to the allocation placed the Suburban Division in an incredibly difficult position. It had three months to complete optioning (which necessarily had to be done secretly) and begin construction, and nine months to complete the towns. No plans had yet been prepared since the land had not yet been acquired. Given the precise stipulation and short deadlines, it seemed utterly impossible that the towns could be completed on time. (In truth they were not.)

As a result of this meeting, the Suburban Division was forced to reduce the number of towns from nine to those five where land optioning had already begun. These were the areas near Milwaukee (Greendale); Beltsville, Maryland (Greenbelt); Cincinnati (Greenhills); Bound Brook, New Jersey (Greenbrook); and St. Louis.

Of these five, only three were built. The St. Louis project was dropped when not all land could be purchased by the deadline,[10] and the RA was forced to abandon the Greenbrook project when court action threatened the entire new towns project and much of the New Deal's relief program. A suit entered by a group in the Bound Brook area was successful in enjoining the RA from proceeding further with the town. More importantly, the District of Columbia Court of Appeals, which heard the case in 1936, challenged the constitutionality of the ERAA given the wide latitude the Chief Executive had in spending the appropriation. Greenbrook was dropped from the program, and the Court's decision was not appealed, thereby avoiding the constitutional question.[11] The loss of Greenbrook was particularly unfortunate. Of all the greenbelt towns, it alone was planned for industry and would have been a much purer expression of the garden city than were the others.

Selection of the original nineteen and then nine satellite cities was determined by careful studies of one hundred American cities over the period of 1900 to 1933. Primary consideration was given to past and projected employment stability. Other important criteria were steady economic growth, enlightened labor policies, higher than average wage levels, and a diverse industrial base. A site on the edge of the city, suitable for building a suburban town, was considered, but it was a final consideration, and not a primary one.[12]

The RA's emphasis on employment stability and steady economic growth in determining where to locate the satellite towns was at variance with an important guideline governing the use of ERAA funds. Projects supported through ERAA monies were to be located in areas of severe unemployment. In fact, several of the ERAA requirements were impossible for the RA to meet and still ensure the success of its program. Guidelines specified that projects were to use large numbers of laborers, to be self-liquidating if possible, noncompetitive with private industry, and planned so that laborers could be put to use quickly and dismissed rapidly when employment in private industry increased.[13] The dilemma for the RA was this: Only if high rents were charged could the towns be self-liquidating, yet charging high rents would defeat one of the major purposes of the program. It would also place the RA in competition with private industry for middle-class tenants. Moreover, the RA believed that decent housing could be provided for workers *only* if maintenance costs were kept low. This required the very best in construction and meant that the towns could not be built quickly just to provide immediate employment. "It is our belief that the highest standards of construction are essential to genuinely low-cost building," Tugwell insisted. "We are asking ourselves most searchingly not 'what is the first cost?' but rather, 'what do the forty-year costs add up to?' "[14]

The greentowns were all built between 1935 and 1938. Work began first on Greenbelt, which was also the first to be completed in the fall of 1937. Greenhills and Greendale were finished over the winter and spring of 1938. When the first residents arrived, the physical accoutrements of the towns were in place. Houses were built, utilities were laid, streets were paved, parks and playgrounds were finished, a business center and a school were constructed. The towns were completed, but hardly as originally conceived. The original plan had been for 1,200 housing units in Greendale, 2,000 in Greenbelt, and 1,000 in Greenhills, but only 40 percent of the dwelling units envisioned in 1935 were constructed. Greendale opened with 572, Greenhills with 676, and Greenbelt with 890.[15]

The high costs of the town due to relief labor meant that optimum populations were continually revised downward in line with what the RA could afford to build. This had several consequences. First, the land was developed and the infrastructure laid for a much higher population than could be accommodated in the reduced number of housing units. This development necessarily had to be done in the earliest stages and so was based on the original optimum populations.[16] It also meant that the original calculations for stores, schools, and other facilities were no longer relevant given the reduced numbers of people.[17] Most importantly, the towns could not be self-supporting entities. Studies for the Suburban Division had demonstrated that for the towns to meet their operating costs alone, each required a minimum of 1,000 units with an average family income of $1,250 per unit. With fewer housing units, the towns could be self-supporting *only* if residents paid more than twenty percent of their income for housing, a percentage which would work a severe hardship on this income group.[18] To exceed the $1,250 average annual income per unit would mean that the housing would go beyond the rental range of those for whom the towns were designed. Ultimately the severely reduced populations meant that the federal government was compelled to hedge on its original promise to sell the project towns. As Arnold writes:

The RA was caught in a dilemma. If the towns were transferred to a private housing corporation rents would have to exceed the amount low- or moderate-income families could afford. This would not only contradict all the announced intentions of the Resettlement Administration, but also might be an illegal use of the project funds under the executive order directing the RA to resettle "destitute or low-income families." On the other hand, if the RA were to sell the towns at a price the residents could afford, the result would amount to a gigantic subsidy for a very small number of people. The third alternative was for the RA to retain ownership of the towns.[19]

The government did this until Congress mandated divestiture in 1949. Public Law 65 which ordered their sale gave preference to present residents and to veterans groups. Greenbelt, in fact, was sold to the Greenbelt Veterans Housing Corporation in 1952. In Greendale, long negotiations with the American Legion Community Development Corporation fell through in 1952 and the houses were sold mainly to tenants. The business district and undeveloped property were sold to the Milwaukee Community Development Corporation, which intended to develop the property along the original lines. Greenhills was sold in 1949, the residences and commercial property purchased by the Greenhills Home Owners Association. Some of the undeveloped land was deeded to a county park district, with the remainder bought by the Cincinnati Community Development Corporation.[20] The public law requiring the sale of the greentowns included no requirements for master planning or future development, but plans were drawn up by PHA to guide private developers.[21] In Greendale, the Milwaukee Community Development Corporation hired Elbert Peets as consultant, making for greater continuity. Peets had been the principal architect in the initial building phase.

The greentown program was shrouded in controversy from beginning to end. Apart from the legal challenge posed by Greenbrook, the program received little public support and outright hostility from the real estate industry. *Nation's Business* was not atypical in its criticism of the RA for the program's cost, alleged overstaffing, ignorance of sound business practices, vague thinking, and disdain for private enterprise.[22]

Not surprisingly, the program was attacked repeatedly for its socialistic overtones. Most of FDR's relief and economic recovery projects were so indicted, but the greentowns were especially vulnerable given the federal government's continued ownership of the towns. Contributing to this public suspicion was Tugwell's reputation as a leftist, and when the press dubbed the greentowns "Tugwelltowns," the connotations were much more unsettling to most Americans than "Hoovervilles" had been. The RA was continually at pains to stress that the towns were not meant to be "federal islands" and the government fully intended to divest itself of them once completed. The RA's inability to do this while still preserving the viability of the cities only supported the contention that the entire program was inspired by communists.

The RA was also compelled to justify the expense of the towns, a frequent point of criticism. Although it was impossible to determine their precise cost,[23] Arnold estimates that the three cities had cost the federal government some 36 million dollars.[24] Critics divided the number of housing units into the total expenditure and reproachfully held up the figures for justification. The National Association of Real Estate Boards said that Greenbelt had cost $10,000 per unit because "dream boys" were building "a little Utopia of their own."[25] *Nation's Business* published an article entitled "$16,000 Homes for $2,000 Incomes: Greenbelt, Maryland."[26]

These unit costs were highly misleading. By far the largest expense had been for labor. At Greenbelt, for which Arnold was able to obtain figures, labor costs were 67.8 percent of land development and construction costs compared to a 30 to 45 percent average for private industry.[27] Moreover, the costs included the infrastructure for many more dwelling units than were built, and in fairness these could not be added to the unit cost. Greendale, for example, had 572 homes, yet utilities were laid for a town of 1,200 families.[28] The total cost also included furniture which the Suburban Division sold to the residents and farm improvements on the greenbelts. Nevertheless, housing in the greentowns was undoubtedly more expensive than private industry would have built since a primary construction objective was to build for the long term.

The controversy over the cost of the cities reflected a much deeper confusion over what the program was to do. Among those connected with the project, there was broad agreement that the towns were to serve as a demonstration and thereby influence the larger culture, but beyond this the program was a melange of multiple and often competing objectives. Was it to be a make-work project for the unemployed? A model of efficient planning and construction? A demonstration in garden city building? An experiment in regional planning? In large-scale development? In housing the low-income family? In fostering "community life"?

Indeed it was all of these. For this study, however, two are important: how the greentowns reflected and interpreted the garden city concept, and how they reflected a much longer tradition in American planning so apparent in the new town of Radburn.

The Greenbelt Program and the Garden City Idea

Garden cities were not specifically mentioned in the early days of the project, nor was the term used in the Suburban Division's policy statement, yet the greentowns bear the unmistakable imprint of Ebenezer Howard's ideas and the towns are far closer to Howard's ends and purposes than most subsequent American new towns ostensibly based on his principles.

The kinship with Howard was largely owing to Rexford Tugwell. Clarence Stein, a consultant to the project, reported that Tugwell "fervently believed" in the garden city concept and was apparently more deeply influenced by Howard then by any other idea in his conception of the new towns he proposed to build.[29] Tugwell's was a vision of socio-economic reconstruction, as was Howard's. Both men were only secondarily interested in physical and spatial arrangements.[30]

The Suburban Division's policy statement suggests how influential Howard's principles were for this program:

> The principal objective of this Division of Suburban Resettlement, so far as it concerns the four major projects now being planned, is as follows:
>
> (a) *to secure a large tract of land*, and thus avoid the complications ordinarily due to diverse ownerships; in this tract to create a community, protected by an *encircling green belt*; the community to be designed for families of *predominantly modest income*, and arranged and administered (managed) so as to encourage that kind of family and community life which will be better than they now enjoy, but which will not involve subjecting them to coercion or theoretical and untested discipline; *the dwellings and the land upon which they are located to be held in one ownership*, preferably a corporate entity to which the Federal Government will transfer title, and which entity or corporation *will rent or lease the dwellings but will not sell them; a municipal government to be set up* in character with such governments now existing or possible in that region; *coordination to be established, in relation to the local and state governments*, so that there may be provided those *public services of educational and other character which the community will require*; and, finally, to accomplish these purposes in such a way that the community may be *a tax-paying participant in the region*, that extravagant outlays from the individual family income will not be a necessity, and that the rents will be suitable to families of modest income.
>
> (b) To develop *a land-use plan* for the entire tract; to devise, under the direction of the Administrator, *a system of rural economy coordinated with the land-use plan for the rural portions of the tract* surrounding the Suburban community; and *to integrate both the physical plans, the economies of the rural area and the Suburban community.*[31] [Emphasis by author]

Many elements of the garden city were attempted in the greenbelt towns. Some were implemented successfully, others were not.

Single Ownership of Land

Like Garden City, the greentowns were based on single ownership of land. While land was not collectively owned, the RA intended for the towns to be sold to a corporate entity, preferably comprised of the residents themselves, with the understanding that this entity would sell neither land nor structures.

As in Garden City, land use was not determined by speculative pressures and individual profit seeking. Indeed, much of the land, particularly in the latter days, was in "uneconomic" use. Since the federal government absorbed all losses from this, implicitly the land was held in trust for the community.

Because the towns were federally owned, the property could not be taxed. The cities could neither generate revenue to finance their own services nor be assessed by county agencies for services they provided. The RA had intended all along that the towns be tax paying participants in their regions, but this was not possible until a mechanism was found to contend with the unique jurisdictional problems the towns posed. The system that was adopted was one of "payments in lieu of taxes." As landlord, the federal government collected rents from residents and commercial lessees. From these receipts sums were paid to the towns and to county governments. The salaries of the town treasurer, solicitor, clerk and director of adult education were paid directly by the government. Salaries of other local employees were paid indirectly through sums annually allocated to the town in lieu of taxes.[32] "Payments in lieu of taxes" were equal to tax revenues the land would have generated under ordinary circumstances. Rents, established from the outset, thus covered the costs of municipal services but were insufficient to redeem the capital costs much less pay the interest on the government's investment.[33] Had the towns housed their planned optimum populations, rental income presumably would have covered all operating and capital cost. This was the notion Howard had outlined with his rate rent system.

All housing and commercial property were leased. Initially this was considered desirable, since those for whom the towns were designed could not afford home ownership, but later the rental concept became *essential*. With a severely reduced population base, residents could not support necessary municipal services. Some federal subsidy was required, but this could be done only if the government retained ownership. The necessity to adhere to the rental concept created a number of problems over the years as residents repeatedly and unsuccessfully sought to purchase their homes. The strong tradition of property ownership in America with its conferred social status meant that residents would inevitably resent this RA regulation. As Douglas Marshall, in a dissertation exploring social integration in Greendale, said:

> It was assumed that Greendale would become a normal, thriving, American community, and yet it was also planned as an area of cheaper rent and a place in which people could never buy their own home. This it seems is a fundamental schism in policy. How on the one hand can one have a stable and progressive community and yet, on the other hand, know full well that a large proportion of the population plan to live there only a few years and then move on to a new community? . . . One can have a relatively integrated community provided that the people are not too unstable, *or* one can have a transitional community if one acquiesces to or even encourages a high turnover of the population.[34]

Population turnover was also encouraged through another policy placing a ceiling on annual earned income as a condition of residency. Since the towns were designed for low- and modest-income families, those who earned in excess of $2,000,[35] the established maximum, faced eviction. Although ceilings were occasionally revised to account for local economic conditions, it was not until 1939 that the Farm Security Administration (FSA), raised all income maximums by 25 percent. Even so, a number of families exceeded the limit and faced eviction. The problem was especially severe at Greenbelt, the home of many government employees. Raises for this group frequently put a family just $100 over the maximum.[36] A special committee created to consider the problem told the FSA that:

> You will not discover one family in Greenbelt which has a feeling of security of tenure which is the essence of home life and of community life because of the fear ... that some day the family will get a raise and have to move.
>
> This is the bed of sand on which we are attempting to build a more integrated community life.... This is the insecure foothold from which we are trying to better our relations with surrounding communities and establish our right to recognition by our county and our state.[37]

In 1942 the policy was changed to permit all families to remain regardless of income and to pay higher rents,[38] a solution residents had proposed from the start. However, no families were permitted to purchase their homes as long as the federal government retained ownership of the towns.

Municipal Control

As the Suburban Division's policy statement clearly indicated, the RA considered local self-governance essential and sought to make the towns legal and political entities.

There were a number of reasons for this. First, Tugwell and other RA officials were committed to building cities, and not mere housing projects. Administratively the program was separate from the WPA Housing Division. Second, one consequence for federal policy of the Bound Brook court decision was to necessitate much greater local control over federally financed projects.[39] Third, the greentowns' vulnerability to allegations of socialism made the RA doubly anxious to foster local independence in the towns. Finally, given the uniqueness of the towns, jurisdictional rights were greatly complicated. Without formal autonomy for the cities, residents were considered federal dependents and deprived of the ordinary rights of state citizenship. Establishing the towns as independent municipalities was necessary to restore these rights, and all three were incorporated between 1938 and 1939.

Like many other cities during those years, the greentowns favored the council-manager form of government. They wanted to establish, as Greendale's manager wrote, "a type of village administration in keeping with the descriptive appelation of 'model' that had been tacked on the community by newspaper writers."[40]

This form of governance was considered greatly advantageous because such a system ostensibly removed important administration from the political sphere and made government more efficient, rational, and scientific. Moreover, conducting city council or mayoral elections on a nonpartisan basis, as was done in Greendale, meant that even the elective posts were protected from political coloration. It was believed that this approach kept nonlocal issues and ideological questions out of local affairs.[41] The system adopted by the greentowns was absolutely consistent with Howard's. Good government in Garden City and the greentowns was defined as good administration, with administration considered "good" to the extent that it was removed from political influence. It was presumed that democracy would be protected in this fashion.[42]

Such a view of politics and government was common in the 1930s and remains so today. In the greentowns, however, the political and the administrative were separated even more sharply due to the intergovernmental nature of the towns. Each had *two* managers, one appointed by the council and one designated by the RA. As landlord, the federal government represented its interests through a manager appointed by and responsible only to the government. The salaries of this "resident manager" and his staff were paid directly by the government, while the salary of the town manager was paid by the town. This latter was only a token payment, since in all instances, *both* positions were held by the same person. This was not required, but neither was it entirely coincidental. Certainly this dual position facilitated "effective administration" and coordination of activities, yet the location of so much authority within one individual presented a number of potential problems. Surprisingly there were remarkably few difficulties arising from overlapping of official responsibility.[43] The managers were all graduates of programs specializing in town administration and the residents considered them capable and helpful administrators.

Population Groups

Howard's intention that Garden City house a cross section of the general population was not possible in the greentowns given the mandate to resettle the destitute and low income. Within the income limitations established for residency, an effort was made in Greenbelt to represent a cross section of the Washington, D.C. population based on the 1930 census. Among Greenbelt's first residents, 70 percent were government workers and 30 percent were nongovernment workers; 63 percent were Protestant, 30 percent were Catholic, and 7 percent were Jewish. In all three towns most initial residents were in their child bearing years, suggesting that "low" or "moderate" income referred more to a stage in the economic life cycle than to a relatively constant economic position. In Greenbelt's early years, most adults were under thirty with the average couple having two to three school-aged children.[44] In Greendale, the "typical" family was a young couple with two children and an average income of $1,600 a year.[45]

In a major way, planning decisions regarding house design determined this age-similar composition of the population. Greendale had the largest percentage of single family homes, with 48 percent of all units in two- and three-bedroom houses.[46] Greenbelt had some apartment units and one-bedroom row houses, making it theoretically attractive to older and childless couples; but in all three towns, two- and three-bedroom units were the rule, which virtually guaranteed that the cities would be populated primarily by young adults with children.

For a family applying to live in one of the greentowns, income floors and ceilings were the first criterion to be met. The most important single eligibility requirement was an annual income between $1,200 and $2,000. Originally the towns were planned for "low-income" families, defined by the federal government as $1,000 to $1,999 of annual income. But due to the downward revisions on optimum populations and the necessity to charge rents adequate to cover the towns' operating expenses, by the fall of 1936 the RA began to call its future tenants "moderate-income" families and changed the eligibility floor from $1,000 to $1,200.[47] There was much irony in this. Many of the relief laborers who had worked on the towns were disqualified from living there by too low incomes. In fact, nearly as many Americans were too poor to qualify as too rich. One half of all city dwellers, Tugwell himself had reported, had incomes below $1,200.[48]

Eligibility requirements beyond income excluded Blacks and families with working wives. It is not known how many Blacks applied and were rejected,[49] but the prohibition against working wives disqualified one-third of all families in the Washington area alone from consideration.[50] Still, there were thousands of applicants for this limited number of homes. All were subjected to rigorous screening and scrutiny. According to Arnold:

> Each family filed an application form giving family size, income, present housing facilities, and other information which allowed the Family Selection Section to screen out those not meeting general requirements. Unfortunately, no copies of the form have survived to provide us with the bases on which 3,400 to 5,700 applicants to Greenbelt were eliminated.... Families accepted for investigation were subsequently interviewed by a five-man family selection committee. Following this a social worker visited each family in its home and filled out a "rating sheet." Families were rated on the conditions of their present

housing and also on personal habits and attitudes. Social workers were to determine whether a family in debt was trying to pay it off or was unconcerned, whether they were members of a "socially acceptable organization" or one "likely to conflict with project objectives," and whether they possessed "questionable family life and social attitudes" or were a "well-integrated family group—normal, home loving, self-respecting." A credit check was made and references from two landlords were reviewed. Finally, a physical examination was required for each family.[51]

This investigative process was owing in part to fearful area residents. As early as 1936, one RA official stated that "Prince George's County [the site of Greenbelt] needn't worry about a disreputable community. The Resettlement Administration will take no chance on the experiment failing because of being peopled by shiftless people."[52] Another RA official promised that families would be selected to ensure long-term occupancy, and that those who posed "any exceptional social problems" would be excluded. The policy of the RA's Management Division was "to make sure, before any family is accepted, that it will fit into the proposed community with benefit both to itself and to the community."[53] The RA's concern seems not to have extended to political philosophies.[54]

This close attention to tenant selection was partly attributable to the watchful monitoring of a largely conservative and frequently hostile press. To ensure the success of its social experiment which cut so deeply against the American grain, the RA apparently felt it necessary to select only the very "best" residents. Had all nineteen cities been built, perhaps the screening process might have been less intensive. This was by far the most distasteful part of the program, and the most disappointing too. In this respect the towns departed widely from garden city principles. Skewing for a predetermined "desirable" population was an engineered exceptionalism utterly foreign to Howard's purposes. In the manner in which it ensured its "success," the greentown program strongly resembled Radburn and most American new towns which followed. By whatever means, only the most "desirable" could qualify; the disqualified became the problems of other cities.

Balance and Economic Self-Sufficiency

Howard believed most daily needs should be met within the city itself. Commercial and educational facilities were provided, and industry was essential to the plan.

When the greentowns opened, all had schools and recreational facilities. The government could not build churches, but sites were provided in the plan.[55] While not extensive, the commercial areas included basic retail and service activities. Many of these enterprises were cooperatively run, giving support to Howard's thesis that such activity would flourish in Garden City.

In fact, the cooperative institutions were one of the most notable elements of the greentown program.

There was no industry (and hence little employment) in the greentowns. This seems to have been intentional and reflected Tugwell's belief that future populations would live in the suburbs. The RA was interested in metropolitan areas where existing employment opportunities were good. Greenbrook alone was to have industry, since it was located where future development prospects were excellent. The RA's policy on tenant income minimums was a major obstacle to industrial development in all of the towns. The possibility of an industrial park in Greendale was examined but discarded almost immediately. There was no money for industrial relocation and a study revealed that Milwaukee area factories employed labor at *less* than the minimum income required to live in Greendale.[56]

Cooperative Activity in the Towns

Howard foresaw the rise of a deep spirit of communitarianism emerging from life within Garden City, and many cooperative programs did develop in the three greentowns. Each had a consumer-owned cooperative which ran many of the retail stores. Greenbelt's was so successful that it survived the sale of the town, as did its credit union.[57] Greenbelt had a consumer-owned health clinic, and Greendale prided itself on establishing the first health care plan in the nation organized on a community (v. industrial) basis.[58] Cooperative credit unions were created in two of the towns. Greendale's newspaper was cooperatively owned. Greenbelt mothers founded a cooperative nursery school. Following a local recession in Milwaukee in 1939, Greendale's residents set up an Exchange of Skills office with a roster of available jobs. In 1940 a special fund was created to help the needy.[59]

The extensive cooperative program was clearly more radical than the physical plan which could be (and has been) duplicated by private industry. The cooperative program touched real social and economic issues: food costs, health care, financial needs, and later on even efforts to buy the towns. In all this activity the RA was most supportive.[60] Influenced by the consumer cooperative movement of the 1930s, RA administrators believed, as Arnold reports, that "the spread of economic cooperation to a majority of consumers, not to mention manufacturers, would force a fundamental change in the American economic system."[61] Residents were equally enthusiastic. Their numbers, proximity, and common vulnerability meant that together they could accomplish what none could do alone.

Cooperative enterprise was a keystone of the cooperative program. The retail and credit union coops were funded by loans from the Consumer Distribution Corporation, and not by the federal government as the RA had intended. Long interested in establishing a consumer cooperative in each of the towns, the RA had hoped to lend the residents funds which would be repaid through stock and proceeds sales.[62] When action was finally initiated on this, the proposal was rejected. By then the RA had been merged with the Department of Agriculture and that department's legal counsel, according to Arnold, "regarded the retail coops as contributing to the rural rehabilitation of the residents 'only by a very tenuous line of argument.' "[63] The FSA then turned to the Consumer Distribution Corporation (CDC), an organization financed by Edward A. Filene to advance the cooperative movement in America. First in Greenbelt and then in the other towns, the CDC agreed to establish a nonprofit subsidiary with the exclusive right to operate all commercial facilities. This amounted to controlled competition as in Garden City. All profits were returned to consumers and ownership of the cooperative was turned over to the residents by a specified date. In Greendale, a food store, variety store, drug store, movie theater, shoe repair and valet shop, barber shop, beauty shop, restaurant-tavern, and gas station were opened by Greendale Cooperative Association. Similar enterprises were operated in the other two towns.[64] The FSA, taking the position that the community was acting as a private business, leased commercial centers to the cooperative groups and they in turn operated them. Rents were paid in proportion to receipts, a standard business practice in private enterprise.[65]

Enthusiasm for cooperative enterprise was greatest in the early years. After the war all of the towns opened their doors to private enterprise. When the coops no longer wished to lease certain stores, the Public Housing Administration (PHA) rented them to private proprietors. Greendale's co-op disbanded in 1948, partly due to an antimonopolistic faction in the community, and partly due to the PHA's refusal to renew leases on cooperative businesses. Greenhills' coop ran into financial trouble during the war and divested itself of all enterprise except its food and drug stores. Greenhills Consumer Services survives today. Between 1954 and 1956 Greenbelt' Consumer Services (GCS) divested itself of its less profitable businesses and consolidated its food, drug, and general merchandise stores. Today GCS is a major business enterprise with thousands of members in the Baltimore-Washington area.[66]

The Greenbelt and the Integration of Rural/Urban Economies

In Garden City, the greenbelt's major function was economic. While it also protected against outside encroachment, it served primarily to integrate town and agricultural economies and to control land values within the city.

The RA also intended to integrate agricultural and town economies and this was attempted in Greenhills and Greendale. Land in Greenbelt was unsuitable for profitable farming. Greenhills had four thousand acres in agricultural use and twenty-eight full-time farmers, mostly dairymen, on the greenbelt.[67] At Greendale thirteen full-time dairy farmers and fifty-three part-time farmers resided on the greenbelt.[68] All three towns made free allotment gardens available on the belt. In Greendale this stimulated further cooperative activity. A garden club was organized which bought supplies in bulk and sold them at cost to members. Later the outside garden lots were leased by management directly to the garden club which prepared and fertilized the land for $1 per lot.[69] A collective farm was proposed for Greendale's greenbelt, but the idea was never executed.[70] Instead the RA improved rural homes and built farmers' markets in town to aid distribution.[71]

Despite the appearance of successful integration, town and country economies remained separate. Greenhills' farmers continued to market their produce almost entirely in Cincinnati[72] and the farmers' markets in Greendale were not successful.[73] As Marshall discovered in his research on Greendale, farmers "take no part in commercial affairs; they often voice the fact that they have no *interest* in the village."[74] Greentown planners had repeatedly argued that the greenbelt would break down "one more barrier that creates strangeness and misunderstanding among different groups of people,"[75] yet Douglas found the contrast between planning assumptions and actuality marked indeed:

> The farmer was to be in an advantageous position; he was to enjoy the conveniences of suburban life and his social and economic life was to be centered largely in the village. This happy state of affairs has not come to pass, and there is little likelihood that it will, *unless something is done to rectify this condition.*[76] [Emphasis by author]

One reason why little was done "to rectify this condition" was that planners viewed the greenbelt's importance differently from RA administrators. At least in its publications, the RA tended to emphasize the *rural* use of the greenbelt,[77] while planners emphasized other functions. At the request of Frederick Bigger, Tracy Augur, an advisor to the program and an RPAA member, did extensive research on the appropriate size of the greenbelt. Size, of course, related to functions which planners thought the greenbelt should perform:

> The width of the protective belt should be such that persons living at the edge of the community will not be tempted to walk across it to shopping facilities which may spring up in the surrounding territory, but will instead find it more convenient to go to their own shopping centers within the community. It should be wide enough and open enough in character that persons crossing it by automobile will distinctly realize that they have left one community and entered another. It should be so wide that private subdividers of adjoining land cannot make a plausible demand that their tracts be connected with the water and

sewer lines and streets of the community. It should be so wide that it would form a natural boundary between school districts so that there would be no temptation to place part of the community in the same school district with unorganized areas outside.[78]

The difference between Howard's and the greentown planners' approach to the greenbelt illustrates how the towns were at once based on garden city principles and at the same time quite foreign to them. Planners saw the greenbelt as a vehicle for centering the lives of residents within the town itself. The greenbelt also served as an expanse of nature preserved for recreation and renewal. But above all, the greenbelt was to be a buffer protecting the town from "undesirable contamination."[79] At Greendale's decennial, Stein warned of the threat metropolitan expansion presented to Greendale's integrity:

> [This metropolitan advance] covers the land with a disorderly wreckage of structures. The roads are lined with an ugly chaotic mixture of gas stations, eating places, and packing-box abodes. Ultimately a specific builder buys a large farm or two just beyond the village border, and erects rows and rows of unsightly, badly constructed houses. They are beyond the jurisdiction of the village, as well as that of the big city. No authority can regulate the construction or maintenance of houses, or highways, or the quality of the utilities. The families who have come in search of space and natural beauty find that they have traded city slums for suburban blight.
>
> Once physical decay and social degeneration has blighted the surroundings, there is no way to keep it from spreading its evil character into the lovely village it surrounds. A wide open area is needed just as much to prevent destruction from the spread of blight, as from forest fire.[80]

The Greentowns and "The Radburn Idea": Social Planning in Greendale

> *Should you ask why we love Greendale,*
> *Find it fun to work and play here,*
> *We all answer, we all tell you . . .*
>
> *It's awakening to bird-song*
> *In the rosy dawn of springtime!*
> *Watching frisky squirrels cavorting!*
> *Romping space for pets and children,*
> *Far from city's threatening traffic!*
> *It's group picnics at grounds southward,*
> *And the suppers cooked o'er charcoal*
> *In one corner of our gardens;*
> *Baby's playpen in the sunshine,*
> *Knowing well that naught can harm him!*
>
> —Vivian Husher, "This is Greendale"

For FDR, the primary purpose of the greentown program had been to create jobs. For Rexford Tugwell, who had conceived the project, an essential purpose was to address the housing needs of the rural and urban poor. Federal initiation of the program, and the large amount of subsidy involved, pointed to the *structural* nature of the housing problem in an industrial economy. The very existence of the greentowns implied a tacit acceptance that the problem could not be solved by unaided private industry. This alone made it an extremely daring venture in socio-economic reform.

The significance of the greentowns was differently interpreted by the planners who executed the project. They cumulatively restated the program's objectives and redefined its importance. In a 1944 report, for example, Greendale's manager asserted that all the greenbelt towns were "an adaptation of the English 'garden city.'"[82] As he interpreted it, this adaptation bore little resemblance to the RA's own policy statement and even less to Howard's ideas. "In the planning of Greendale," the author wrote, "perhaps the primary objective was to show how better conditions and a full community life could be developed in a suburban town." A second objective was "to give [Greendale's] residents some advantages of both city and country life in a community so protected that time would not produce the usual run-down neighborhood." A third purpose was "to provide for families of modest income, good housing at low rents in an environment conducive to healthful, wholesome living"; and finally, "to ease the severe unemployment that existed in the building trades and allied industries at the time of construction."[83]

This last "objective" subtly distorts an important aspect of the program, since the towns were funded to create work for *unskilled* labor. But the point is larger. It shows the extent to which the American interpretation of the garden city departed from the economic and institutional changes outlined by Howard. The garden city was instead directed towards the much more elusive goals of fostering "community life" and "good living." In this the program was influenced by RPAA philosophy. Whereas Rexford Tugwell initiated the project, basic decisions and key policy statements regarding the actual planning of the towns was the responsibility of Chief of Planning Frederick Bigger, an RPAA charter member and close associate of Clarence Stein. Stein served as consultant to the project. Other RPAA members were directly involved in planning the towns. The RA had the pick of the finest planners in America; during the Depression years even the most eminent found work scarce.

The redirection of the program followed the path of Radburn.

Physically "The Radburn Idea" meant the superblock, with its interior parks, curvilinear streets and cul-de-sacs; the separation of pedestrian and vehicular traffic; specialized and single-use roads; houses turned inward; and the park as the backbone of the neighborhood. Not all the towns conformed precisely to this physical plan, but all planners were influenced by it.[84] The concept was developed most fully at Greenbelt where the superblock was extensively used.[85] It was used to some extent in Greenhills, but not at all in Greendale. The variation from city to city was due to the autonomy accorded each planning team. Separate teams, coordinated by a general planning director, worked on each of the towns.

Elbert Peets and Jacob Crane, Greendale's planners, favored conventional streets and traditional architecture. Roughly half of the housing units in Greendale were detached single-family homes with an average yard area of 5,000 square feet.[86] Row houses were more numerous in the other towns, permitting planners to group them and thus open up interior parks.

Despite differences in physical design, all three towns were based on similar philosophical assumptions. In this they evoked the social planning which lay behind "The Radburn Idea" and revealed the extent to which the towns were at once forward-looking and inspired by a longing for the past.

Greentown planners sought to restore and preserve a type of community they believed had existed in an earlier America. Significantly, it was not the preindustrial *city* that provided their model. "Orderly development" and "preindustrial" were contradictory concepts. The preindustrial city was highly compact and congested. It was a walking city by necessity, not choice. Land use was highly mixed, with shops, homes, and manufacturing scattered throughout. Social classes were not segregated spatially, and homes of the poor bordered those of the well-to-do. A jumble of sounds, smells, structures and activities, the city was scarcely harmonious. Politically it was aristocratic, with a small elite dominating urban affairs. With few exceptions, preindustrial cities grew by accretion, not by design.[87] The greentowns were modelled not after the preindustrial *city* but after an idealized conception of the preindustrial *village*. To planners, "community" was virtually synonymous with "village."

Physically, the preindustrial village was limited in size and scale by the distance a person could walk. The natural contours of the land determined the form of the town. The village was low in density. Its focal point was the town center, the heart of the community's social, political, commercial, and religious life.

With her colonial architecture, freestanding houses and white-washed picket fences, Greendale especially had the look of a village. Nevertheless, *all* the greentowns emulated the physical landscape of the bygone village. All were of walking dimensions with low residential density. Each had a center intended to be the cultural focus of community life.[88] And each was carefully designed in accord with natural topography. In Greendale, the indigenous shape of the ground had determined the location of roads, paths, and buildings. Greenbelt's crescent-like shape was similarly decided by natural landforms, as was the form taken by Greenhills.[89] These were truly communities of homes in the midst of nature. In Greendale, grazing cattle and great fields of grain permanently framed and embraced the houses.[90]

Within the physical form of the village, planners emphasized family life, friendly association and cooperation, and simple pleasures—presumed *social* elements of village society. In this conception of the good community as a simple, democratic and harmonious village, planners were surely influenced by the theories of urban sociologists, and particularly those of Louis Wirth.[91] Relationships in urban societies, Wirth observed, were segmentalized, superficial, anonymous, transitory, formal, impersonal, and "secondary." By contrast, relationships in rural and folk societies were spontaneous, personal, informal, holistic, and permanent. Contacts were "primary," determined by blood and geographical propinquity. Urban and rural societies were further distinguished by differences in size and density.[92] For greentown planners, controlling *size* was to become the single most important tool for creating and preserving village society.

Theories of folk/urban contrast similarly shaped assumptions about village polity. RA administrators paid much closer attention to political institutions in the towns than did planners who tended to believe that face-to-face informal interaction (made possible by the village environment) obviated the need for formal, intervening political mechanisms or institutions. It was assumed that citizens would resolve their differences through informal communication. For this reason Radburn planners and so many associated with the greentown project heartily approved of citizens' associations and preferred them to more formal governmental structures. Citizens' associations were the counterpart of the village's town meeting.

Planners only partially based "the good city" on the preindustrial village. They wished to recreate the village physically, socially, and politically, but not economically and only partly technologically. Leisure and a high standard of living, economic byproducts of the industrial process, were not only welcomed but helped define the good city. Smokestacks and concrete slabs were foreign to the towns, but the automobile was common, and necessary to the scheme. Decentralization, which enabled the realization of the good city, was absolutely dependent on the automobile. Planners wished to accommodate progress within a vision of village life. They wanted what Stein wished for Greendale: that the town might "grow and prosper—without losing [its] delightful character as a small neighborly village."[93]

RA officials may have shared this image of the good community as village, but if so, they chose different means to realize it. If restoring the lost age meant removing "barriers," then barriers for RA administrators were economic and institutional. For planners, in contrast, barriers were mostly physical and spatial.

Equations between social goals and technical means were a fundamental part of greentown planning. As late as 1967, Albert Mayer, principal architect for the Greenbrook Project, revisited the greentowns for the readers of *The Journal of Housing* and drew attention to the relationship between physical design, nature, and emotional stability. He correlated the greenbelt with the low incidence of juvenile delinquency in Greenhills, and quoted a Cincinnati judge as saying:

> I believe the interior parks have helped every child grow emotionally in every possible way. I am impressed with the overall stability and the very many great achievements of those now adult and known to me.... No doubt another very significant factor... is the close contact every youngster has with nature and its animal life, to some extent in the parks but especially in the greenbelt.[94]

One cannot overstate the role greentown planners assigned to comprehensive planning in addressing major social problems. They argued repeatedly that comprehensive design enabled working-class families to enjoy all the amenities of an upper-middle-class suburban community at rents well within their means.[95] Because planning was efficient and economical, broad social goals could be served without sacrifice or without challenge to entrenched and special interests. Distributional problems became *engineering* problems, and planning itself became a *technical* method for achieving social goals.

This correspondence between social ends and technical means is nowhere better illustrated than in the manner in which planners sought to protect the simple democratic life they were confident had been created in the towns. The *greenbelt* and the *neighborhood* unit were their most important tools. Both were used to control *size*, the pivotal variable in maintaining village society. Unlike Howard, greentown planners favored controlled size for *social*, not economic reasons. Size affected neighborliness and interaction. "A community must be small enough to permit friendly association," Stein told an audience at Greendale. "It is only in small places that everyone can know everybody and associate with as many as he wants."

Stein attributed magical, transforming qualities to the small city. "It does something to folks.... Getting up and talking and being listened to at the town meeting gives a fellow self-confidence that affects his business as well as social life."[96] Smallness also meant increased opportunities for individual recognition and greater participation in civic affairs. Greendale's manager observed that the Citizens' Association had been a training laboratory for citizenship. "The people have opportunities to express themselves on community affairs, and many who never before stood on their feet to talk before a crowd are acquiring a new ability that can make them more useful citizens."[97]

Planners likewise assumed that small cities would produce better citizens. As one observer reported, Greendale's planners recognized that "living conditions and environment greatly influence the attitude of families toward community affairs, and that families living in big cities often lose nearly all contact with community affairs and become indifferent to their responsibilities as citizens."[98] It was necessary to build small cities to *preserve* the democratic future. New towns, so interpreted, were the noblest of patriotic efforts.

How then was Greendale to reach her optimum population—"to grow and prosper without losing her delightful character as a village"? The answer lay in carefully integrating neighborhoods into the larger city. As in Radburn, the neighborhood unit was the building block for this. The neighborhood was determined by the elementary school within it, its size limited by the distance a child might conveniently walk to school. This distance was assumed to reflect the geographical span of friendly contact.

Design encouraged this place-based definition of community. Each "neighborhood village" (as Stein called them) was to be organized around its own center. Open space separated and clearly delineated one neighborhood from another. Residents were to find their primary associations within the neighborhood unit. A wider frame of reference was encouraged only where necessary. Libraries, swimming pools, a large shopping center required the combined support of many neighborhoods. In the greentowns, Howard's "clustered cities" concept was applied *within* the city itself. As far as possible, each neighborhood was to be socially autonomous.

Through building new and discrete neighborhoods whereby place-based relationships were induced, the city might continue to grow without losing its village character. But even this growth had a final constraint. The greenbelt resolutely limited the city's physical expansion and form. This was "the greatest advantage of the greenbelt," according to Stein, because only with a limited size (which the greenbelt ensured) "[could] the neighborly character be sustained—and the common interest of all in their community affairs be kept alive."[99] Together with carefully orchestrated neighborhoods, the greenbelt thus guaranteed the timeless harmony of the village. Change from *within*, as well as from without, was restrained.

While the physical design of the greentowns was innovative for the times and represented a major departure from conventional urban form, the philosophy behind it could only be described as conservative—and extremely so. As greentown planners viewed it, planning was neither perceived nor used to direct change; it was used to *restrain* it. Those elements of the garden city which appealed to planners were those which assisted them in recreating and preserving an era which had been lost with industrialism. A park and playground, a limited size, a belt of encircling green—these were simple tools which promised such great social ends.

On the decennial of their town, Clarence Stein assured Greendale's residents their greenbelt protected them and would continue to do so as long as they chose to preserve it. In truth the choice wasn't theirs. Their greenbelt could be sustained only under a system of land valuation resistant to market economies. This required either public ownership of, or permanent control over, the land. The greentowns never had common land ownership, but they did have single ownership and a land use system not determined by market pressures. When the federal government sold the towns, land within them was no longer so protected. Given multiple ownership and the towns' proximity to developing metropolises, land in the greentowns succumbed to the pressures of speculative development and rising taxation. Greendale lost its greenbelt and its village character because change could not be so easily restrained.

6

Levittown, New Jersey: "More House for the Money"

Easterners have long known Levitt & Sons as one of the largest builders on the East Coast, but to other Americans the firm is probably best known for its three "Levittowns," communities built on Long Island, New York; in Bucks County, Pennsylvania; and in Burlington County, New Jersey. The best of these, as well as the most significant for this study, is the third Levittown, begun in 1958 and built largely in the 1960s. As a venture of private capital, the firm was not interested in building garden cities; in fact, it was only secondarily interested in building communities. Above all, Levitt & Sons was in the business of building houses, and through offering "more house for the money," a phrase synonymous with a Levitt house, the firm discovered its metier. The Levitt house had tremendous appeal. "All this for $10,000," said one truck driver who toured the second Levittown. "I'd work like a dog for the rest of my life if only I could live here."[1]

Despite the profitmaking nature of the enterprise, Levittown, New Jersey is certainly within the garden city tradition. The town is included here to illustrate one of the central themes of this study: that American planned cities, given all their variety, are remarkably more alike than different, and most are philosophically closer to one another than to Howard's idea of the garden city. Second, while Levitt & Sons had no intention of emulating Ebenezer Howard's social ends, Levittown, New Jersey contained at least one feature which placed this town closer to Howard than most American "garden cities" have been: the town was a recognized legal and political entity. To understand its relationship to the garden city it is necessary to consider the town's two predecessors as well as the Levitt approach.

Abraham Levitt became the largest builder on the East Coast by applying the principles of mass production to housing. He used specialized labor, held to an exacting time schedule, and was meticulous in his attention to detail—to the point where "eight pounds of yellow nails [were] delivered (on time) to every seventh house—which happens to have yellow siding."[2] Houses were built from precut lumber, and wherever possible everything was packaged in house-size units. Highly specialized crews moved from house to house, each attending to a specified task. It was thus possible to construct a Levitt house within a short time with no sacrifice in quality. The lower housing costs were made possible because houses were similar. All had the same basic floor plan. (In the second Levittown the floor plans were identical; in the third there were several housing types.) Variation was achieved through color, location of carports, and siting of the house on the lot.

The Levitt firm first learned these cost saving techniques during World War II when the firm built more than 2,000 houses for the Navy in Norfolk, Virginia.[3] After the War, knowledge gained from the Navy contract was applied in the building of "Levittown," the first of the mass-produced suburbs which would make the firm famous.

Levittown, New York, was built on Long Island between 1947 and 1951. Intended to supply rental housing primarily for veterans, the new community quickly attracted a wave of interested buyers, most of them middle class. The Levitts, of course, had not anticipated the great demand for home ownership that followed World War II. Initially they planned to construct a few thousand homes in the area, yet by 1950 they had built more than 15,000 homes and the town had grown to a population of 60,000. For its time it was the largest community ever built by a single developer.

The town was built in classic subdivision style, with the firm acquiring additional land only as sales progressed. There was no master plan; instead, parcels of land were developed as needed. The resulting improvisational form of the community meant that Levitt-built homes abutted non-Levitt property and houses, making for some difficulties in administering recreational facilities and confusing irregularity in street layout.

Despite the absence of a master plan, however, the first Levittown clearly demonstrated Levitt's intent to provide more than mere housing in his communities. Homes were grouped around "Village Greens" consisting of neighborhood shops, a playground and a swimming pool. Each of these "neighborhood" shopping areas contained grocery, drug, barber and specialty shops, and a filling station. (No large shopping center was built, although Levitt & Sons soon came to regret the omission. Another developer built a center nearby and reaped handsome profits from patronage by Levittowners.) Levitt did not build elementary schools, as he did in his later towns, but sites were set aside for them, and also for churches.

The early and rapid success of this development prompted the firm to plan another community, Landia, also to be located on Long Island. Landia was to be a totally planned community of 6,500 people in 1,750 homes built on 675 acres of land. It was to include not only residential, but commercial, industrial, educational, and recreational facilities.[4] The inclusion of industry is important, since there had been none in the first Levittown. The firm considered this attempt to provide employment for the residents "a great step forward."[5] All land had been acquired, a major improvement over the first Levittown, which meant that the firm was able to plan "right down to the last tree and shrub."[6]

Unfortunately, Landia was never built. With the advent of the Korean War the housing industry was diverted into defense housing, and following the war the firm went on to other things. Although Landia was never built, the town merits close attention given its conceptual importance to subsequent Levitt-built towns and its clear connection with the American garden city tradition.

The community's features and planning assumptions were carefully explained by Alfred S. Levitt, one of the principals in the firm, in an article published in the *Journal of the American Institute of Planners.*[7] Alfred had designed Landia. Trained in architecture and greatly interested in promoting better planning, Alfred was much impressed with the work of the Regional Plan Association of New York and acknowledged its influence on his ideas for the town. While not specifically acknowledged, the influence of Clarence Stein is also apparent in Landia.

Like other Levittowns, Landia was designed for young families in their child bearing and rearing years, families with an annual (1950) income of $5,000. There were no apartments in the community. All houses had three bedrooms, a feature which additionally inclined the population towards young families. Had the community been built in 1951 as planned, the Landia house would have cost $13,000 making it a slightly more expensive model than most other Levittown houses. But where else could one buy so much for so little? The house included three bedrooms, two baths, a living room, dining area, kitchen and two-car garage. The kitchen was completely equipped with refrigerator, range, dishwasher, clothes washer, and freezer. The house had built-in shelves and drawers, a three-way fireplace, bookcases in the living room, exhaust fans and a picture window. It was situated on a lot at least 80' x 100' which was completely landscaped. Here, as in subsequent houses, all Levitt homes were surrounded with greenery. Each had an average of five fruit and shade trees, a dozen or so evergreens, a lawn, and additional shade trees between the sidewalk and the street.[8]

Beyond "more house for the money," the public and community facilities planned for Landia were considerable, indicating once again the firm's intent to build communities and not mere housing projects. These included 22 miles of roads, 43 miles of sidewalks, two drainage basins, six miles of concrete drainage sewers, 27 miles of water mains, 57 acres of parks and parkways, 38 acres of land for school sites, and ten acres for prospective churches. Levitt & Sons also planned to build a complete shopping center, a railroad passenger and freight station, parking lots, a professional-size baseball field with grandstands and dressing rooms, a preschool nursery, swimming pools, and a town hall.[9]

Levitt also planned for social and recreational needs. In addition to swimming pools, playgrounds and the baseball field, Landia was to have tennis courts, parks, and a pond suitable for ice skating. A town hall was also planned which Alfred intended as "the center of community life." The hall was to contain an auditorium capable of seating 600, a completely equipped kitchen, and offices for a community manager.[10] In the absence of a taxing authority or government, provision for maintaining recreational facilities was also worked out. The Levitt organization proposed to form the Landia Association, consisting of all homeowners, to which these facilities would be given. Through an annual assessment members would support the maintenance of these jointly owned facilities. Alfred Levitt calculated that this maximum assessment would not exceed $36 a year, but in any event, the maximum would be fixed by a clause in the deed.[11] Actual upkeep would be the responsibility of a manager hired by the Association.

The Landia Association differed in scope, but certainly not in kind, from the Radburn Association. There were other commonalities between the two towns, most notably, the similarity between "planning principles" governing Landia's design and "The Radburn Idea." As Albert listed them, these were:

(1) The residential area is divided into seven separate neighborhoods, with no through streets in any neighborhood.
(2) The 30-acre industrial area is an integral part of the community, but is separated from the rest of Landia by a wooded shelter belt.
(3) Landia has only one through street in its interior; all community facilities are located on it and the seven neighborhoods are connected to it by means of circumferential drives which surround each neighborhood.
(4) Parks serve as part of the separation scheme of the neighborhood.
(5) Parks are located at the end of major streets.
(6) The sites for the two public schools are so located that children can walk to school, thus eliminating the expense of school buses.[12]

In other physical characteristics, and especially in the language used to justify them, Landia was reminiscent of Radburn. Some examples: Landia eliminated the gridiron street pattern, which "[meant] greater convenience, safety, quiet, and peace." "Landia [was] designed for neighborhood living both because it [was] good planning and because people like to belong to a neighborhood." "Separated from the rest of the community by a shelter belt of trees is the industrial area where two or three light industries [would] be located." "Parks and playgrounds [would] be placed at intervals along the drive, so every house [would] be near at least one park and playground." "Natural features of the land determined the boundaries wherever possible."[13]

Alfred Levitt paid close attention to siting in Landia. The town hall was located adjacent to the shopping center in order to share a common parking lot. The railroad station and baseball field also shared common parking space. Playgrounds were planned near the shopping center so play space would be convenient for shopping mothers. Alfred justified these and other locational decisions on the basis of economy and efficiency, values which were not so very different from those Stein celebrated in writing of Radburn's significance.

The Levitt organization planned to build Landia after the war, but the town was never begun. Instead the firm went on to build a second Levittown in lower Bucks County, Pennsylvania. The decision to build in Pennsylvania followed a successful lobbying effort by the Levitt firm in which the federal government declared the area a Critical Defense Housing Area. Such a designation meant relaxed credit restrictions for home buyers and gave additional government support for mortgages, thereby reducing the builder's risks.[14] Begun in 1951, Levittown, Pennsylvania, was based largely on Landia.

The second Levittown was built in part to provide housing for steelworkers. In 1950, U. S. Steel announced its intention to build a new plant, Fairless Works, in lower Bucks County, a semirural area. Immediately other steel-related industries, hoping to supply Fairless Works, moved into the area. Of course all these workers required shelter. To avoid the problems of company towns, U. S. Steel for many years had called upon John Galbreath, a Columbus real estate agent, to provide housing for its employees. The company financed the work while Galbreath built the houses and sold them directly to their owners. Asked by the steel company to build the Bucks County homes, Galbreath bought up 2,000 acres on which he planned to construct 4,000 prefabricated houses.[15] This activity naturally brought much speculation in land, with many small developers bidding against one another. A group of area farmers, determined to sell to one person or not at all, banded together, and Levitt bought his land from this group. He paid a great deal for it, too: $2.5 million for his first 2,000 acres and even more for the remainder.[16]

Hence there were two adjacent developments in the area—Galbreath's Fairless Hills and Levitt & Sons Levittown. Levitt planned for a population of 60,000 in 16,000 homes to be built by 1954.[17] Besides providing housing for Fairless Works employees and other steel-related industrial workers, the firm hoped to cash in on the housing potential continued industrial suburbanization would bring.[18] Levittown, Pennsylvania, is about twenty miles from Philadelphia.

As with Landia, the land in Levittown #2 was all contiguous, permitting a master plan. "Here is a town that has been planned in its entirety," *House and Home* quoted Bill Levitt as saying. "We bought 5,000 acres and we have planned every foot of it."[19] The firm planned for the residential, commercial, light industrial, educational, and recreational needs of the community.

The basis of the plan was the neighborhood unit, as it was with Landia. The firm proposed a series of eight "master blocks," each a mile square, and each containing about 1,400 houses. This master block was not unlike Stein's superblock, with boundary streets carrying through traffic and residential streets relatively traffic free. At the heart of the master block was the elementary school (a change from Landia where schools were placed between neighborhoods). Children did not cross traffic, and no child had to walk more than one-half mile to school. Block centers held recreational facilities with a swimming pool and playground in each. Each master block contained four neighborhoods of 300 to 400 families each. These neighborhoods were arranged on curved streets, with houses all facing the block, reminiscent of Radburn.

As in Landia, an area was designated for light industry in order to enrich the tax base. The industrial area was separated from the residential area by a strip of greenbelt and located at one end of the town.[20]

The Levitt organization sought to concentrate commercial facilities in a large shopping mall located at one end of the city. This was to attract non-Levittowners as well. Small neighborhood shops, as in Levittown #1, were kept to a minimum. This time the firm intended to profit from the drawing power of a regional shopping center.

Community facilities were also considerable. The firm built a complete water and sewage system, a railroad station for commuters, and a community building. A professional-size baseball field was constructed. In addition to pools and playgrounds, Levitt planned for "some 250 acres of "forest preserves"—heavily wooded sections clean of underbrush but otherwise as natural as possible."[21] There were plans to transform a gravel pit into a community lake after construction was completed. Covering the plan, *House and Home* concluded that "no other city of comparable size in the country will have as much usable recreation space."[22]

The city was generously landscaped, with twenty feet of "greenbelt" on either side of the parkways bordering the master blocks. The standard number of trees and shrubs were planted on each home lot, and even the shopping mall was lined with thousands of trees interspersed between parking strips. The planting bill alone came to five million dollars.[23]

There were no apartments in the town. All houses had three bedrooms and sold for $9,900 the first year and $10,500 the second year.[24] At the request of the steelworkers union, Levitt during the first year held back 1,500 houses for rent at $65 a month.[25] There were 500 houses which sold for $17,000, houses modeled after those the firm had earlier built in the country club district of Long Island. A 1954 report of the Institute for Urban Studies at the University of Pennsylvania profiled the early residents: There were "a large proportion of children, most of them between the ages of 0 and 5, almost no teenagers, few young adults, but a very heavy representation of adults between the ages of 25 and 35, few middle-aged adults, and almost no old people at all."[26] There were no Blacks.[27]

Despite the studied master planning and the careful orientation toward the neighborhood unit, the second Levittown shared a drawback of the first. Because of the way land had been acquired, the Levitt property straddled four political units. This meant that residents paid taxes and voted in different localities, some of which (due to proximity to Fairless Works) were decidedly more affluent than others. The multijurisdictional fabric of the community meant horrendous problems for the developer who had to deal separately with each unit and thus became embroiled in the political disputes of all. But it meant far more serious problems for the community. Since the town was located in four civil divisions, there were complicated problems with respect to police protection, tax assessment, the administration of recreational facilities, the growth of the community into areas zoned for other uses—and particularly problems centering on the schools.

Levittown was designed around the neighborhood school concept. However, since the community was located in several different civil divisions, school districts did not correspond with the lines of the site plan. Children had to walk excessive distances to schools outside their neighborhoods. The problems raised for education by multiple jurisdictions were known from the beginning, but the Levitt organization did not consider them insurmountable and very early pursued redistricting. The recommendation to redistrict was made when the area was still undeveloped and Levitt was the sole owner. However, by the time the changes were made, the general area was occupied and property owners in the more well-to-do townships objected to efforts to move them into a less well-to-do political unit. They brought the matter to court, and the court ruled in their favor. The inability to change existing political boundaries negated many of the advantages of Levitt's site and master planning.[28]

The third Levittown, begun in New Jersey in 1958, was a direct result of the success of the first two. Despite earlier problems, the Levitt firm had found both towns profitable and intended to continue large-scale development. Then too the firm was learning more all the time. In fact, major jurisdictional difficulties in the second town were what made the third site such a desirable one: Levitt's purchase essentially coincided with the township unit. Levittown #3 was located in Willingboro Township on sparsely settled agricultural land seventeen miles from Philadelphia and within ten miles of the second Levittown, making it a prime site for industrial development. Aside from small farmers, the land was almost uninhabited. A small Quaker settlement of five hundred people, the village of Rancocas, was located in the township, but after Levitt had purchased his land, he had the boundaries changed to incorporate the village into a neighboring township. This meant that Levitt & Sons had a virtual *tabula rasa* on which to construct their third city. Additionally, since the town would correspond with the township's boundaries, Levittown, N.J., could have its own government.

The firm announced its purchase and its intention to build a third town in 1955. By that time William Levitt was the principal figure in the organization, father Abraham having retired and brother Alfred having sold his interest to brother William. Unlike Alfred, William had little patience with professional planners, and in fact did not hire one until a decade later when the firm was building developments worldwide. Gans notes that William's goals with the New Jersey town were to "build another profitable development and a better community, more comprehensively planned in advance and more completely stocked with public facilities."[29] While the Levitt firm had always emphasized the house in its marketing, William strengthened this approach and downplayed the importance Alfred had placed on "community." Nevertheless, fearful that charges of "homogeneity" and "massiveness" levelled against the first two Levittowns might hurt sales in the third, William sought to answer his critics in a piece written for *Good Housekeeping*.[30] His sensitivity to the criticism of planners led him to mix house types on the same block—a heretical concept, but one which tended to minimize age and income homogeneity.

Since Levitt owned the land, and since there was but a single governmental entity to deal with, a fairly complete master plan was quickly developed. The first residents of Levittown, New Jersey arrived in October of 1958. Levitt intended to build 12,000 houses by 1965,[31] but only 6,000 were built by that date. This slowed growth is sometimes attributed to the racial integration of the town, begun in 1960 when a court order mandated the enforcement of a state antidiscrimination law, but it was more likely due to the relative saturation of the area's housing market. Gans reports that no market research was done before the third town was planned. In late 1963 the township voted to change the town's name from Levittown to Willingboro, as it is legally known today.

In physical form, Levittown #3 did not differ markedly from Levittown #2. In fact, the third master plan was almost identical to the Bucks County one. Twelve neighborhood "parks," as they were called, each containing some 1,200 homes, were organized around an elementary school, playground, and swimming pool complex. A regional shopping center, Willingboro Plaza, was located at the edge of town to attract both local and nonlocal business. Through traffic was kept out of the neighborhoods; interior "lanes" were designed for local transit, while parkways surrounding the master blocks carried heavier traffic. Houses were located on cul-de-sacs and sited to face greens as often as "lanes." The industrial area was located at one end of the town and separated from the rest of the community by a strip of green. The entire town was completely landscaped, as in the earlier ones, but here "conservation areas," or green strips, ran through each neighborhood.

As before, Levitt planned to construct a full range of community facilities, including water and sewage plants and a government building/community center which was donated to the community. Church sites, scattered throughout the neighborhoods, were set aside and given to congregations who sought them.[32]

Like the second Levittown, the third development appealed to the lower-middle-class buyer. Herbert Gans's research on the first three thousand families who moved to the new town indicates that these early residents were young families who settled there to raise their children. Most homeowners were under forty, and roughly half were between thirty and forty. The median family size was 3.9 people. One-third of the families had only preschool children, whereas only five percent had a majority of their children in high school. Fifty-six percent of the men were white-collar workers, 26 percent were blue collar. The median family income was $7,125. House size and cost largely determined the class structure of the town, for Levitt discriminated only against Blacks and sold to all who could pass the credit check.[33]

There were some noteworthy differences, however, between this Levittown and its predecessors. First, in the New Jersey town Levitt sought to appeal to a higher class of buyer. In Pennsylvania, the Levitt staff had become concerned about the "marginal buyer" who could not really afford the house. The company did not want such owners in the third town, and so attempted to attract middle-, and even upper-middle-class buyers.[34] This accounts for the firm's decision to offer several different house types and neighborhoods of varying densities.

Second, and over the strong objections of his staff, Levitt insisted upon mixing house types in the same block. This was done to diffuse the criticisms of urban planners. As a result, the three house types—ranging from $11,500 to $14,500[35]—were scattered throughout the town. This decision was significant. It prevented the emergence of three separate types of neighborhoods and this in turn made it more difficult to form solid neighborhood coalitions on political issues. Gans says, for example, that mixing house types made it far more difficult for segregationists to "find one another" when the town was going through the first stages of racial integration, and the Levitt decision probably made that transition much smoother.[36]

Third, the schools in the New Jersey community were built by the firm and "donated" to the town, their cost included within the price of housing. Until 1961 Levitt subsidized the operation of the elementary schools. Thereafter he could do so only in new neighborhoods under construction and not yet on the tax rolls.[37]

Fourth, Levitt concentrated on building and marketing *houses*, while leaving the planning of local institutions and facilities to the residents-to-be.[38] While not unmindful of the community, Levitt's overriding interest was in homebuilding, not in institutional development.[39] It was, after all, primarily for housing that people moved to the town, and it was housing that Levitt did best. In marketing, the firm's major emphasis was on the size and value of the house,[40] with ads stressing the size of the down payment and monthly payments. Since all appliances were included, and no additional cash outlay was necessary, many young people found the Levitt house extremely attractive. As before, the firm sought to reach this clientele.

Finally, the most critical difference between the third Levittown and its two predecessors was the community's location within a single jurisdictional area. For the developer this meant that negotiations were necessary with only *one* governmental unit, but for the community it meant much more than this. Fundamentally it meant that the political and legal unit was coincident with the town's geographical boundaries, and that the residents were, in fact, a *citizenry*—with legal rights and legislative control over municipal matters. Technically it also meant that the citizenry could influence the developer and the direction of his plan—a situation almost without precedent in new town planning. While this did not happen, the important point is that it *could* have. It did not happen because the township's planning board and its consultant planner were in accord with and cooperated with Levitt's plan,[41] and because Levitt, as the principal actor in the township urbanization drama, was always listened to and usually deferred to. Nevertheless, of profound significance for this study is that Levittown, New Jersey, was an American planned town with a *polity*; it was a recognized legal and political entity. In this, Levittown was closer to Howard's Garden City than were Radburn and Columbia—which ostensibly were based on Howard's principles.

In one other feature Levittown was closer to Howard's purposes than most subsequent new towns have been. Most have been upper-middle-class communities. Levitt, on the other hand, offered housing at an affordable price, thus making home ownership possible for income groups often excluded from American new communities.

Of course Levittown was not a garden city and the comparison can only be carried so far. In the final analysis the limits of Levittown in contending with the distributional problems of industrial society are the limits of private enterprise and mass production. The fact that Levitt could provide housing for otherwise excluded income groups was not owing to superior planning or efficient management. *It was due to a change in government practices.* Ultimately it was a *political* change, and not a technical one, which addressed the distributional nature of the housing problem, for without FHA and VA support, no Levitt could ever have succeeded in providing housing for those who found their homes in these communities.

7

Columbia, Maryland: "A Garden for People to Grow In"

Following the Greenbelt program, nearly thirty years elapsed before the new town concept again took hold in America. Few new cities were built in the 1940s and 1950s, but in the 1960s they proliferated. The Urban Land Institute counted no fewer than 160 new towns, either planned or in the construction stage, in 1965.[1]

Several timely factors accounted for this rush to build new towns. First, the children of the postwar baby boom had begun to enter the housing market, creating a vastly enlarged demand for shelter. An expanding economy in the 1960s made large-scale investments attractive, and many developers were willing to experiment with larger units like the big subdivision or the new community. Also, by the early 1960s, American planners were aware of Britain's successful use of new towns in postwar reconstruction and in framing a national urban policy. As the "urban crisis" was discovered in America, the British experience with physical and social planning took on new significance. Finally, and largely in response to market trends, developers sensed the profit to be made in the planned unit. "Community" in the 1960s became, like so much else, a packaged consumer product. It was no longer sufficient to sell houses; it became necessary to sell a way of life.[2]

Few of the developments the Urban Land Institute called "new towns" truly qualified as such. Only a handful were fairly self-contained entities with a diverse economic base, jobs for residents, and those commercial, educational, and other facilities and services normally supplied by a city. Most were little more than bedroom communities with some recreational facilities, or else special-use communities, like those designed for leisure or retirement.

Perhaps twenty of the new communities built during the decade could legitimately claim to be "new towns," for although undertaken by private enterprise to produce a profit, they nonetheless represented efforts to build "complete" cities. These towns became eligible for HUD-backed loans when the federal government moved to support the fledgling new town movement in the late 1960s.

Still, there were wide differences between and among the new communities. They differed not only in their degree of dependence on nearby municipalities,[3] but in character as well. Soul City, for example, was premised on Black capitalism and worker-owned industry, whereas Irvine Ranch was prosperous and almost exclusively white and middle class. ("When it comes to low- and moderate-income housing," Irvine's mayor lamented, "our people don't want any more housing at all."[4]) Reston, Virginia was owned and managed by a major energy corporation in contrast with Fort Lincoln, D.C., where plans were to be developed by a nonprofit corporation with profits reinvested in the community.[5] Differences between the new towns were frequently more noteworthy than similarities.

One extremely significant commonality, however, was the financial difficulty encountered by new town developers. The League of New Community Developers estimated in 1974 that:

> a community of 70,000 people requires a minimum of $700 million in mortgage loans for 20,000 dwelling units; another $400 million is required for capital outlay, public services and buildings; and about $400 million is needed for industrial and commercial development. Thus the total is about $15 billion.[6]

These sums were beyond the reach of even the wealthiest of real estate entrepreneurs, and developers very early turned to large pools of private capital for investment funds. They also pressured Congress for federal aid.

The earliest legislation to assist the embryonic new towns movement came in 1966 with the passage of the Demonstration Cities and Metropolitan Development Act. Title IV, "Land Development and New Communities," made guaranteed loans available to developers whose projects met specific criteria. The proposed community's contribution to the "sound and economic growth of the area" was emphasized.[7] In 1968 Congress passed more encompassing legislation in the New Communities Act. Guidelines were expanded to *require* social and economic integration. Two hundred and fifty million dollars in federally guaranteed loans were made available to developers who qualified by the following definition of "new community":

> In determining whether a given undertaking, otherwise eligible for assistance and consistent with the purposes of the Act, is a new community, the Secretary will apply the following general criteria:
>
> (a) A new community must include most, if not all, of the basic activities normally associated with a city or town: Housing, education, cultural facilities, transportation, commerce, industry, and recreation.
>
> (b) It must combine these varying activities in a balanced and harmonious whole, with a view to creating an environment that is an attractive place to live, work, and shop.

(c) It must have a favorable impact upon the growth and development of the area within which it is located in terms of conserving land, minimizing transportation problems, extending the range of housing choice for all who live or may in the future live in the area, promoting needed economic development, and creating new job opportunities.

(d) It must be designed for the fullest possible range of people and families of different compositions and incomes and must be open to members of all national, ethnic, and racial groups.[8]

The New Communities program was expanded under Title VII of the 1970 Housing Act, and under the 1968 and 1970 acts, an average of $22 million each in government-backed loans were issued to developers of fifteen "Title VII" communities.[9] The New Communities program remained in effect until January of 1975 when the Ford administration announced it would accept no new loan applications. While HUD promised to honor its commitments to those already in the program, many observers regarded this decision as fatal for the new towns movement.

Nevertheless, many of the better known new towns of the decade were built entirely with private capital (Reston, Virginia; Columbia, Maryland; Lake Havasu City, Arizona; and Irvine Ranch, California); and more than a few developers believed it was possible to serve broad social ends with new cities developed by private industry. Foremost among them was James Rouse, developer of Columbia, one of the first new cities and widely considered to be the best among them. Rouse in particular believed bold public goals could be realized while still ensuring profitability. In fact, he considered Columbia's financial success as the city's major contribution to the urban design process.[10] Columbia was also closer to Howard's Garden City than any of the other new communities imagined or begun during the period, and within the limits of private enterprise, Columbia is perhaps as close as one can come to attaining the ideals which Howard outlined.

The History of Columbia

Although largely the creation of James Rouse, Columbia was a joint venture of the Rouse Company and Connecticut General Life Insurance (now CIGNA Corporation). Through the Rouse Company, one of the largest mortgage banking and shopping center development firms in the country, Rouse supplied the talent, ideas, and plans for the city, whereas Connecticut General provided much of the capital. In 1985 CIGNA sold its interest to the Rouse Company who will develop the remainder of the community on its own.

Rouse's decision to locate the community in rural Howard County, Maryland, followed an exhaustive search of the entire Eastern Seaboard.[11] Of the several areas studied, the Maryland site, situated midway between

Baltimore and Washington, was considered the best given its growth potential, and on this basis Rouse convinced Connecticut General to invest in the project.

Acting in strict secrecy and through dummy corporations, Rouse began acquiring land in mid-1962 and within nine months he had successfully completed 175 transactions to acquire 14,000 acres of land. With the exception of a few holdout farmers and a small subdivision already developed within the area, all the land designated for the city itself had been assembled and acquired and at an average price of $1,500 an acre! This was a stunning real estate coup.[12] Rouse astounded not only the citizens of Howard County but the real estate industry as well when he announced in October 1963 that he now owned nearly one-tenth of the county. To an astonished press and a wary county, he outlined his plans to build a city complete with industry, jobs, shopping, recreation, schools, health care, and a range of housing. Columbia was to be an alternative to congested cities, suburban development, and the sprawl between them. Rouse's objectives in proposing this new city were to build a complete city, to provide an environment conducive to "the growth of people" (a recurrent phrase in his speeches), to respect the land, and to make a profit. The presumed complementarity of these goals was an important planning premise in Columbia and remains so today.

The Plan of Columbia

Columbia's general plan was developed between October 1963 and November 1964. Rouse assembled a gifted planning staff under William B. Finley, former staff director of the National Capital Planning Commission and chief author of Washington's "Plan for the Year 2000." Finley recruited a Commission colleague, Morton Hoppenfeld, to serve as chief of design. Hoppenfeld proposed that Rouse form a consulting group of behavioral scientists to advise on social matters. This was done, and the deliberations of this "work group" greatly determined the city's physical form and many of its institutions.

The neighborhood is the nucleus of the Columbia plan. Each neighborhood holds about 3,000 people and each is a mile wide. Its size, as with Radburn, was determined by the distance a child might walk to school. Housing is clustered around a neighborhood center which includes a kindergarten through fifth grade school, a multipurpose meeting/community room, a convenience store and snack bar, a park, playground, and swimming pool.

From two to four neighborhoods comprise a village which contains 10,000 people. Neighborhoods cluster around a village center, the heart of which the is the secondary/middle school. Village centers also contain more frequently used services (such as a bank, supermarket, pharmacy) and more recreational facilities (such as athletic clubs, ice rinks, tennis courts), as well as interfaith religious centers.

The nine villages are clustered around an urban core. Each village is separated from the others by open space, streams and valleys, but tied together by the city's minibus transportation system. The bus travels on its own right-of-way and moves from village to village, to industrial parks, and to downtown.

Land use is organized into eight categories: low-, medium-, and high-density residential; commercial areas; employment centers; permanent open space; bus land; roads/utilities/miscellaneous. Pedestrian and vehicular traffic are separated through under- and over-passes. A pathway system enables people to cycle and walk "free of attack by the automobile,"[13] and only access roads enter the neighborhoods.

Overall, the city plan reflects "The Radburn Idea."

For a full year, after evolving the plan, Rouse and his staff made numerous presentations to county groups explaining and arguing the desirability of Columbia and seeking to assuage residents' and politicians' fears. Suspicious of urban encroachment, Howard County had been engaged in a "stop urbanization" campaign, and citizens were highly skeptical of Columbia's effect on the county. Rouse made his critical presentation to county officials in November 1964. This presentation was crucial because a special zoning ordinance was required if the city were to be built.

Rouse based his arguments on the inevitability of growth. Howard County's choice was not between development and no development, he argued, but between good and bad development. Columbia, however, provided "a balanced and effective set of solutions" to the challenges of growth.[14] Columbia also offered "outstanding tax advantages": the city "would have the theoretical effect of a 40 percent reduction in present taxes."[15]

After nearly a year of discussion, review and modification, county commissioners voted approval of the zoning variance and land was prepared and construction begun in June of 1966. Columbia's first residents moved into the village of Wilde Lake a year later.

Originally, Columbia's development was phased over a fifteen-year period, with a population ceiling of 110,000. This was revised over the years and today the city is targeted for completion by the end of the '90s. Columbia's optimum population is now set at 100,000. As of 1985, the city was home to 65,000 people living in nine villages in 21,000 homes ranging from rental units to apartment condominiums to townhouses and single-family detached homes. Over 1,600 businesses and industries were located in Columbia, providing more than 39,000 jobs. The city has an extensive recreational program with numerous facilities for play. Columbia houses a hospital and health maintenance organization, branches of several colleges and universities, a shopping mall, an interfaith cooperative ministry, and a symphony.[16] This is an impressive testimonial to the vision of James Rouse.

The Planning Philosophy of James Rouse

Enormously influential among planning professionals from its beginnings, Columbia has often been cited as America's most successful new city and a bold model for future urban development. In the early days the city was dubbed "the next America" and the name has endured. In many ways Columbia does represent a striking departure from conventional urban planning; in terms of safeguarding the ecological system, in progressive efforts at social and economic development, in planning to accommodate certain future growth, in regional integration, in rethinking the entire city-building process—the city deserves every accolade bestowed upon it. In other ways, however, Columbia is very much within the mainstream tradition, particularly in continuing the premises and suppositions so evident in Radburn's planning: the historic definition of good planning as municipal conservation and protection of one's investment, the perception that ineconomy and inefficiency are major impediments to realizing the "good city," and the belief that proximity to physical nature is beneficial for moral character. The image of the desired future, although couched in different language, is essentially the same as in Radburn: the small town of a bygone America where individual opportunity presumably flourished and democratic cooperation was spontaneous and harmonious, obviating the need for formal mechanisms of political and social control. Columbia's planners, like Radburn's, sought to preserve individualism from a variety of urban constraints.

In good measure this continuation of "The Radburn Idea"—physically[17] and especially socially—was the work of the consulting group Rouse hired to advise him on social matters. However, Rouse himself shared many of the sociological and philosophical premises of Clarence Stein. His thinking reflected the same communitarian sentiments, free enterprise ideology, City Beautiful tradition, and reverence for nature that underlay the planning philosophy of Clarence Stein and other members of the Regional Planning Association of America.

James Rouse was a respected and shrewd real estate professional long before he began work on Columbia. He was also a man of extraordinary civic mindedness. Over the years these characteristics led to his active involvement in urban renewal efforts in Baltimore and Washington. With Nathaniel Keith he wrote *No Slums in Ten Years* dealing with redevelopment in Washington. He headed ACTION (American Council to Improve Our Neighborhoods);

held the presidency of Urban America; was a member of Eisenhower's Advisory Committee on Housing, and chaired a subcommittee that recommended the urban renewal program embraced in the Housing Act of 1954. In the early 70s he became involved in HUD's efforts to provide large numbers of low-cost housing units across the country.[18] Having sold the Rouse Company, James Rouse today heads a new real estate development firm and a foundation concerned with housing for the poor. Given his background, it is not surprising that during the 1970s Rouse became the unofficial spokesman for the new communities movement. Because of his stature and influence, it is important to consider the planning philosophy James Rouse brought to the development of Columbia.

Like Clarence Stein before him, Rouse proposed the new town as an alternative to the old city. The traditional negative view of the city expressed so clearly by Stein and other members of the RPAA was given academic respectability in the 1960s by a substantial literature of urban criticism. During the decade, this urban indictment came to embrace a *suburban* critique as well. Once the answer to the ills of urban congestion, the suburbs came to be identified with "sprawl," whose connotations were nearly as unpleasant as those associated with "slum" fifty years before.

In addition to inefficiency, "sprawl" came to convey loneliness and sterility as the suburban indictment expanded to encompass a sociological critique of suburban *life* given expression by two influential books of the period: Whyte's *The Organization Man* and Reisman's *The Lonely Crowd*.[19] This critique characterized the suburbs as the home of transient organization men obsessed with career and material gain. This had given rise to the "bedroom community," a state of affairs thought to be producing a matriarchal society, a generation of potentially homosexual sons and alcoholic housewives, and a country so conformist, shallow, and materialistic that the nation was dangerously prey to a communist takeover.

Rouse's rationale for Columbia also drew from this suburban development critique. Columbia would provide, he explained to a United States congressman, an alternative both to urban decadence and the "economically stratified, automobile straitjacketed, culturally sterilized, massive suburbs."[20] Nevertheless, the city basically favored the suburban trend. As with Radburn, Columbia offered not a rejection of suburbanism, but an *improvement* upon it. The city represented a continued attempt to realize the best of town *and* country, the best of nature *and* culture. The *suburban* setting was critical. As Edwin M. Baker, head of the Columbia Planning Department of the Rouse Company, explained,

> There are important things that you can't get anywhere except in a big city. But there are other things that you can't get unless you're far enough away from that big city to have the

land for them, and the open space, the social contact, the interaction of a variety of kinds of people—the really important things.[21]

One of these "really important things" was physical nature, which dominates the city visually and actually. This was a conscious planning decision. In Columbia the eye encompasses nature wherever it rests. The city appears to be planted among fields and trees. Housing is clustered to create internal parks in neighborhoods. There are three artificial lakes with over 500 acres of water surface, three golf courses, and a hunting preserve. Stream valleys and small ponds appear here and there. Picnic groves and camping sites are scattered throughout, and many miles of bridle paths interlace the city. Over 2,300 acres are designated permanent open space. More land is devoted to open space than to industrial and commercial uses combined. Parks dominate at each level of the city, and downtown Columbia is surrounded by a 40-acre oak forest and a 32-acre lake. The intent was to evoke Copenhagen's Tivoli Gardens.

Such reverence for nature and the physical environment was a fundamental element of Rouse's planning philosophy. Determined to respect the land,[22] Rouse undertook extensive site studies in the early days. A professional forester was hired to analyze timber areas and prepare trees for transplant, and roads were altered to maintain a magnificent stand of trees. The area's three major stream valleys were preserved, as were 3,000 acres of forest. "We invited the land to impose itself as a discipline on the form of the community," Rouse said,[23] and Chief of Design Morton Hoppenfeld confirmed that:

> Choice locations for various activities such as schools, industry, low- and high-density housing and lake sites were virtually dictated by the land and the critical economics of "proper usage" (that is, in harmony with nature.)[24]

The "garden" setting Rouse sought to create was perhaps best expressed in a word-picture he painted while Columbia was still in the idea stage. One is reminded of the words of Clarence Stein on his spring walk through Radburn:

> Coming upon a village, the visitor will first be aware of a sense of quiet orderly neighborhoods, of attractive homes on lots ranging up to several acres. Others are clustered along lakefronts or golf courses. The road is clean and safe, its borders landscaped and planted. Under or over the road pass pedestrian walkways. Private driveways do not open onto this road to the village; homes are grouped along quieter streets that serve only for parking and access. The visitor will be conscious of the continually attractive setting of the village. Trees are abundant and cared for; streams flow clear and fresh; even the sign which marks the road seems to complement the place.

> Among the houses, he catches here and there the glimpse of a swimming pool, a playing field, a shaded bench. Along a lake, people fish or picnic. Sailboats and canoes dot the water. Ahead is a cluster of buildings, designed to fit into the landscape. The broad playing fields of a high school, the spires of churches, the peaceful stirring of activity, signal the arrival at the village center...[25]

One of the more celebrated of Rouse's goals was "to provide the best possible environment for the growth of people," and this goal especially placed Columbia within the social planning tradition of Radburn.

Rouse spoke eloquently and frequently on this point. Before a congressional subcommittee in 1966, he said:

> The ultimate test of a civilization is whether or not it contributes to the growth and improvement of mankind. Does it uplift, inspire, stimulate, and develop the best in man? There really can be no other right purpose of community except to provide an environment to develop better people. The most successful community would be that which contributed the most by its physical form, its institutions, and its operation to the growth of people.[26]

Before a symposium on "The City of the Future," he explained Columbia's purpose as:

> nourish[ing] and support[ing] the growth and dignity of the individual human being and his family. This is the only legitimate purpose for our cities or our civilization—to grow better people—more concerned, inspired, fulfilled—more loving people.[27]

The idea is extremely significant when placed within the intellectual history of urban planning and the persistent view that cities are "bad" to the extent they constrain, thwart or limit the individual's freedom, whereas "good" cities are those which promote the individual's interests. In this context, frequent references to "proper scale," "containing megalopolis," and "accommodating future growth" have connotations beyond their descriptive meanings. Rouse argued, for example, that urban growth had created "noncommunities" so "huge and irrational" they were "out of scale with people—beyond their grasp and comprehension—too big for people to feel a part of, responsible for, important in."

> The richness of real community—in both its support and its demands—is largely voided. Variety and choice are reduced to a sort of prepackaged brand-name selection of recreation, culture, and education. The individual is immersed in the mass. What nonsense this is.[28]

Securing individualism required central attention to scale—*defined* scale, but especially small scale. The task of urban planning, therefore, was to

> identify the circumstances under which man, woman, and family can grow in their individual personality, character and spirit and then... to find the way to shape services, institutions, land, buildings, and communication systems to create communities that will provide maximum support for the people who live there.[29]

For most of American history, individualism and autonomy were associated with physical nature or the small town but not with cities. Cities implied anonymity, interdependence and constraint. As Rouse perceived the city, Columbia involved *restoring* what was lost with urbanism, and Rouse found his model in the small town of America's past. As he told the officials of Howard County, "all of the opportunities that were once possible only in very small towns will be part of the rich fabric of life in Columbia."[30]

> The villages permit a scale of life reminiscent of the small towns which form such a rich heritage of America. In place of monotonous, sprawling suburbs stretching in endless ranks across much of the County, the villages of Columbia will offer a vitality and a scale of living too often sacrificed today.[31]

As urbanism had threatened individualism, Rouse believed it had also destroyed the *community life* so common in earlier times. Columbia was thus an attempt to recapture a more "natural" social state of smaller scale which was absent in both cities and suburbs:

> I believe that many of the most serious problems of our society flow from the fact that the city is out of scale with people; that it is too big for people to comprehend, to feel a part of, to feel responsible for, to feel important in. I believe this out-of-scaleness promotes loneliness, irresponsibility, superficial values. People grow best in small communities where the institutions, which are the dominant forces in their lives, are within the scale of their comprehension and within reach of their sense of responsibility and capacity to manage. A broader range of friendships and relationships occurs in a village or small town than in a city; there is a greater sense of responsibility for one's neighbor and a greater sense of support by one's fellowman. I believe that self-reliance is promoted, that relationship to nature—to the out-of-doors—to the freer forms of recreation and human activity is encouraged in a smaller community.[32]

As Morton Hoppenfeld summarized Rouse's planning philosophy, it was one that "believes that people can have a good life and can live together in brotherhood. It looks upon everything short of that as a malfunction to be corrected and not a condition to be worked around."[33]

Like the social philosopher John Dewey, who feared the urban public was so inchoate and dispersed it could not find itself, Rouse came to emphasize the importance of the primary group and face-to-face communication in safeguarding democracy:

> The real breakdown in urban life is the breakdown in communication. The inability of people to relate one to another, to relate to groups, to be able to speak under circumstances where they could be heard and where results might occur, we believed to be the most fundamental reasons for the basic urban malaise...
>
> There is a sense of aloneness, a sense of the whole thing being bigger than I am and that there is nothing I can do about it. There is a sense of frustration and oppression on the part of little people. But even on the part of the well-to-do, there is a sense of being incapable of bringing about results through the existing processes of community. Out of this basic lack of effective communication among people come the conditions that breed the hostility and fear and separation and division and conflict. There is this inability of people to change their institutions because they cannot get at the institutions without other people who think as they do because they cannot find these people. People of likemindedness do not have the opportunity to find themselves in natural association.[34]

The physical plan of Columbia, the hierarchical organization of the city, and, of course, its size—all reflected an attempt to recreate a sense of community within the vast impersonal Eastern megalopolis of today.

Social Planning in Columbia: The Work Group

Columbia's physical plan was a direct product of the consulting group[35] Rouse hired to sketch out ideals in education, social services, government, recreation, and so on. Donald Michael, a social planner and futurist, chaired the group of behavioral and social scientists. Michael had written *Cybernation: The Silent Conquest* and other works treating the social consequences of abundance and advanced technology. His interest in these topics would profoundly affect the premises and recommendations of the work group.

The idea for such an advisory group was truly novel. Rouse assembled these experts because there was "absolutely no dialogue in the United States today between the people who have developed knowledge about people—the teachers, the ministers, the psychiatrists, sociologists—and the people who are designing and building our cities."[36] The work group was asked to consider, "What works best for people? Which arrangements of facilities and institutions will enhance or inhibit the life of the community?"[37] Rouse asked them to suggest ideal systems, to recommend how things might be if starting anew with no financial or institutional constraints. This charge is important, since the group ultimately recommended another Radburn. Moreover, the group's guiding assumptions and visions were not unlike those of James Rouse. They shared Rouse's concern with proper scale and size, and sought to strengthen an identification with place and give people roots in a defined community. The group labored to reinstitute the walking city of America's past and to combine home, school, work, and social networks within the radius of a few miles. They based much of the town on an individualistic self-development ethic, and attempted, like Rouse, to diminish conflict and dissension. In so doing they also embraced many of the planning assumptions of Clarence Stein.

The work group met twice monthly for two days and a night over a six-month period. During these brainstorming sessions, no consensus was sought. Instead, the group sought to express the needs and wants of people in physical planning terms. Rouse directed them to "devise a physical setting that will endow each resident with a sense of membership in a coherent community, and simultaneously offer him the greatest possible choice of styles for his own life."[38] Chairman Michael believed this to be possible: "A good physical plan," he said, "can actually encourage social activities and encourage individual growth."[39]

The collective results of these meetings became known as the "Gladstone Papers." Although they were never published or codified,[40] it is clear that the ideals which emerged presumed the imminent emergence of a "postindustrial society" defined by affluence and freedom from economic constraints. The group foresaw a future where leisure would become a way of life, with consumership the sole economic activity for increasing numbers of people. In their presumption of a service-based economy in which theoretical knowledge assumes a new centrality, the group drew from the ideas of Daniel Bell and Herman Kahn and other futurists in the just-emerging field of future studies.

The presumption of postindustrialism so defined led the work group to emphasize education, the productive use of leisure time, and self-development and interpersonal relations. Their "pivotal planning decision," according to Hoppenfeld, was the decision to "acknowledge learning as the basic foundation for a human community."[41] In physical terms, this meant that schools were made the focal point for each level of community life. The group also emphasized education as a means to fill expanding leisure time productively, and the arts were given much attention. In fact, the first public building constructed in Columbia was the Meriweather Post Pavilion, the summer home of the Washington Symphony Orchestra.

The three-tiered organization of the city into neighborhood, village, and city-as-a-whole followed from the work group's views about proper social organization.[42] As with Radburn, each neighborhood and village was limited in size, with optimums determined by considerations of individual freedom and community interaction.[43] Overall, the optimum size of the city was no larger than that needed to support desired services and amenities.

The consultants recommended the neighborhood as the nucleus of the community. Just as the family was considered the building block of society, so *the neighborhood of families* was considered the building block of the city. As with Radburn, neighborhood size was determined by the distance a child could safely walk to school. This distance defined the limits of the neighborhood and hence the political unit. The limits of the village were similarly determined by the distance middle- and secondary-students could walk to school.

The work group favored small and decentralized schools over larger and consolidated ones. They chose, as Hoppenfeld said, "to adopt a system of relatively small schools within walking distance to surrounding residents as a focus of communities."[44] This decision was made partly from considerations of safety, as in Radburn, and partly because it was economical (it made busing unnecessary). Still, there were significant *social* reasons for this choice. The consultants wanted to break "the community down into groups small enough for people to feel an identity and an involvement."[45] As one staff member put it,

> In the smaller group there would be more chance for Johnny to be president of his class; therefore, he would have a more continuing interest in his school. That would lead to an identity with his community, because his community also had a size that was identifiable.[46]

Howard County officials were later persuaded to adopt a decentralized school system based on this idea and organized into K-5, 6-8, and 9-12 grades. Rouse explained that:

> We made a decision to try to sell Howard County, and we have succeeded now in doing it, in abandoning in Columbia the consolidated high school and going to small high schools and small junior schools, 800 to 1,000 each, where there could be more team captains, more debaters, more members of the drama club, more winners, fewer losers in the community, and at the same time to be able to make the high school and the junior high school reach centers of the village with a sense of proprietorship by the people and use by the people, so that each of these areas of communities of 10,000 to 15,000 people has a village center.[47]

In Columbia, said Wallace Hamilton, project historian for the Rouse Company, "nobody need feel like a nobody."[48]

Considerations of size and scale were also related to perceived participation in community affairs and cooperative association. The work group believed, much like Stein and Rouse, that *defined* (and especially small) space fostered this involvement. The clear separation of villages one from another was also advised by the consultants who feared that individuals would take no interest in local affairs without such distinct boundaries.[49] Similar reasoning lay behind the group's recommendation that the city be enclosed within a greenbelt, although this was not done.

Also at their suggestion, each level of Columbia was organized around a center designed to perform specific and appropriate functions. Thus the *city center* provides facilities and services that can only be supported by a large population, and here Columbia's cultural and commercial life is centered, while *village centers* offer services related to household needs like the supermarket and pharmacy, as well as interfaith centers where various religious groups worship. But the *neighborhood centers* are the heart of the Columbia plan. The work group considered them the "prime device for drawing residents into the life of the community."[50] Neighborhood centers were so important to Columbia's social planning that each was built prior to, or concurrent with, the development of the neighborhood itself.[51] Like their counterparts at the turn of the century, these were created as a functional means for fostering civic improvement and responsibility. Richard Crenshaw, Project Design Coordinator for Neighborhood Centers, called them "the most essential part of Columbia."[52]

While the entire city of Columbia was and is family- and child-centered,[53] the neighborhood center is particularly so. This was by design. The consultants wanted to offer "a point of orientation for families and young children"[54] and especially for housewives, "the most place-bound members" of an urban community."[55] The group recommended that each center contain:

> a nursery and tot lot for infants, a kindergarten and playground for preschool children, a school and play field for children in the first four grades and a general store which would answer a minimum of shopping needs. This store would also serve as administrative nucleus for the neighborhood and its recreational facilities. The store manager should receive special training for his role. His duties would include maintaining a neighborhood bulletin board, keeping an eye on recreation facilities and issuing sports equipment.[56]

This recommendation was followed literally and each neighborhood center has an elementary school, a swimming pool, a children's park, a community center, and a nursery school and childcare center. Each also has a general store, modeled after the country store of a bygone America. The elementary school, however, is *the* focal point of the neighborhood center. Indeed, *all* of Columbia was predicated upon the elementary school. Hoppenfeld notes how virtually all other decisions about housing cluster, size of neighborhoods and villages, etc., were derived from this single decision about the proper size and location of elementary schools. As in Radburn, the city was determined primarily by children.

Governance in Columbia

Columbia has two levels of government: the village associations and the Columbia Association (CA). Residents (whether renters or owners) elect representatives to the village associations. These are essentially homeowners associations, with no real power or authority. Residents also elect Council

Representatives from each village who comprise the Board of Directors of the Columbia Association, which is the central community institution in the city.

A nonprofit organization, the CA has broad powers to operate programs in recreation, childcare, park service and transportation and the authority to assess a tax to support them. Since the beginning, the CA has offered an extensive recreation and maintenance program for parks, pools, tennis and golf courses, lakes, the minibus service, and community buildings. It has supported a swim club, an ice and roller skating rink, tennis clubs, a horse center, bowling lanes, an athletic club, and a comprehensive recreation program for all ages. The Association is heavily involved in early childhood education programs and partially subsidizes nursery school and daycare programs. Some of these services are free to Columbians; others are supported by a combination of Association revenues and user fees.

The CA is a classical association, with no direct influence over the development of Columbia. It has no control, for example, over whether or not a given piece of land allocated for residential multifamily housing should be used instead for low-income (or high-income) housing.[57] The Association does have a great deal of influence over what is "public" in Columbia, and "public" is virtually synonymous with recreation and leisure. The CA owns and controls all open space, roughly 20 percent of the city's total acreage. It owns community centers and facilities and holds first lien on all 14,000 of the city's acres regardless of the use to which the land is put. This provision enables the association to borrow capital to finance community facilities.

The CA also has the right of taxation. Through the creation of a special Community Improvement District (also an idea of the work group), the CA is empowered to assess an annual charge of 75¢ per $100 assessed valuation. This has proven to be a highly lucrative source of revenue. The CA has already invested more than $20 million in facilities and equipment and is scheduled to spend more than $10 million for new facilities during the next ten years.[58]

The Columbia Association remains the only formal governmental entity within the city. In this it virtually mirrors the Radburn experience and again illuminates certain tacit assumptions of urban planners. Formal citizen influence over matters of recreation and open space, *and over these matters alone*, reveals the overwhelming importance of leisure and nature in defining "the good city." More importantly, however, the congruence of recreation and governance, together with the absence of a recognized polity, implies that an entity such as the CA is wholly adequate for governing the city. Clearly Columbia was not planned on the premise that a city is defined in good measure by an unstable pluralistic polity; that various and conflicting goals develop over time; and that mechanisms for adjudicating differing and competing value hierarchies are essential to a successful community. Was the planning supposition that conflict and discord were unlikely in such an environment? Were no mechanisms created for arbitering differences because of a shared presumption that no important differences would exist that could not be resolved face-to-face?

One of the more prevalent and troubling features of American new towns built in the 1960s is the absence of political institutions in their conceptualization and design. Such a widespread omission forces a reconsideration of what "city" has come to mean to many planners. Is the city a physical structure? an economic unit? a legal and political nexus? a locus of friendship? a site for homes?

The "city" of Radburn, for example, was conceived more as structure and locus for social intercourse than as legal or political entity. This conception did not trouble Radburn's planners—indeed, one could argue that such was exactly what was sought. Economy was not essential to Radburn. It certainly was, and is, to Columbia. But in Columbia, as in Radburn, polity appears to be incidental, even unnecessary. Direct democratic interaction through social activity apparently substitutes for formal, political mechanisms of democratic control.

Columbia is not a city in the legal and political sense. It was not incorporated. Citizens lack the usual municipal control over schools, public safety, sanitation, transportation, land use, revenue raising and allocation, and civic welfare. Only in matters of recreation is there a significant citizen voice. The city's school system, health and police protection, water and sewer services, and even libraries are under the jurisdiction of Howard County to whom Columbians also pay their taxes.

To a degree, the developer's reluctance to incorporate Columbia was understandable, reflecting an old and complex problem in the history of new town building. Democracy at too early a stage can upset the delicate zoning policy that is necessary to build any new town, and besides, the people who will eventually live there are not present when crucial decisions are made and cannot therefore be "represented." Also, early democracy can be used as a tool to exclude certain groups from the city.[59] Hence the more critical problem of democracy in a new town involves the *transferring of power* from the developer to the citizenry after crucial planning decisions have been made. This has been done effectively with the Columbia Association. Developer appointed in the early days, the directors of the CA are now entirely residents. However, there is neither provision for altering the city nor for incorporating it at some future date.[60] Legally and politically, Howard County will govern in Columbia. To be sure, the potential problems with this arrangement have been mitigated by the city's growth. Columbians now constitute a sizeable plurality in the county and can effectively represent their interests before that county government. Nevertheless, the concept of the political city is absent in Columbia's design as it was absent in Radburn's.

Columbia and the Garden City

Is Columbia a garden city as Howard defined it?

Certainly there is no common ownership of land, the axial principle on which Garden City was premised. But the single ownership of the substantial open space acreage, coupled with the careful master planning, serves to minimize speculative behavior and therefore helps to control land values, which was Howard's intent. Like Howard, Rouse did not believe that individual greed accounted for this elevation in land values, but rather the city-building process itself where thousands of small separate decisions made with little or no relation one to another could have enormous impact on the whole. Unlike Howard, however, Rouse believed that sound planning *within* market realities could produce the good city.

Columbia most clearly approaches Howard's ideals in the extent to which the city is fully a city, supplying the commercial, recreational, educational, social, and employment needs of a diverse population. In this respect Columbia's social and economic development have been remarkable and singular in the history of American new town planning. As of 1985 there were 1,600 firms doing business in the city, supplying 39,000 jobs.[61] Twenty-eight percent of Columbia's workforce was employed within the city.[62] Commercial needs were supplied by nearly 300 stores. Columbia was home to one of the finest public school systems in the country, with 25 preschool programs, 11 elementary, 4 middle and 3 high schools. There is a Community College and programs offered by Johns Hopkins University, Towson State University, Loyola College, and The University of Maryland. Columbia has a 180-bed hospital and a health maintenance organization. There are commuter buses to Washington and Baltimore and a citywide bus system.[63]

Despite its plentiful offerings, Columbia remains economically and socially integrated within its greater region, as Rouse intended from the start. In this respect the city follows lines suggested by Howard in his clustered cities concept and given strong advocacy by Lewis Mumford and the RPAA. Like Howard, Rouse also related new city development to the revitalization of old metropolitan areas. Baltimore would not be hurt by Columbia's growth, he said; on the contrary, new towns like Columbia would actually help Baltimore by directing "irrational, piecemeal [and] inefficient sprawl" away from the city's borders, thus permitting the city to concentrate on more pressing needs:

> Baltimore's task, and that of every other American city, is to correct its obsolescence; get rid of its slums; to address itself to the urban renewal opportunity through comprehensive planning large enough to re-form the center of the City into a beautiful, efficient, powerful economic force, and to reshape the older areas around downtown into a system of healthy, slum free communities.[64]

More than any other American new town, Columbia has seriously attempted to counter the race and income segregation so characteristic of our cities. Rouse, who deplored the stratified suburbs, wanted the interaction of many social groups in his city, and Columbia has been enormously successful in attracting racial minorities. Rouse refused to discriminate racially, a courageous decision for the time, and today the city's population is 22 percent nonwhite.[65] 1980 census data show that 19 percent of Columbia's population is Black with the remaining nonwhite classified as "other," including Hispanics, American Indian, Eskimo, and Oriental. *Newsweek*, covering the town for a twenty year retrospective, called it a veritable "integrated Xanadu in conservative Howard County."[66]

Contributing to this heterogeneity is the range of housing available in the city. Thirty-nine percent of all homes in 1984 were single family, 28 percent were townhomes, and 33 percent were apartments (both condominium and rental)[67]—a distribution that has promoted a rich mix of family types. A 1985 survey of Columbians indicated that only 41 percent of families consisted of two adults and children, the conventional nuclear family. One-fifth of all households were single adults living alone, 5 percent were single parents, and the remainder were adults living together.[68]

Columbia was designed as a series of relatively homogeneous neighborhoods, however. This was a decision of the work group. Rouse wanted to combine housing types at the neighborhood level and therefore to mix social classes, but the work group strongly cautioned against such an approach, warning that divisiveness followed when neighborhoods were socially diverse.

Ironically, the city's very success as a working plural community is responsible for the failure of the neighborhood concept in which individuals were encouraged to develop close relationships with their like-minded neighbors. Because of the diversity that does exist and the various institutions the city has developed, one's friends can be drawn from one's religious or interest group associations, not simply one's immediate neighborhood.[69] This is the conclusion of Burkhart's study on the politics of race and class in Columbia. She found that the social integration that has taken place has not been on the terms originally conceived:

> Rouse and his team of innovative planners, committed as they were to a mixed and balanced community, saw assimilation as the only viable alternative to social fragmentation and hostility. The residents of Columbia, albeit unwittingly, have taken the raw materials provided by the ideology of integration and molded the dimensions of the community into a stable and working pluralism that respects and builds on the variations in its population. One well-known example of this is the Interfaith Center, a large modern structure planned and built to house numerous different religious groups. These different groups indeed occupy the center today, but they do not form one comfortable

interdenominational effort; rather, each competes, at times rather fiercely, for an equitable share of the expenses and the resources available to them as tenants of one physical structure.[70]

Economic integration along the lines Howard envisioned has been a much more difficult goal. Rouse wanted to supply housing for all who worked in the city—"from the company janitor to the company president"[71]—but this has proved difficult in practice. Analysis indicates that over half of the jobs in the city are held by nonresidents,[72] suggesting that housing price barriers have prevented the realization of this goal. In 1985 single family dwellings sold for $89,900 to $300,000; townhomes, $75,500 to $139,000; and condominium apartments, $58,750 to $95,000. Rental units ranged from $535 to 685 per month for townhomes to $359 to $740 for apartments.[73]

Columbia does have low-income housing distributed in pockets in several neighborhoods, where the income range is least marked. About 7 percent of the total housing in the city is subsidized for low income (elderly and welfare recipients).[74] The Columbia Interfaith Housing Corporation has been the major force behind this effort, although other builders have supplied and administered federally supported programs as well.

Not surprisingly, Columbia marketing data confirm that those who can afford to live in the city are overwhelmingly middle and upper-middle income families. Average monthly housing expenditures in 1984, for example, were $558 for owners and $402 for renters, with average household income reported at $45,880. The lowest household income reported was $31,775.[75]

The nature of jobs available in the city further dissuades the less affluent and less educated from living there. Heavy industry was zoned out of the plan, and such manufacturing as exists in Columbia is light manufacturing. The preponderance of employment is in high-technology fields with the city's major employers engaged in research and development, electronics, engineering, and consulting,[76] the tertiary and quaternary economic activities that are the postindustrial economy's growth industries. This followed from a conscious planning decision made in the early days:

> The program of business development will be directed largely at research and development and science-oriented companies.... It is expected that such firms, with a high percentage of skilled, professional employees, will make up the bulk of new industry in the community.[77]

And this has come to pass. Nearly 70 percent of Columbia's full-time workers are in professional, technical, managerial, or administrative occupations. Sixty-two percent of the city's adults hold four-year degrees, and 29 percent have advanced or professional degrees, indicating again the highly educated workforce required by the postindustrial economy.[78] One brochure claims Columbia as having "the largest concentration of scientists and engineers in the country."[79] Columbia embodies postindustrial society as the work group perceived it: affluent, educated, and leisured. And as close as Columbia comes to realizing the Garden City as Howard conceived it, it is for this very reason that the city is not a viable model for American urbanization. The most portentous aspects of postindustrialism simply are not conveyed by images of abundance, choice, and high technology. Postindustrialism in this sense has emerged for only a very few. What postindustrialism raises for American society is not the spectre of a rich leisure but the emergence of a new class structure based on knowledge, the dominance of a meritocratic and technocratic elite, and an increasing disparity between the haves and have nots.[80] The advent of postindustrialism perforce raises *distributional* questions about wealth, power, and status—and especially questions of equity and opportunity, justice, and community. It is surely one of the cruelest hoaxes of postindustrial society that the poor lack the skill and education necessary to compete for the good life postindustrial cities like Columbia offer. In the final analysis, Columbia is an exceptional city with an exceptional population and an exceptional economic base. There is no place in "the next America" for either the industrial worker or industrial era problems of inequality, competition, scarcity, poverty, environmental degradation. These have been addressed not by their resolution but by their transcendence. The flotsam and jetsam of industrial society have been left to other cities to contend with. Because of this Columbia does not point the way to a new urban pattern, for in a nation of Columbias so conceived, where are the postindustrial anachronisms and misfits to go? The knotty problems of industrial society may be temporarily evaded by reference to a new post-industrial future, but they may not be transcended. Distributional questions are intensified, not minimized, by such economic and technological changes. Howard understood this in proposing Garden City, for he argued that generating new wealth was vital to a better civilization—but its just distribution was equally essential. The two could not be separated.

The limits of Columbia as a model for the future are by no means the fault of James Rouse, whose city is exemplary in so many ways and whose own efforts have been herculean. As a business venture undertaken with the expectation of profit, Columbia simply could not, nor could Rouse be expected to, significantly affect some of the most entrenched problems of urban-industrial society. "These are essentially problems of poverty and racism," Hoppenfeld acknowledged in discussing Columbia's capabilities, and they require "major national decisions concerning the distribution of wealth and the provision of jobs and adequate environment for currently 'uneconomic' families."[81] The limits of Columbia are the limits of private enterprise in addressing deep structural problems in urban America.

Columbia also reveals the limits of urban planning as Americans have practiced it, in particular the limits of *technique* and *space* in effecting broad social change. James Rouse once said "the shape and form and richness and values and standards of our civilization will depend on the kinds of cities that we unfold."[82] To this process Columbia has contributed greatly, certainly, but we await urban reform that addresses *structural* issues such as Ebenezer Howard outlined in *Garden Cities of Tomorrow* nearly a century ago.

8

New Towns as Social Inventions

Settlement patterns reflect a society's goals, economic conditions, political structures, cultural history, and visions of the future. This study has attempted to elucidate these patterns through an examination of four widely influential experiments in new community building, and through this to discern the underlying values and embedded meanings contained within the new towns movement in twentieth-century America. Each of these new towns has embodied a conception of what "the good city" is, how it was to be brought into being, and how maintained and preserved. Each has carried implicit assumptions about society, economy, polity, technology, the natural world, human nature and purpose. And while each has expressed "the good city" concept in different ways, several common themes emerge from the overall social vision they collectively communicate.

American planners have interpreted Ebenezer Howard's garden city proposal in keeping with distinctly American cultural traditions. While new town planners have been progressive, they have simultaneously sought to restore an earlier America of presumed simplicity, innocence, harmony, and democratic community. Their ambivalence towards change and complexity continues a long standing and deep seated attitude in American intellectual history, that of ambivalence toward the city and living in community. Consistent with this cultural belief, planners have advanced a landscape ethic, not a *land* ethic,[1] and an economizing mode, not changes in the economy. Land use considerations and structures have dominated in their "good cities" while institutions and structural reform have been given minimal attention.

In consonance with the diminished role assigned institutions, new town planners have defined "the city" not in terms of its economy or polity or legal basis, but in terms of the "natural unit" of the individual, the primary group, and the friendship network. Thus "the city" is defined by, and organized as, a series of *family neighborhoods* carefully integrated with one another.

The new towns also carry an indictment of diverse urban life with its irreducible value differences. Planners have implicitly defined diversity and conflict as "evil" and indicative of the "false community" believed to characterize conventional cities. "True community" has been perceived as synonymous with agreement, accord, and spontaneous cooperation and sought through eliminating or transcending heterogeneity and disorder. Community has thus been defined in ways which avoid confronting the issues of pluralism, justice, and equity in a democratic society.

From its first expression through its flowering in the scores of new communities undertaken in the 1960s, the direction the garden city in America has taken has been that first articulated by Clarence Stein: that of building "contemporary new cities for present day good living." The model for this has more often been Radburn than Columbia, however. Most new towns have not been communities with diverse populations and a sound economic base; instead they have been leisure "cities" which provide a pleasant environment for middle-class families in a setting which assures the protection of one's investment. Although proposed as vehicles for social change, new towns in America have accommodated to the culture more than they have reformed it.

A critique of the new towns movement is not merely, or even largely, of historical interest. Its value lies in future directions for American urban planning in general and for subsequent new town development in particular. As a concept, the new town idea has been a valuable "social invention."[2] Social inventions are innovations in cultural practices which change the way people relate to themselves or one another. From a "futures" perspective, their value lies in opening the future to "otherness" and to fresh possibility, and in conceiving tomorrow in ways not narrowly circumscribed by present day practices or beliefs. Garden City was a social invention par excellence, directing urban planning along new lines. Howard's major contribution in advancing this social invention was to free the future from fidelity to present trendlines and to enlarge the cultural "imaging stock."[3] In this context, the new town concept is highly relevant. As social inventions capable of leading to new approaches and images of the future, new towns have a special potential in redirecting urban-industrial civilization along more humane and sustainable lines. This is a goal which Howard outlined in 1898, the realization of which is *urgently* needed today.

Two Views of the Future

Among futurists and future-oriented policy analysts, there is widespread agreement about the nature, character, and evolution of industrialism as a worldwide social and economic phenomenon. There is, however, fundamental disagreement over its long-term direction and sustainability. In fact, the basic axis of difference among professional futurists is over this very issue: whether things as they are can (and should) continue, or whether things as they are can (and must) change.[4]

One school of thought views the future in terms of continued growth of a high technology, materially affluent service society, as described by Herman Kahn's "Basic Long-Term Multifold Trend." This view holds that developed societies have been shaped by, and will continue to reflect, the following dominant forces and trends:[5]

1. Increasingly sensate (empirical, this-worldly, secular, humanistic, pragmatic, manipulative, explicitly rational, utilitarian, contractual, epicurean, hedonistic, etc.) cultures.

2. Bourgeois, bureaucratic, and meritocratic elites.

3. Centralization and concentration of economic and political power.

4. Accumulation of scientific and technical knowledge.

5. Institutionalization of technological change, especially research, development, innovation, and diffusion.

6. Increasing military capability.

7. Westernization, modernization, and industrialization.

8. Increasing affluence and (recently) leisure.

9. Population growth.

10. Urbanization, recently suburbanization and "urban sprawl"—soon the growth of megalopoli.

11. Decreasing importance of primary and (recently) secondary occupations; increasing importance of tertiary and (recently) quaternary occupations;

12. Increasing literacy and education, and (recently) the "knowledge industry" and increasing role of intellectuals.

13. Innovative and manipulative social engineering—i.e., rationality increasingly applied to social, political, cultural, and economic worlds as well as to shaping and exploiting the material world.

14. Increasing universality of the multifold trend.

15. Increasing tempo of change in all the above.

In the culture at large, this view of the future predominates, but large numbers of professional futurists are increasingly convinced that a quite different future is not only to be preferred but is more likely as well. They point to the unsustainability of the industrial paradigm given fundamental incongruities between its premises (limitless growth, dominion over nature, consumption and material affluence as the highest good) and present and emerging realities: a world population approaching six billion people, most of them hungry, poor and with little hope for future improvement; worldwide poverty coexisting with abundance and *causally* related to it; the Third World's insistence on a new international economic order; a challenge to the legitimacy of western values and consumption patterns by nonindustrialized, nonwhite peoples who comprise the overwhelming majority of the earth's citizenry; the rapid depletion of fossil fuels on which industrialism depends; the alarming threat to the earth's *renewable* resource base—the air, water, soil and plant and animal life that are the planet's life-support system and which undergird all economic activity; the environmental costs of worldwide economic growth; and the human and social costs of technological *dis*employment and structural unemployment as more and more human labor becomes incidental to the economic system. These problems comprise "the crisis of industrialism" and are *endemic* to all advanced industrial societies, whether capitalist or socialist.[6] Willis Harman has identified the *intrinsic* failures and anomalies of the industrial paradigm which portend its breakdown. He writes:

> An interrelating set of fundamental dilemmas of industrial society, growing steadily more pressing, seems to require for its ultimate resolution a drastically changed social paradigm. We seem able to tolerate neither the ecological consequences of continued material growth nor the economic consequences of a sudden stoppage. We fear the implications of greatly increased control of technological development and application, yet sense that such control is imperative. We recognize the fatal instability of economic nationalism and a growing gap between rich and poor nations, yet seem completely unable to turn the trend around. We seem unable to resolve the discrepancy between man's apparent need for creative, meaningful work and the economic imperatives that cause much human labor to become superfluous or reduce it to make-work.[7]

These very dilemmas have led many professional futurists to question the future viability of Kahn's "Long-Term Multifold Trend," premised as it is on accelerating material growth. This group instead advocates a reversal, or a modification, of the "modernization" trend of the last two centuries, and urges movement toward a more decentralized and ecologically oriented society addressing the full range of human needs. In contrast to the "Post-Industrialism-as-a-Service-Society" outlined by Kahn, Michael Marien has described this counter view of "Post-Industrialism-as-a-more-Self-Reliant-Society." Its major features include:[8]

1. Greater spirituality, with cultural movement toward a synthesis of spiritual and secular, "rational" and "nonrational," East and West traditions.

2. Industrial era paradigms underlying much "knowledge" questioned, as is reductionist trivia; more use of holistic methods to cope with complexities.

3. Institutionalization of technology assessment; more emphasis on appropriate technologies and calculation of total costs.

4. Increasing emphasis on self-help, participation, and questioning of professionals; growing stress on learning needs and ignorance.

5. Increased efforts to reverse the trend to militarism in all cultures; development of global peace-keeping structures and arms control agreements.

6. Increasing effort to limit domination of Western culture and allow survival of indigenous cultures.

7. Decreasing material affluence as costs of overdevelopment exceed benefits; broader quality of life measures developed and employed.

8. Decreasing rate of world population growth.

9. Declining urbanization in rich nations and growth of nonmetro areas relative to metro areas; in poor nations, efforts to stem growth of rural-urban migration.

10. Environmental costs included in new and more holistic measures of "progress" and "growth."

11. Stability or decline in service sector; more emphasis on self-reliance, self-service, part-time employment, job sharing, small farms or partly self-sufficient homesteads; new occupational categories necessitated.

12. Emphasis on new human needs-oriented definition of "progress"; serious consideration of preferred alternative futures replacing forecasting.

13. Increasing universality of this multifold trend and increasing tempo of change in all of the above.

New Directions for New Towns

As a social invention with great potential for advancing this new social paradigm, the new town has special relevance. Historically, urban planning has reflected the culture more than it has reformed it, and with few exceptions has reinforced trends toward "modernity." The new towns have been exceptions to this rule. They, more than any other urban planning initiative, have embodied an *alternative* view of the future based on *qualitative* growth and human-centered institutions. They have served an important *demonstration* function, physically communicating what Bertrand de Jouvenel in another context called "exhibits of achievable ends."[9] Because they are tangible and can be seen and assessed, they permit two crucial tests which are antecedent to any lasting change: the tests of "likelihood" and "likeability."[10] Observers can apply both objective and subjective tests as to the system's feasibility and desirability. Studies in the psychology of change emphasize the importance of this subjective element, although it is frequently overlooked in "evaluating" future proposals. One of the greatest contributions of demonstration projects is their ability to elicit both rational and emotional responses.

Because the new towns approximate whole systems, with the interaction of people, place, and institutions, they are especially promising for advancing this new social paradigm. Their holistic nature permits men and women to "see" "otherness" as both workable and appealing. The towns can embody positive images of the future that are capable of persuading large numbers of ordinary citizens that other paths are possible, other choices exist.

The strategic importance of positive images of the future in effecting cultural change has been thoroughly explored by Frederick Polak in his lengthy study, *The Image of the Future*, and by Elise Boulding, who has translated his work from the Dutch and extended it significantly.[11] Together they (and others who have followed in this pioneering research[12]) have documented the extent to which our ideas about the future influence the future, and how *the image of the future* that guides behavior in the present is in no small way the "cause" of the present. Boulding in particular has taken these ideas and applied them to public policy issues, urging the generation of innovative, positive future images capable of breaking with the "stale strategies" that so often impede purposive change in the present.[13]

Because they present positive alternatives to current patterns, because they are holistic, and because they are demonstrations of achievable ends, the new towns can be powerful leaders in directing the culture along new lines. This is their potential. But the next generation of new towns must be reconceived if this potential is to be realized. It is clearly beyond the scope of this study to outline the next generation of new communities. Nevertheless, conclusions drawn from this analysis bear on the general direction the movement must take if it is to contribute to civilizational reform, at once its legacy from Ebenezer Howard and its nascent potential today.

American new towns in this century have ostensibly advanced decentralized and human needs-centered social visions. As this study has attempted to show, such advancement has often been more apparent than real. While embracing "human scale" as related to spatial considerations, new town planners have seldom struggled with the decentralization of economic institutions, which is at the heart of the new social paradigm outlined by Marien. Unlike the traditional right-left political axis concerning the control of production, Marien says, the axis of difference between the "Service Society" and "Self-Reliant Society" views concerns *the scale and purpose of production.*[14]

Economic decentralization means more than the provision of local jobs for new town residents. It means community self-determination, which in turn means a certain degree of independence from national and international economic forces. American new towns have been tightly integrated with the national economy and are therefore as vulnerable as any other "traditional" city to economic cycles, fluctuations in food and energy costs, and labor force requirements. The next generation of new towns must become more self-reliant cities. For if we can no longer "grow" our way out of old problems, "solving" them by economic aggrandizement, then planners must begin to think in terms of indigenous resources, both material and human, and meeting local needs largely (but not exclusively) with local effort. Indeed, the extent to which capital is retained within the community to do real productive work, rather than exported to other cities in an unfavorable "balance of payments," is the true measure of a community's economic health.

In the new decentralist social paradigm, there can be no exceptional cities with the misfits and problems of urban-industrial society relegated to others to contend with. The new towns must provide a viable economic development model which incorporates the needs and realities of the growing numbers of people who do not fit the requirements of a "high-tech," service society. Thus the *purpose* of production, as well as its scale, is a *social* issue in the new paradigm. Proponents of this view argue the importance of work beyond the provision of products and services for consumption and emphasize its essential role in realizing one's humanity and in building community among men and women. For social, psychological and economic reasons, they advocate community development through a mix of technology choices, including substantial investment in "appropriate technologies."[15] Because they are low cost, easily understood and maintained, rely on local resources, foster self-help and local control, and have minimal adverse environmental impact, "appropriate technologies" are especially suited to problems of "underdevelopment" and "overdevelopment" alike. They address the need for economic development and meaningful work simultaneously.

The next generation of new towns must advance a genuine ecological ethic, not a "landscape ethic" such as has been pronounced in community development over the last decades. A much more sophisticated approach is needed in understanding and minimizing the impact of settlement and activity patterns on the environment. Worldwatch Institute has identified three threats to civilization which are environmental in nature: the erosion of soil, the deterioration of biological systems which provide the resource underpinnings for human life as well as the industrial economy, and the rapid depletion of oil reserves before adequate substitutes can be developed.[16] These are worldwide phenomena in which developed societies like the United States are heavily implicated. Among the changes required to address these problems are strict conservation measures, superior land use planning, preservation of prime agricultural land, efforts to safeguard water and air quality, reliance on renewable energy resources, protection of topsoil, reduced consumption and waste, and the crafting of an environmental ethic. Adoption of these practices and values within the industrialized nations would address not only their particular problems but those of the less-developed world as well. The affluence and waste of the First World nations figure decisively in the poverty and environmental degradation of Third World countries. Many people in these nations are unable to feed themselves because the land, water, and credit resources have been geared away from food sufficiency to export commodity agriculture—such as flowers or strawberries or coffee, which fill "needs" of the wealthy nations. The American insatiable appetite for burgers has similarly hastened the destruction of the world's tropical rain forests, as entrepreneurs have responded to this market by clearing forests for grazing lands.[17] As the forests are in jeopardy, so too is the vast reservoir of genetic material contained in its rich plant and animal life, and so too is the earth's climate since the storage and discharge of water is importantly regulated by the tropical rainforests. These are but two examples of the ecological interdependence of all life on earth. New town planners can assert leadership in fostering this awareness, in broadening public understanding of the local-to-global dimensions of lifestyle and consumption patterns, and in developing new technical and social systems which support living harmoniously with natural systems.

Finally, the next generation of new town planners must confront the meaning of community in all its diversity. New towns cannot be used for isolationist ends but must instead embrace the entire human family with all its variety and conflicting differences. Distributional issues, and those of justice and equity, must be central to any social planning. Developing trust and new modes of relating to others is vital to the new social paradigm, but these goals cannot be presumed to follow effortlessly from mere face-to-face interaction. Institution-building is essential to this process. In many ways, new town planners of the last decades have not realized their social goals because they advanced visions but failed to develop the institutional support to sustain them. Community development necessarily requires cooperative institutions, and community self-determination absolutely requires political ones.

Should the next generation of new communities be crafted on this emerging social paradigm of urban self-reliance,[18] these cities would look remarkably like the conceptual basis of Garden City as Howard outlined it nearly a century ago. And like the two garden cities he actually saw constructed, future new towns organized on decentrist, human-needs lines can be powerful influences in redirecting the entire city-building and social reform process.

As social inventions anticipating the new century and its requirements for building a sustainable society, these new towns must perforce be highly experimental. Howard's reflections on this process remain relevant. "It is quite true that the pathway of experiment towards a better state of society is strewn with failures," he wrote. "But so is the pathway of experiment to any result that is worth achieving. Success is, for the most part, built on failure."[19] And the road of innovation is *always* paved as it is walked.

Figure 1. An Underpass at Radburn, New Jersey, 1985
(Photo: © David L. Ames)

Figure 2. Interior Park within a Superblock at Radburn, New Jersey, 1985
(Photo: © David L. Ames)

Figure 3. Houses Turned to Face the Interior Park, Radburn, New Jersey, 1985
(Photo: © David L. Ames)

Figure 4. Multifamily Housing, Radburn, New Jersey, 1985
(*Photo: © David L. Ames*)

Figure 5. The Elementary School and Its Surrounding Park. Radburn, New Jersey, 1985
(Photo: © David L. Ames)

Figure 6. Swimming Pool within the Superblock and near the Elementary School, Radburn, New Jersey, 1985
(Photo: © David L. Ames)

Figure 7. Underpass at Greenbelt, Maryland, 1942
(Photo: Courtesy of Library of Congress)

Figure 8. Aerial View of Greenbelt, Maryland, during Early Construction, 1936
(Photo: Courtesy of Library of Congress)

Figure 9. Aerial View, Greenhills, Ohio, 1938
(Photo: Courtesy of Library of Congress)

Figure 10. Housing and Open Space, Greenbelt, Maryland, 1942
(Photo: Courtesy of Library of Congress)

Figure 11. Greendale, Wisconsin, 1939
(Photo: Courtesy of Library of Congress)

Figure 12. Tree-lined Streets in Levittown (Willingboro), New Jersey, 1985
(Photo: © David L. Ames)

Figure 13. Housing in Levittown (Willingboro), New Jersey, 1985 (Photo: © David L. Ames)

Figure 14. Neighborhood School and Recreation Center, Levittown (Willingboro), New Jersey, 1985 (*Photo: © David L. Ames*)

Figure 15. Downtown Columbia, Maryland, 1985
The city fronts on a lake.
(Photo: © David L. Ames)

Figure 16. Fishing in Downtown Columbia, Maryland, 1985
(Photo: © David L. Ames)

Figure 17. Columbia, Maryland, 1985
(Photo: © David L. Ames)

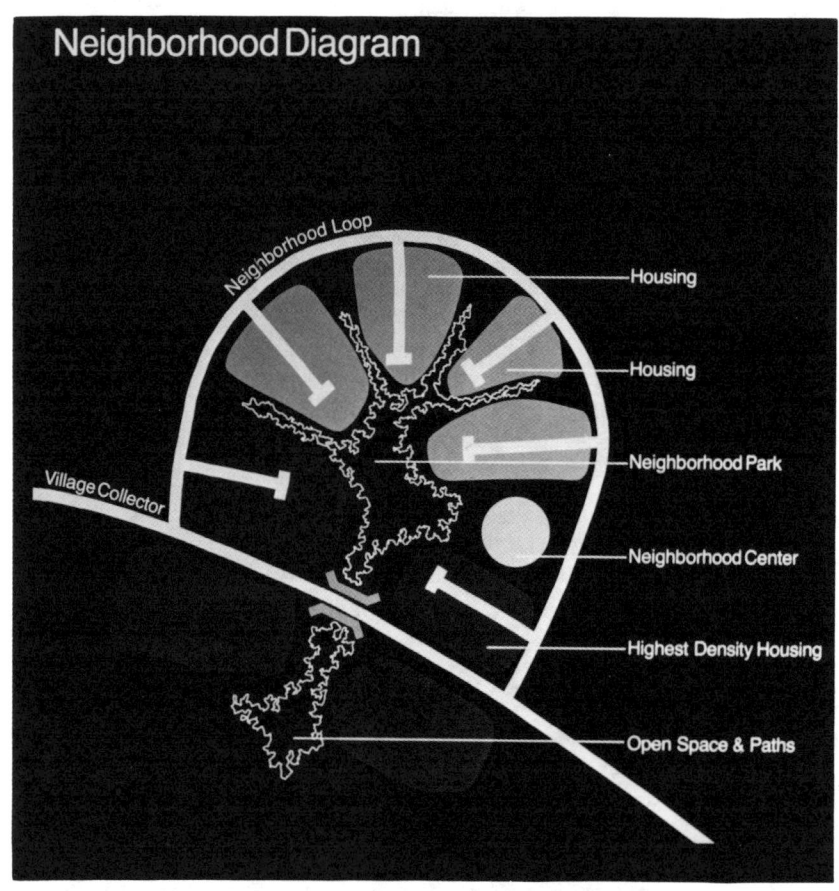

Figure 18. The Neighborhood Concept at Columbia, Maryland
(Photo: © David L. Ames)

Figure 19. Open Space, Columbia, Maryland, 1985
(Photo: © David L. Ames)

Figure 20. Open Space and Condominium Housing, Columbia, Maryland, 1985
(Photo: © David L. Ames)

Notes

Introduction

1. Ebenezer Howard, *Garden Cities of Tomorrow: A Peaceful Path to Real Reform* (Cambridge, Mass.: MIT Press, 1965).
2. J. Ross McKeever, "Private Development by Private Interests," *Urban Land*, April 1965, p. 2.
3. Frederick L. Polak, *The Future of Man*, as quoted in Don Fabun (ed.), *The Dimensions of Change* (Beverly Hills, Calif.: Glencoe Press, Macmillan Co., 1971), p. 32.
4. Lewis Mumford, *The Story of Utopias* (New York: Viking, 1962).
5. George Kateb, "Utopias and Utopianism," *International Encyclopedia of the Social Sciences*, vol. 16, 1968, p. 269.
6. For this clarification of the utopian tradition I am indebted to J. C. Davis, "Utopia and History," *Historical Studies*, April 1968. Davis usefully distinguishes between utopia, the Perfect Moral Commonwealth, and the millenarian and arcadian traditions.
7. Kateb, p. 269.
8. Jane Jacobs, *The Economy of Cities* (New York: Random House, 1969).
9. Yi-Fu Tuan, *Topophilia, A Study of Environmental Perceptions, Attitudes, and Values* (Englewood Cliffs, N.J.: Prentice-Hall, 1974).
10. Sylvia Thrupp, "The City as the Ideal of Social Order," in Oscar Handlin and John Burchard (eds.), *The Historian and the City* (Cambridge, Mass.: MIT Press and Harvard University Press, 1963).
11. Sennett argues persuasively that the city is necessary for human *psychological* maturity. Richard Sennett, *The Uses of Disorder: Personal Identity and City Life* (New York: Alfred A. Knopf, 1970).
12. These intentional societies are discussed by Mark Holloway, *Heavens on Earth, Utopian Communities in America, 1680–1880* (New York: Dover, 1966); Ruth E. Sutter, *The Next Place You Come To, A Historical Introduction to Communities in North America* (Englewood Cliffs, N.J.: Prentice-Hall, 1973); Arthur E. Bestor, Jr., *Backwoods Utopias* (Philadelphia: University of Pennsylvania Press, 1950); and Charles Nordhoff, *The Communistic Societies of the United States* (New York: Schocken, 1875, 1965).

13. Bestor.
14. Clarence S. Stein, "Indications of the Form of the Future," in *Toward New Towns for America* (Cambridge, Mass.: MIT Press, 1966), pp. 217-227.
15. Davis.

Chapter 1

1. Arthur M. Schlesinger, "The City in American Civilization," in *Paths to the Present* (Cambridge, Mass.: Riverside Press, 1949, 1964).
2. As quoted in Roderick Nash, *Wilderness and the American Mind* (New Haven, Conn.: Yale University Press, 1973), p. 146.
3. U.S. Census Bureau, as quoted in F. J. Turner, "The Significance of the Frontier in American History," in *The Frontier in American History* (Huntington, N.Y.: Robert E. Krieger Publishing Co., 1976), p. 1.
4. Frederick Jackson Turner, "The Significance of the Frontier in American History," in *The Frontier in American History* (Huntington, N.Y.: Robert E. Krieger Publishing Co., 1976), p. 1.
5. Schlesinger, p. 219.
6. Zane Miller, *The Urbanization of Modern America* (New York: Harcourt, Brace, Jovanovich, 1973).
7. Ibid., p. 15.
8. Richard C. Wade, "The City in History—Some American Perspectives," in Werner Z. Hirsch (ed.), *Urban Life and Form* (New York: Holt, Rinehart and Winston, 1963).
9. Ibid.
10. Miller, p. 13.
11. Wade.
12. Howard P. Chudacoff, *The Evolution of American Urban Society* (Englewood Cliffs, N.J.: Prentice-Hall, 1975), p. 29.
13. Wade.
14. Miller, p. 31.
15. See Robert H. Wiebe, *The Search for Order, 1877-1920* (New York: Hill and Wang, 1967).
16. Schlesinger, p. 209.
17. Ibid., p. 210.
18. Wade.
19. Ibid.
20. Turner, p. 29.
21. Stephan Thernstrom, *Poverty and Progress, Social Mobility in a Nineteenth-Century City* (New York: Atheneum, 1972).
22. Schlesinger, p. 207.

23. Ibid.
24. See Raymond Vernon, *The Myth and Reality of Our Urban Problems* (Cambridge, Mass.: Harvard University Press, 1962, 1966).
25. William Jennings Bryan, "Cross of Gold" speech, July 8, 1896, Democratic National Convention, Chicago, Illinois. Reprinted in George B. deHuszar, Henry W. Littlefield and Arthur W. Littlefield (eds.), *Basic American Documents* (Ames, Iowa: Littlefield, Adams & Co., 1956), p. 229.
26. As quoted in P. L. Ford (ed.), *The Works of Thomas Jefferson*, IX (New York, 1904), pp. 146-147.
27. Barbara Novak, *American Painting of the Nineteenth Century; Realism, Idealism, and the American Experience* (New York: Praeger, 1969).
28. Ibid.
29. John W. Ward, "The Politics of Design," in Laurence B. Holland (ed.), *Who Designs America?* (Garden City, N.Y.: Doubleday-Anchor, 1966), p. 61.
30. Louis H. Sullivan, *The Autobiography of an Idea* (New York: Dover Publications, 1924, 1956), p. 290.
31. David W. Noble, *Historians Against History* (Minneapolis: University of Minnesota Press, 1965); *The Eternal Adam and the New World Garden* (New York: Braziller, 1968); *The Progressive Mind: 1890-1917* (Chicago: Rand McNally, 1970).
32. Walter Allen, *The Modern Novel in Britain and the United States* (New York: E. P. Dutton & Co., 1964, 1965), p. xv.
33. Richard Chase, *The American Novel and Its Tradition* (Garden City, N.Y.: Doubleday Anchor, 1957).
34. Samuel Clemens, *Adventures of Huckleberry Finn* (New York: W. W. Norton & Co., 1961, 1962), p. 226.
35. Nash, p. 85.
36. Novak.
37. Sam Bass Warner, Jr., *The Urban Wilderness, A History of the American City* (New York: Harper and Row, 1972), Chapter 2.
38. Ibid.
39. Daniel J. Boorstin, *The Lost World of Thomas Jefferson* (Boston: Beacon Press, 1948).
40. Miller, p. 26.
41. John W. Ward, *Andrew Jackson—Symbol for an Age* (New York: Oxford University Press, 1953, 1955).
42. Henry David Thoreau, "Where I Lived and What I Lived For," *Walden*, in Norman Foerster (ed.), *American Poetry and Prose*, Part I (Boston: Houghton-Mifflin, 1957), p. 569.
43. Henry David Thoreau, *Excursions, The Writings of Henry David Thoreau*, IX (Boston, 1893), p. 287.
44. As quoted in Nash, p. 87.

Notes for Chapter 2

45. As quoted in Perry Miller, *Consciousness in Concord* (Boston: Houghton-Mifflin, 1958), p. 46.
46. Emerson, as quoted in Bliss Perry (ed.), *The Heart of Emerson's Journals* (Boston, 1937), p. 208.
47. Morton and Lucia White, *The Intellectual and the City* (New York: New American Library, Mentor Books, 1969), p. 37.
48. E. W. Emerson (ed.), *The Complete Works of Ralph Waldo Emerson*, III (Boston: 1903-04), pp. 153-54.
49. As quoted in White and White, p. 36.
50. Ibid.
51. Samuel P. Hays, "Business Elite and the Centralization of Decision-Making," in Bruce M. Stave (ed.), *Urban Bosses, Machines and Progressive Reformers* (Lexington, Mass.: D. C. Heath & Co., 1972).
52. Richard Hofstadter, *The Age of Reform* (New York: Vintage Books, 1955).
53. Wiebe.
54. Ward, "The Politics of Design."
55. John Dewey, *The Public and Its Problems* (New York: Holt, 1927).
56. Noble, *The Progressive Mind*.

Chapter 2

1. Sam Bass Warner, Jr., *Streetcar Suburbs, The Process of Growth in Boston 1870-1900* (New York: Atheneum, 1962, 1973).
2. Zane W. Miller, *The Urbanization of Modern America* (New York: Harcourt, Brace, Jovanovich, 1973), p. 164.
3. Mel Scott, *American City Planning Since 1890* (Berkeley, Calif.: University of California Press, 1969), p. 80.
4. Ibid., p. 17.
5. Roderick Nash, *Wilderness and the American Mind* (New Haven, Conn.: Yale University Press, 1973), p. 106.
6. Ibid., p. 155.
7. Ibid., p. 106.
8. Ibid., p. 155.
9. Scott, p. 107. See also Roy Lubove, *The Urban Community, Housing and Planning in the Progressive Era* (Englewood Cliffs, N.J.: Prentice-Hall, 1967).
10. Scott, p. 66.
11. J. Horace McFarland, "The Nationalization of Civic Improvement," *Charities and the Commons,* XVII (1906), p. 231, as quoted in Scott, p. 67.
12. Charles M. Robinson, *Modern Civic Art* (New York, 1904), p. 27, as quoted in Scott, p. 68.

Notes for Chapter 2   161

13. Civic League of St. Louis, *A City Plan for St. Louis* (St. Louis, 1907), p. 53, as quoted in Scott, p. 73.
14. Ibid., pp. 37-39.
15. Marshall B. Clinard, *Slums and Community Development* (New York: The Free Press, 1966), p. 40.
16. Ibid., p. 41.
17. Scott, p. 7.
18. Clinard, p. 32.
19. Ibid., p. 32.
20. Scott, p. 10.
21. Clinard, p. 33.
22. Ibid.
23. Glenn H. Beyer, *Housing and Society* (New York: MacMillan Co., 1965), p. 453.
24. Scott, p. 10.
25. Clinard, p. 37.
26. *City Planning*, U.S. 61st Congress, 2nd Session, S. Doc. 422 (1910), p. 59, as quoted in Scott, p. 96.
27. Edith Elmer Wood, *Housing of the Unskilled Wage Earner* (New York: MacMillan, 1919), p. 7.
28. Adna F. Weber, "Growth of Cities in the United States: 1890-1900," *Municipal Affairs*, v (June 1901), p. 375.
29. *City Planning*, U.S. 61st Congress, 2nd Session, S. Doc. 422 (1910), p. 59, as quoted in Scott, pp. 98-99.
30. B. C. Marsh, "City Planning in Justice to the Working Population," *Charities*, xix (Feb. 1, 1908), p. 1516, as quoted in Scott, pp. 85-86.
31. For an excellent discussion of Marsh's role in early planning history, see Harvey A. Kantor, "Benjamin C. Marsh and the Fight Over Population Congestion," in Donald A. Krueckeberg (ed.), *The American Planner* (New York: Methuen, 1983), pp. 58-74.
32. Scott, pp. 166-167.
33. American Institute of Architects, *City Planning Progress* (Washington, 1917), p. iii, as quoted in Scott, pp. 166-67.
34. Scott, p. 121.
35. Ibid., p. 124.
36. George E. Kessler, *A City Plan For Dallas*, 1910, p. 8, as quoted in Scott, p. 124.
37. Scott, p. 152.
38. Ibid., p. 155.
39. Ibid.

40. Ibid., p. 162.
41. Charles H. Cheney, "Districting Progress and Procedure in California," *Proceedings of the Ninth National Conference on City Planning*, p. 185, as quoted in Scott, p. 161.
42. Frederick L. Ackerman, "Where Goes the City-Planning Movement?", *Journal of the American Institute of Architects*, VII (December 1919), pp. 519–20.
43. John Nolen, *Replanning Small Cities* (New York: B.W. Huebsch, 1912), p. 2, as quoted in John Hancock, "John Nolen: The Background of a Pioneer Planner," in Donald A. Krueckberg (ed.), *The American Planner* (New York: Methuen, 1983), pp. 44–45.

Chapter 3

1. Ebenezer Howard, *Garden Cities of Tomorrow* (Cambridge, Mass.: The MIT Press, 1965).
2. Ibid., p. 19.
3. Ibid., p. 37.
4. Ibid., p. 127.
5. Ibid., p. 138.
6. Ibid., p. 106.
7. Ibid.
8. In formulating his scheme, Howard drew from Herbert Spencer the principle of tenancy as the only land tenure, and from Thomas Spence the concept of a single-rate rent administered by the community. The specific application of common ownership of land to an urban setting was an extension of J.S. Buckingham's early-nineteenth-century proposal for a model industrial town. He drew his concepts of social balance from the proposals of E.G. Wakefield and Alfred Marshall. All of these sources were explicitly acknowledged. For an analysis of these and other influences on Howard, see W.A. Eden, "Ebenezer Howard and the Garden City Movement," *Town Planning Review*, Summer 1947. See also F.J. Osborn, "Sir Ebenezer Howard, The Evolution of His Ideas," *Town Planning Review*, October 1950.
9. Howard, p. 136.
10. F.J. Osborn, Preface to Howard, p. 26.
11. Lewis Mumford, "The Garden City Idea and Modern Planning," introductory essay in Howard, pp. 34–35.
12. Howard, p. 148.
13. Ibid., p. 147.
14. Ibid., p. 158.
15. Ibid., p. 138.
16. Ibid., p. 131.
17. Ibid., p. 123.
18. Ibid., p. 138.

19. Mumford in Howard, pp. 37-38.
20. Ibid., p. 38.
21. For an overview of the British experience, see Frederic J. Osborn and Arnold Whittick, *The New Towns, The Answer to Megalopolis* (New York: McGraw Hill, 1965); Ray Thomas and Peter Cresswell, *The New Town Idea* (Milton Keynes, U.K.: The Open University Press, 1973); Sir Frederic J. Osborn, "Britain's Place in Town Planning," in H. Wentworth Eldredge (ed.), *Taming Megalopolis*, Vol. II (Garden City, N.Y.: Anchor Books, Doubleday & Co., 1967). Information about recent decisions affecting the new towns can be found in *Town and Country Planning*, special issue on new towns, vol. 52, no. 11 (November 1983), and vol. 53, no. 11 (November 1984).
22. J.B. Cullingworth, *Town and Country Planning in Britain* (ninth edition) (London: George Allen & Unwin, 1985), ch. 9.
23. Thomas & Creswell, p. 14.
24. Ibid., pp. 18-19. Also Cullingworth, p. 407.
25. Thomas and Creswell, p. 24.
26. Ibid., p. 17.
27. Ibid., pp. 48-49.
28. Ibid.

Chapter 4

1. For a history of the RPAA, see Roy Lubove, *Community Planning in the 1920s: The Contribution of the Regional Planning Association* (Pittsburgh: University of Pittsburgh Press, 1963) and Carl Sussman (ed.), *Planning the Fourth Migration: The Neglected Vision of the Regional Planning Association of America* (Cambridge, Mass.: The MIT Press, 1976).
2. Eugenie Ladner Birch, "Radburn and the American Planning Movement: The Persistence of an Idea," in Donald A. Krueckeberg (ed.), *The American Planner* (New York & London: Methuen, 1983).
3. Sussman, p. 21.
4. Lewis Mumford, "The Fourth Migration," *Survey Graphic* 7 (May 1925): pp. 130-33, quoted in Sussman, p. 59.
5. Ibid., p. 61.
6. Ibid., p. 56.
7. Clarence S. Stein, "Dinosaur Cities," *Survey Graphic* 7 (May 1925), pp. 134-38.
8. Lewis Mumford, "The Fate of Garden Cities," *Journal of the American Institute of Architects* 15 (February 1927), p. 39.
9. Clarience S. Stein, *Toward New Towns for America* (Cambridge, Mass.: MIT Press, 1950, 1957, 1965), p. 220.
10. Geddes Smith, "A Town for the Motor Age," as quoted in Stein, *New Towns*, p. 44.

11. Stein, *New Towns*, p. 21. For the evolution of Sunnyside Gardens and Radburn, and the changes made over the planning years, see Alexander M. Bing for the Board of Directors, "Annual Report[s] of the City Housing Corporation, nos. 4–10" (New York: The Corporation, 1928–1934).

12. Stein, *New Towns*, p. 21.

13. Lubove, p. 33.

14. Stein, *New Towns*, p. 22.

15. Ibid., p. 34.

16. Ibid., p. 28.

17. Ibid., p. 37.

18. Ibid., p. 22.

19. Ibid., p. 40. While there was no industry, provision was made for stores and shops. See Clarence S. Stein and Catherine Bauer, "Store Buildings and Neighborhood Shopping Centers," *Architectural Record*, February 1934.

20. Robert B. Hudson, *Radburn: A Plan of Living. A Study Made for the American Association for Adult Education* (New York: American Association for Adult Education, 1934), p. 13.

21. Ibid., pp. 11–12.

22. Ibid., p. 12.

23. Stein, *New Towns*, p. 68.

24. Sussman, p. 18.

25. Stein, *New Towns*, p. 67.

26. For plans, illustrations, maps, and descriptions of the physical and social features of "The Radburn Idea," see, in addition to Stein, Louis Brownlow, "Radburn: A New Town Planned for the Motor Age," in *International Housing and Town Planning Bulletin*, February 1930; James Bailey (ed.), *New Towns in America, The Design and Development Process* (New York: John Wiley & Sons for the American Institute of Architects, 1973), p. 8; Arthur C. Comey and Max S. Wehrly, *Planned Communities. Part I of Urban Planning and Land Policies, Vol. II, of the Supplementary Report of the Urbanism Commission to the National Resources Commission* (Washington, D.C.: Government Printing Office, 1939), pp. 97 ff.; and Henry Wright, "The Radburn Plan," *National Real Estate Journal*, September 30, 1929.

27. Stein, *New Towns*, p. 41.

28. Geddes Smith, as quoted in Stein, p. 44.

29. Stein discussed the overhead factor in "Dinosaur Cities," *Survey Graphic* 7 (May 1925), pp. 134–38. Also reprinted in Sussman, pp. 65–74.

30. Stein, *New Towns*, p. 48.

31. James Rouse, "The City of Columbia," in H. Wentworth Eldredge (ed.), *Taming Megalopolis* (New York: Anchor, 1967), p. 844.

32. Stein, *New Towns*, pp. 218-19.
33. Ibid., pp. 217-18.
34. Ibid., p. 218.
35. ibid., p. 217.
36. Ibid., p. 218.
37. See Ruth E. Sutter, *The Next Place You Come To, A Historical Introduction to Communities in North America* (Englewood Cliffs, N.J.: Prentice-Hall, 1973), pp. 50-54.
38. Stein, *New Towns*, p. 218.
39. Charles H. Cooley, *Social Process* (New York: Charles Scribner's Sons, 1918), p. 192.
40. Stein, *New Towns*, p. 218.
41. Lewis Mumford, "The Garden City Idea and Modern Planning," in Ebenezer Howard, *Garden Cities of Tomorrow* (Cambridge, Mass.: MIT Press, 1965), p. 38.
42. Stein, *New Towns*, p. 60.
43. Hudson, p. 85.
44. Stein, *New Towns*, p. 63.
45. Stein was disturbed that children frequently played in the lanes behind rather than on the greens in front of the house. In trying to account for this, he concluded that their wheeled toys went better on the pavement of the lanes, but that a solution to this problem probably required a change in the house plan. Since the living room was placed in the front of the house and the kitchen in the rear, mothers presumably kept their children out back where they could watch them. Since Stein preferred not to change the reposeful location of the living room, he decided that the kitchen/dining area should be extended the length of the house so that mother could easily keep a watchful eye on children playing on the park side. In his discussion of this problem, Stein gave no mention of factors other than design. It apparently did not occur to him that the allure of streets for children was frequently due to the activity there. Even the lightly-traveled rear lanes brought human activity frequently more interesting than trees or flowers. Stein, *New Towns*, p. 52.
46. Hudson, p. 9.
47. Stein, *New Towns*, p. 51.
48. Ibid., p. 41.
49. Hudson, p. 85.
50. Ibid., p. 38.
51. Stein, *New Towns*, pp. 218-19.
52. Robert E. Park, et al., *The City* (Chicago: University of Chicago Press, 1925).
53. Louis Wirth, "Urbanism as a Way of Life," *American Journal of Sociology*, vol. 44, July 1938, pp. 1-24.
54. Albert Z. Guttenberg, "City Encounter and 'Desert' Encounter: Two Sources of American Regional Planning Thought," *Journal of the American Institute of Planners*, vol. 44, no. 4, October 1978, p. 400.

55. As quoted in Guttenberg, p. 402.
56. Stein, *New Towns*, p. 219.
57. Hudson, p. 12.
58. Ibid., p. 3.
59. Ibid., p. 5.
60. Stein, *New Towns*, p. 60.
61. Ibid.
62. Ibid., p. 187.
63. Richard Sennett, *The Uses of Disorder: Personal Identity and City Life* (New York: Alfred A. Knopf, 1970).
64. Ibid., p. 70.
65. Ibid., p. 80.
66. Stein, *New Towns*, p. 61. For a fuller explication of the Radburn Association, see "Radburn, Protective Restrictions and Community Administration," (New York: City Housing Corporation, 1929).
67. Stein, *New Towns*, p. 62.
68. Hudson, p. 54.
69. Stein, *New Towns*, p. 62.
70. Hudson, p. 54.
71. Ibid., p. 80.
72. Ibid., p. 15.
73. Ibid., p. 88.
74. Stein, *New Towns*, p. 60.
75. Ibid., p. 63.
76. Ibid., p. 60.
77. Ibid., p. 34.
78. Ibid., p. 218.
79. Ibid., p. 218.
80. Stein, as quoted in Sussman, p. 15.
81. Ibid.
82. Stein, *New Towns*, p. 66.
83. Hudson, p. 12.
84. Stein, *New Towns*, pp. 68–69.
85. Hudson, pp. 24–25.

86. Stein did acknowledge Olmstead's influence on his work. (The separation of pedestrian and vehicular traffic in Radburn was directly derived from Olmstead's plan of Central Park.) Stein, *New Towns*, p. 44.
87. Stein, *New Towns*, p. 66.
88. Ibid.
89. Hudson, p. 12.
90. Stein, *New Towns*, p. 226.

Chapter 5

1. Joseph L. Arnold, *The New Deal in the Suburbs, a History of the Greenbelt Town Program, 1935-1954* (Columbus, Ohio: Ohio State University Press, 1971). Another valuable source is Paul K. Conkin, *Tomorrow a New World: The New Deal Community Program* (Ithaca, N.Y.: Cornell University Press, 1959).
2. Arnold, p. 42.
3. Ibid., p. 112.
4. Ibid., p. 29.
5. Ibid., p. 26. See also Rexford G. Tugwell, "Down to Earth," *Current History*, July 1936. For a fuller analysis of Tugwell's philosophy, see David Myhra, "Rexford Guy Tugwell: Initiator of America's Greenbelt New Towns, 1935-36," in Donald A. Krueckeberg (ed.), *The American Planner* (New York & London: Methuen, 1983), p. 225-49.
6. Jonathan Mitchell, "Low-Cost Paradise," *New Republic*, September 18, 1935, p. 152.
7. Rexford G. Tugwell, "The Meaning of the Greenbelt Towns," *The New Republic*, February 17, 1937, p. 42.
8. Arnold, pp. 42-43.
9. Ibid.
10. Ibid., p. 44
11. See Arnold, p. 63 ff. After the U.S. Court of Appeals decision, a group of building and loan firms in the Milwaukee area announced their intention to file suit to stop both PWA and RA housing projects in Milwaukee County. Although the suit was filed, it was never heard. Since the land was already in the government's possession, it was immune from injunction by the terms of the Bound Brook decision which had related to land acquisition.
12. Arnold, pp. 38-39.
13. Ibid., pp. 40-41.
14. As quoted in Arnold, p. 89.
15. Arnold, pp. 96, 118.
16. On changing optimum sizes, see Arnold, p. 91.
17. Ibid., p. 118.
18. Ibid., pp. 126-27; also Clarence S. Stein, *Toward New Towns for America* (Cambridge, Mass.: MIT Press, 1957, 1965), pp. 169-73.

19. Arnold, p. 127.
20. "Greentowns All Sold by Federal Government," *The American City*, March 1953, p. 113; "Veterans Seek Purchase of Greendale," *The American City*, January 1949. See also Robert R. Poston, "Communique on National Housing Front," 4th issue, January 6, 1947, a report of the Special National Committee on Veteran's Housing of the American Legion.
21. Albert Mayer, "Greenbelt Towns Revisited," *The Journal of Housing*, April 1967, p. 157.
22. Warren Bishop, "A Yardstick for Housing," *Nation's Business*, April 1936, p. 70.
23. Arnold, p. 194.
24. Ibid., p. 119.
25. As quoted in Arnold, p. 194.
26. George Morris, "$16,000 Homes for $2,000 Incomes: Greenbelt, Maryland," *Nation's Business*, January 1938.
27. Arnold, p. 117.
28. Ibid., p. 96.
29. Stein, *New Towns*, pp. 120, 130.
30. Arnold, p. 47. In fact, Tugwell initially refused to hire planners, relying instead on engineers to draw up plans for the towns. He distrusted professional planners, considering them too "utopian."
31. U.S. Resettlement Administration, "Greenbelt Towns," p. 1.
32. Arnold, p. 149.
33. Stein, *New Towns*, p. 121.
34. Douglas Marshall, "Greendale: A Study of a Resettlement Community," unpublished Ph.D. dissertation, University of Wisconsin, July 31, 1943, pp. 71-72.
35. The ceiling was actually graduated according to family size.
36. Arnold, p. 157.
37. Ibid.
38. Ibid.
39. Ibid., p. 76.
40. Sherwood L. Reeder, "A Report on the First Two Years of the Greendale Community," Greendale, Wis., April 30, 1940, p. 6.
41. Walter E. Kroening, "The Story of Greendale, a Government Demonstration in Community Planning and Public Housing," April 1944, p. 3. Mimeo.
42. It can be argued that the centralization of power in fact *restricts* democracy. See Samuel P. Hays, "Business Elite and the Centralization of Decision-Making," in Bruce M. Stave (ed.), *Urban Bosses, Machines, and Progressive Reformers* (Lexington, Mass.: D.C. Heath & Co., 1972).
43. Arnold, p. 149.
44. Stein, *New Towns*, p. 128.

Notes for Chapter 5

45. Reeder, p. 4.
46. "The Story of Greendale," in "This is Greendale," brochure prepared for Greendale's decennial celebration, 1948, p. 13.
47. Arnold, pp. 138-39.
48. U.S. Resettlement Administration, "Greenbelt Towns: A Demonstration in Suburban Planning," Washington, D.C., September 1936.
49. Arnold, pp. 142-43.
50. Ibid., p. 142.
51. Ibid., p. 141.
52. As quoted in Arnold, p. 140.
53. As quoted in Arnold, pp. 140-41.
54. Arnold, p. 142.
55. Reeder, p. 17.
56. Arnold, p. 93.
57. Ibid., p. 173.
58. Reeder, p. 17.
59. Arnold, p. 167.
60. See, for example, Rexford G. Tugwell, "Cooperation and Resettlement," *Current History*, February 1937.
61. Arnold, pp. 162-63.
62. Ibid., p. 173.
63. Ibid.
64. Ibid., pp. 180-82.
65. Reeder, p. 15.
66. Arnold, p. 7, 181-83.
67. Stein, *New Towns*, p. 131.
68. Reeder, p. 13.
69. Ibid., p. 18.
70. Arnold, p. 92.
71. Albert Mayer, "Greenbelt Towns Revisited," *The Journal of Housing*, February/March 1967, p. 85.
72. Stein, *New Towns*, p. 131.
73. Mayer, "Greenbelt Towns Revisited," p. 85.
74. Marshall, p. 67.
75. Stein, "Greendale and the Future," p. 21.

76. Douglas, p. 67.
77. Arnold, pp. 91–92.
78. As quoted in Arnold, pp. 92–93.
79. Stein, "Greendale and the Future," p. 21.
80. Ibid., pp. 20–21.
81. Vivian Husher, prose poem, "This is Greendale," in "This is Greendale," brochure prepared for Greendale's decennial celebration, 1948, p. 9.
82. Kroening, p. 1.
83. Ibid.
84. Mayer, "Greenbelt Towns Revisited," April 1967, p. 160.
85. Stein, *New Towns*, p. 177.
86. Reeder, p. 4.
87. See Howard P. Chudacoff, *The Evolution of American Urban Society* (Englewood Cliffs, N.J.: Prentice-Hall, 1975); Gideon Sjoberg, *The Preindustrial City* (New York: The Free Press, 1960); Raymond Vernon, *The Myth and Reality of Our Urban Problems* (Cambridge, Mass.: Harvard University Press, 1962, 1966).
88. Arnold, pp. 94–95.
89. Stein, "Greendale and the Future," pp. 19, 127.
90. Ibid., p. 19.
91. During the Roosevelt administration, Wirth and his colleagues at the University of Chicago frequently prepared testimony for congressional committee hearings on urban-related matters. Although "Urbanism as a Way of Life" was not published until 1938, Wirth served as an early consultant (from 1935 to 1943) to the National Resources Planning Board. See Albert J. Reiss, Jr. (ed.), *Louis Wirth on Cities and Social Life* (Chicago: University of Chicago Press, 1964), p. 338.
92. Louis Wirth, "Urbanism as a Way of Life," *American Journal of Sociology*, July 1938, pp. 1–24.
93. Stein, "Greendale and the Future," p. 22.
94. Mayer, p. 83.
95. See Mitchell.
96. Stein, "Greendale and the Future," p. 22.
97. Reeder, p. 12.
98. Kroening, p. 1.
99. Stein, "Greendale and the Future," p. 21.

Chapter 6

1. "Biggest New City in the U. S.," *House and Home*, December 1952, p. 81.
2. Ibid. For further details, see "PB Reveals Levitt's Building Methods," *Practical Builder*, August 1959.
3. Alfred S. Levitt, "A Community Builder Looks at Community Planning," *Journal of the American Institute of Planners*, Spring 1951, p. 80.
4. Ibid., p. 82
5. Ibid.
6. Ibid., p. 81.
7. Ibid.
8. Ibid., p. 87.
9. Ibid., p. 82.
10. Ibid., p. 85.
11. Ibid., p. 87.
12. Ibid., p. 82.
13. Ibid., p. 84.
14. Institute for Urban Studies, University of Pennsylvania, *A Study of Urbanization, Suburbanization and the Impact of the Fairless Works Steel Plant in Lower Bucks County, Pennsylvania*, Volume I (Philadelphia: The Institute, September 1954), p. 4.
15. See "New Towns: Industry's Move to Uncongested Land Outside the Cities," *Architectural Forum*, November 1951.
16. Ibid.
17. *House and Home*, p. 84.
18. Institute for Urban Studies, p. 4.
19. *House and Home*, p. 84.
20. *Architectural Forum*, p. 139.
21. *House and Home*, p. 90.
22. Ibid.
23. William J. Levitt, "What! Live in a Levittown?", *Good Housekeeping*, July 1958, p. 175.
24. *Architectural Forum*, p. 138; *House and Home*, p. 89.
25. *Architectural Forum*, p. 87.
26. Institute for Urban Studies, p. 12.

27. In 1958 a white family sold its home to a Black family, triggering a racial disturbance in the town. It was not until 1960, and then in the third Levittown, that more systematic attempts at integration took place. For that story, see U.S. Housing and Home Finance Agency, "Changing a Racial Policy, Levittown, New Jersey," in *Equal Opportunity in Housing*, June 1964.

28. Institute for Urban Studies, p. 40.

29. Herbert J. Gans, *The Levittowners* (New York: Vintage Books, 1967), p. 6.

30. William J. Levitt, pp. 47, 175–76.

31. Gans, p. 11.

32. Levitt donated sites to churches, including many minor denominations, requiring only that congregations build within a year of organization or forfeit the land. Fundamentalist groups were not given free land. Gans, pp. 8–9.

33. Gans, pp. 22–23.

34. Ibid., p. 9.

35. Ibid., pp. 6–7.

36. Ibid., pp. 136–37.

37. Ibid., p. 97.

38. Ibid., p. 136.

39. Apparently this was a sound decision. In his study, Gans found that 84 percent of the residents came to Levittown primarily because of house-related factors. Only a few considered the facilities and social quality of the community to be primary factors. Gans, p. 34.

40. Ibid., p. 13.

41. This relationship makes for a fascinating footnote in the Levittown story. While hired by the township, the planning consultant identified absolutely with Levitt's plan. In this he was not improperly influenced. On the contrary, his support of the plan reflected his firm belief in its soundness. As I've attempted to show, the site plan did not depart greatly from conventional planning practise, and the consultant himself subscribed to the conventional wisdom of the day. When the consultant drafted his own development plan in 1959 (it was adopted in 1965), it too corresponded with Levitt's. The incident points up how planning-as-free-enterprise-activity and planning-as-municipal-conservation are more often congruent than not. See Herbert H. Smith Associates, "Suggested Development Plan, Willingboro Township, New Jersey," prepared for the Willingboro Township Planning Board, May 1964.)

Chapter 7

1. J. Ross McKeever, "Private Development by Private Interests," *Urban Land*, April 1965, p. 2.

2. See Werthman, et al. (1965). In their study of planned communities in California, the authors found that "planning" and "community facilities" were closely related to a person's "class image" of the community. Also, see Edward P. Eichler and Marshall Kaplan, *The*

Notes for Chapter 7   173

   Community Builders (Berkeley: University of California Press, 1967). They note how developers have advantageously incorporated the concept of "planning" into their sales approaches. "Planning" sells houses.
3. Some were free-standing new towns set in rural areas, such as Lake Havasu City, Arizona, and Soul City, North Carolina. Others were satellite cities built near major metropolitan areas, such as Jonathan, Minnesota, and The Woodlands (near Houston), Texas. Still others were new-towns-in-town, like Cedar-Riverside, Minnesota, and Fort Lincoln, Maryland.
4. Quoted in Thomas W. Lippman and Bill Richards, "New Towns: Realities Dim Dreams," *Washington Post,* Jan. 12, 1975.
5. Regrettably, Fort Lincoln was never built as planned.
6. Lippman and Richards.
7. A critique of these early criteria is found in Carl Feiss, "USA: New Communities—or Their Simulacrum?", *Town and Country Planning,* January 1967.
8. "General Criteria for New Communities," Section 31.5 of the Regulations for the New Communities Act of 1968, as reprinted in Charles M. Haar (ed.), *The End of Innocence, A Suburban Reader* (Glenview, Ill.: Scott, Foresman & Co., 1972), pp. 219–20.
9. These were Jonathan (near Minneapolis), Minnesota; St. Charles (near Washington, D.C.), Maryland; Park Forest South (near Chicago), Illinois; Flower Mound (near Dallas), Texas; Maumelle (near Little Rock), Arkansas; Cedar-Riverside (in Minneapolis), Minnesota; Riverton (near Rochester), New York; Harbison (Columbia), South Carolina; The Woodlands (near Houston), Texas; Granada (near Rochester), New York; Soul City, North Carolina; Newfields (near Dayton), Ohio; San Antonio Ranch, Texas; Beckett (near Philadelphia), New Jersey; and Shenandoah (near Atlanta), Georgia.
10. James W. Rouse, "Great Cities for a Great Society," *Inland Architect,* May 1965. Also, Rouse, "Communication in Columbia," *Columbia Life,* July 14, 1971.
11. James Bailey, "Only in Columbia—the Next America," *Architectural Forum,* November 1967, p. 43.
12. The best account of the land acquisition process is in Gurney Breckenfeld, *Columbia and the New Cities* (New York: Ives Washburn, 1971).
13. James Rouse letter to Congressman Robert W. Kastenmeier, October 14, 1966. This and other correspondence can be found in the Howard County library where Rouse has placed many papers pertinent to Columbia's history.
14. Community Research and Development, Inc., "Columbia: A Presentation to the Officials and Citizens of Howard County, Maryland" (Columbia, Md.: CR & D, Inc., November 11, 1964), pp. 1–2.
15. Ibid., p. 46.
16. The Rouse Co., *1985–86 Newcomers Guide to Columbia.*
17. See Rouse, "A Garden for People to Grow In," p. 96, where Columbia's neighborhood spatial organization is likened to Radburn's. See also Community Research and Development, pp. 24 and 38.

18. J. W. Anderson, "A Brand New City for Maryland," *Harper's Magazine,* November 1964; James Rouse, "Communication in Columbia," *Columbia Life,* July 14, 1971.

19. David Reisman, *The Lonely Crowd* (New Haven: Yale University Press, 1950); William H. Whyte, *The Organization Man* (New York: Simon & Schuster, 1956).

20. Rouse letter to Kastenmeier, p. 5. Also, Rouse's efforts to provide jobs within the city for those who lived there was motivated in part by his concern over "the effect upon children of life in communities deserted during daylight by the adult males." (Quoted in Anderson, p. 100.)

21. Edwin W. Baker, "Land Planning and Development for Columbia, Maryland," *Building Research,* January/March 1970, p. 61.

22. Robert Tannenbaum, "Planning Determinants for Columbia," *Urban Land,* April 1965, p. 4.

23. James Rouse, "Cities that Work for Man—Victory Ahead," address before the Lions International/University of Puerto Rico symposium on "The City of the Future," San Juan, Puerto Rico, October 18, 1967, p. 6. Offprint.

24. Morton Hoppenfeld, "The Columbia Process: The Potential for New Towns," *Architects Yearbook,* offprint, n.d., p. 5.

25. Community Research and Development, p. 20.

26. Hoppenfeld, pp. 3-4.

27. Rouse, "Cities That Work for Man—Victory Ahead," p. 10.

28. James W. Rouse, Statement before the Housing Subcommittee, Housing Banking and Currency Committee on H.R. 1296, Title II, Land Development and New Communities, March 25, 1966. As quoted in H. Wentworth Eldredge (ed.), *Taming Megalopolis,* Vol. II (Garden City, N.Y.: Anchor Books, 1967), p. 840.

29. As quoted in Hoppenfeld, p. 15.

30. Community Research and Development, p. 25.

31. Ibid., p. 20.

32. James Rouse, as quoted in Gurney Breckenfeld, *Columbia and the New Cities* (New York: Ives Washburn, 1971), pp. 175-76.

33. Hoppenfeld, p. 16.

34. Rouse, "Communication in Columbia," p. 7.

35. The group was composed of experts in sociology, psychology, government, recreation, economics, education, health, housing, transportation and communication. It included such well-known names as Herbert Gans, Christopher Jencks, Nelson Foote, and Leonard Duhl. For a total listing, see Hoppenfeld, "The Columbia Process," p. 16.

36. As quoted in Bailey, p. 44.

37. As quoted in Hoppenfeld, p. 5.

38. Anderson, p. 100.

39. As quoted in "Can These Thinkers Help Put Across a Vast New Town?" *House and Home,* December 1964, p. 84.

Notes for Chapter 7

40. Hoppenfeld, p. 6.
41. As quoted in Bailey, p. 44.
42. Tannenbaum, p. 5.
43. Donald Canty, "A New Approach to New-Town Planning," *Architectural Forum*, August/September 1964, p. 196.
44. Hoppenfeld, p. 9.
45. Edwin W. Baker, "Techniques of Construction and Design at Columbia," *Building Research*, January/March 1970, p. 81.
46. Ibid.
47. Rouse, "A Garden for People to Grow In," p. 95.
48. As quoted in *House and Home*, p. 85.
49. Ibid., p. 86. See also Reuben Clark and Paul J. Mode, Jr., "The Transfer of Power in New Communities," in Shirley F. Weiss, Edward J. Kaiser, Raymond J. Burby, III (eds.), *New Community Development: Planning Process, Implementation, and Emerging Social Concerns*, Volume II (University of North Carolina: Center for Urban and Regional Studies, New Towns Research Seminar, 1971).
50. Canty, p. 196.
51. Baker, "Land Planning and Development for Columbia, Maryland," p. 62.
52. Everett Sherbourne, "Columbia's Neighborhood Centers," *Columbia Today*, June/July 1969, p. 9.
53. According to a 1984 survey, 46 percent of all households contained children. Another 20 percent contained two adults. The Rouse Company, "Consumer Research, Columbia Residents," August 1984.
54. *House and Home*, p. 88.
55. Hoppenfeld, p. 8.
56. As quoted in *House and Home*, p. 88.
57. See Clark and Mode. See also the Rouse Co., "What is the Columbia Association?", October 26, 1971 (Mimeo).
58. Columbia Association, *Columbia, Maryland*, January 1985.
59. For this reason the FHA and VA were actively involved in Columbia. As a condition for approving Columbia for FHA and VA loans, these agencies required that the developer not transfer power too quickly. Additionally, they would not permit any amendment to the by-laws or articles of incorporation of the Columbia Association without their prior consent. This was to ensure that certain objectives, notably the access of nonwhite and low-income groups into the community, were achieved. See Clark and Mode.
60. Although the right of amendment is provided for in Columbia, it requires approval of 90 percent of the residents, a percentage so high as to make change virtually impossible. See Clark and Mode, p. 20.
61. The Rouse Company, "The People of Columbia," Brochure 1985.

62. The Rouse Company, "Consumer Research: Columbia Residents, Columbia, Maryland," August 1984.
63. "The People of Columbia."
64. Rouse, Statement before the Housing Subcommittee, March 25, 1966, as quoted in Eldredge, p. 843.
65. Conversations with Betty Moore, Columbia Information Center, June 1985.
66. "A Town Built on Dreams," *Newsweek*, May 27, 1985, p. 11E.
67. "Consumer Research," August 1984, p.4.
68. Ibid.
69. Lynne C. Burkhart, *Old Values in a New Town* (New York: Praeger, 1981), p. 151.
70. Ibid., p. 152.
71. Rouse, "A Garden for People to Grow In," p. 90.
72. This estimate was not obtained from the Rouse Company, but was deduced from other data compiled by the firm. See "Consumer Research," August 1984.
73. Columbia Marketing Department, "Status Report as of March 31, 1985," *Columbia Maryland Quarterly*, p. 1.
74. Conversations with Betty Moore, Columbia Information Center, June 1985.
75. Consumer Research, August 1984, p. 3.
76. *1985-86 Newcomers Guide to Columbia*, pp. 66-67.
77. Community Research and Development, p. 33.
78. Consumer Research, August 1984, p. 3.
79. The Rouse Company, "Columbia, Maryland . . . Where Business Grows," Brochure, ca. 1984.
80. See Daniel Bell, *The Coming of Post-Industrial Society* (New York: Basic Books, 1973).
81. Hoppenfeld, p. 4.
82. Rouse, "A Garden for People to Grow In," p. 89.

Chapter 8

1. See the conservationist writings of Aldo Leopold, particularly *A Sand County Almanac* (New York: Oxford University Press, 1949).
2. D. Stuart Conger, *Social Inventions* (Saskatoon, Saskatchewan, Canada: Modern Press for Saskatoon Newstart, 1974).
3. The phrase has been popularized by Elise Boulding.
4. See Carol A. Christensen, "Thinking About the Future" and "Revising the Future," in Sandra Chizinsky and Peter Whitten (eds.), *Time's Harvest: Exploring the Future*, two volumes (Lexington, Mass.: Ginn Publishing for the International University Consortium for Telecommunications in Learning, 1984).

5. Herman Kahn and Bruce Biggs, "The Long-Term Multifold Trend of Western Culture" (Croton-on-Hudson, New York: The Hudson Institute, 1972). Also found in Willis W. Harman, *An Incomplete Guide to the Future* (New York: W.W. Norton, 1976, 1979), p. 13.

6. See Gerald O. Barney, *The Global 2000 Report to the President* (Washington, D.C.: U.S. Government Printing Office, 1981); Lester R. Brown, et al., *State of the World 1985* (New York: W.W. Norton, 1976, 1979); Donella Meadows, et al., for The Club of Rome, *The Limits to Growth* (New York: Universe Books for Potomac Associates, 1972); see also various other reports to The Club of Rome, synopses of which are available from the U.S. Association for The Club of Rome, 1325 G Street, NW, Washington, D.C. 20005.

7. Harman, p. 114.

8. Michael Marien, "Which Long-Term Direction for Post-Industrial Society?", in *Future Survey Annual 1983* (Bethesda, Md.: World Future Society, 1984), p. viii.

9. Bertrand de Jouvenel, "Utopia for Practical Purposes," in Frank E. Manuel (ed.), *Utopias and Utopian Thought* (Boston: Beacon Press, 1965, 1966), p. 226.

10. de Jouvenel.

11. Frederick L. Polak, *The Image of the Future*, translated and abridged by Elise Boulding (Amsterdam and New York: Elsevier Scientific Publishing Co., 1973); Elise Boulding, "The Dynamics of Imaging Futures," *World Future Society Bulletin,* September/October 1978, pp. 1–8.

12. Wendell Bell and James A. Mau, "Images of the Future: Theory and Research Strategies," and "A Paradigm for the Analysis of Time Perspectives and Images of the Future," in Bell and Mau (eds.), *The Sociology of the Future* (New York: Russell Sage Foundation, 1971). See also the work of Warren L. Ziegler and The Futures Invention Associates, 2026 Hudson St., Denver, Co. 80207.

13. Elise Boulding, "The Dynamics of Imaging Futures," *World Future Society Bulletin.*

14. Marien, p. viii.

15. See E. F. Schumacher, *Small is Beautiful: Economics as if People Mattered* (New York: Harper & Row, Perennial Library, 1973); Hazel Henderson, *Creating Alternative Futures* (New York: Berkley Windhover Books, 1978); Amory B. Lovins, *World Energy Strategies* (New York: Harper Colophon Books, 1973, 1975, 1978); Lester R. Brown, *Building a Sustainable Society* (New York: W.W. Norton, 1981); Marilyn Ferguson, *The Aquarian Conspiracy: Personal and Social Transformation in the 1980s* (Los Angeles, Calif.: J. P. Tarcher, 1981); Gary J. Coates, "Future Images, Present Possibilities: Revisioning Nature, Self, and Society," in Gary J. Coates (ed.), *Resettling America: Energy, Ecology and Community* (Andover, Mass.: Brick House Publishing Co., 1981); Tom Bender, "Sharing Smaller Pies," in Coates, pp. 53–88.

16. Lester R. Brown, *Building a Sustainable Society,* p. 6.

17. *The Global 2000 Report to the President.* For an eloquent exploration of these interdependencies, see Pierre Pradervand, *Development Education—The Twentieth Century Survival and Fulfillment Skill* (Bern, Switzerland: Swiss Federal Department for Foreign Affairs, 1982, 1985).

18. See the work of The Institute for Local Self-Reliance (2425 18th St., NW, Washington, D.C. 20009), especially David Morris, "The Rise of the New City-States," (Washington, D.C.: The Institute for Local Self-Reliance), reprinted in Coates, pp. 240–62. See also Michael

Freedburg, "Sweat Equity in New York City"; Daniel Goldrich, et al., "Community-Controlled Economic Development and Environmental Enhancement: The Case of the Whiteaker Neighborhood, Eugene, Oregon"; Peter Calthorpe with Susan Benson, "Beyond Solar: Design for Sustainable Communities"; William and Helga Olkowski, "Urban Agriculture: A Strategy for Transition to a Solar Society"; Marshall Hunt and David Bainbridge, "The Davis Experience"; Dennis R. Holloway, "The Appropriate Technology Vision and the Future of Our Communities"; Peter van Dresser, "Goals for Regional Development"; George Burrill and James Nolfi, "Strategies for Bioregional Food Systems"; Earle A. Barnhart, "Agricultural Landscapes: Strategies Toward Permanence"; and Wes Jackson, "New Roots for Agriculture," all within the Coates volume.

19. Ebenezer Howard, *Garden Cities of Tomorrow* (Cambridge, Mass.: MIT Press, 1965), pp. 112–13.

Bibliography

Ackerman, Frederick L. "Where Goes the City-Planning Movement?," *Journal of the American Institute of Architects,* VII, December 1919.
Allen, Walter. *The Modern Novel in Britain and the United States.* New York: E.P. Dutton & Co., 1964, 1965.
American Institute of Architects. *City Planning Progress* (Washington, 1917).
American Legion Community Development Corp. *Greendale, the Answer to the Veterans Housing Problem, a Plan Offered by the American Legion Development Corporation.* Greendale, Wis.: The Corporation, 1948.
Anderson, John W. "A Brand New City for Maryland: A Big Bold Dream in Making," *Harper's Magazine,* November 1964.
Armytage, W.H.G. *Yesterday's Tomorrows.* London: Routledge & Kegan Paul, 1968.
Arnold, Joseph L. *The New Deal in the Suburbs, a History of the Greenbelt Town Program, 1935–1954.* Columbus, Ohio: Ohio State University Press, 1971.
Augur, Tracy B. "Radburn: The Challenge of a New Town," *Michigan Municipal Review,* February 1931, pp. 19–22; March 1931, pp. 39–41.
Bailey, James (ed.). *New Towns in America, The Design and Development Process.* New York: John Wiley & Sons for the American Institute of Architects, 1973.
———. "Only in Columbia—the Next America," *Architectural Forum,* November 1967, pp. 42–47.
Baker, Edwin W. "Land Planning and Development for Columbia, Maryland," *Building Research,* January/March 1970, pp. 61–62.
———. "Techniques of Construction and Design at Columbia," *Building Research,* January/March 1970, pp. 80–82.
Ball, Nelson and Associates. "Reconnaissance Study, Village of Greendale, Wisconsin." Milwaukee, Wis.: Nelson Ball & Associates, 1959.
Banfield, Edward C. *The Unheavenly City: The Nature and Future of Our Urban Crisis.* Boston: Little, Brown & Co., 1968.
Barney, Gerald O. *The Global 2000 Report to the President* (3 vols.). Washington, D.C.: U.S. Government Printing Office, 1981.
Barnhart, Earle A. "Agricultural Landscapes: Strategies Toward Permanence," in Gary J. Coates (ed.), *Resettling America: Energy, Ecology and Community.* Andover, Mass.: Brick House Publishing Co., 1981.
Bauer, Kurt W. "A Backward Glance: Greendale, Garden City in Wisconsin." Southeastern Wisconsin Regional Planning Commission Technical Report, Part II, August/September 1964.
———. "A Greenbelt Town Grows Up," *American City,* October 1959, pp. 143–147.

Bell, Daniel. *The Coming of Post-Industrial Society.* New York: Basic Books, 1973.
Bell, Wendell and James A. Mau. "Images of the Future: Theory and Research Strategies," and "A Paradigm for the Analysis of Time Perspectives and Images of the Future," in Bell and Mau (eds.), *The Sociology of the Future.* New York: Russell Sage Foundation, 1971.
Benevolo, Leonard. *The Origins of Modern Town Planning.* Cambridge, Mass.: MIT Press, 1967.
Bennett, C.B. and R.B. Fernbeck. "Greendale—the General Plan, Discussion," *Planner's Journal,* November 1937, pp. 160–161.
Berger, Bennet M. "The Myth of Suburbia," in Charles M. Haar (ed.), *The End of Innocence, A Suburban Reader.* Glenview, Ill.: Scott, Foresman & Co., 1972.
Bestor, Arthur Eugene, Jr. *Backwoods Utopias.* Philadelphia: University of Pennsylvania Press, 1950.
Beyer, Glenn H. *Housing and Society,* New York: Macmillan Co., 1965.
"Biggest New City in the U.S.," *House and Home,* December 1952, pp. 80–91.
Bing, Alexander M. "Community Planning for the Motor Age: How the City Housing Corp. Separates Pedestrian and Motor Traffic in its Unique Experiment at Radburn," in *National Association of Real Estate Boards, Annals of Real Estate Practice,* 1929.
Birch, Eugenie Ladner. "Radburn and the American Planning Movement: The Persistence of an Idea," in Donald A. Krueckeberg (ed.), *Introduction to Planning History in the United States* (New Brunswick: Center for Urban Policy Research, Rutgers University, 1983), pp. 122–151.
Bishop, Warren. "A Yardstick for Housing," *Nation's Business,* April 1936.
Bloch-Laine, Francois. "The Utility of Utopias for Reformers," in Frank E. Manuel (ed.), *Utopias and Utopian Thought.* Boston: Beacon Press, 1965.
Boguslaw, Robert. *The New Utopians.* Englewood Cliffs, N.J.: Prentice-Hall, 1965.
Boorstin, Daniel J. *The Lost World of Thomas Jefferson.* Boston: Beacon Press, 1948.
Boulding, Elise. "The Dynamics of Imaging Futures," *World Future Society Bulletin,* September/October 1978.
Boulding, Kenneth E. *The Meaning of the Twentieth Century.* New York: Harper and Row, 1964.
Branch, M.C. *Selected Bibliography of New Town Planning and Development.* Monticello, Ill.: Council of Planning Librarians, 1973.
Breckenfeld, Gurney. *Columbia and the New Cities.* New York: Ives Washburn, Inc., 1971.
Brooks, Richard. "Social Planning in Columbia," *AIP Journal,* November 1971, pp. 373–378.
Brown, Lester R. *Building a Sustainable Society.* New York: W.W. Norton, 1981.
Brown, Lester R., et al. *State of the World 1985.* New York: W.W. Norton, 1985.
Brownlow, Louis. "Radburn: A New Town Planned for the Motor Age," in *International Housing and Town Planning Bulletin,* February 1930.
Bryan, William Jennings. "Cross of Gold" speech. July 8, 1896. Democratic National Convention, Chicago, Illinois. Reprinted in *Basic American Documents.* George B. deHuszar, Henry W. Littlefield and Arthur W. Littlefield, eds. Ames, Iowa: Littlefield, Adams & Co., 1956.
Buder, Stanley. *Pullman, An Experiment in Industrial Order and Community Planning.* New York: Oxford University Press, 1967.
Burchard, John and Albert Bush-Brown. *The Architecture of America.* Boston: Little, Brown & Co., 1961, 1966.
Burchell, Robert W. and George Sternlieb (eds.). *Planning Theory in the 1980s.* New Brunswick, N.J.: The Center for Urban Policy Research, Rutgers University, 1978.
Burkhart, Lynn C. *Old Values in a New Town.* New York: Praeger, 1981.
Burrill, George and James Noffi. "Strategies for Bioregional Food Systems," in Gary J. Coates (ed.), *Resettling America: Energy, Ecology and Community.* Andover, Mass.: Brick House Publishing Co., 1981.

Calthorpe, Peter with Susan Benson. "Beyond Solar: Design for Sustainable Communities," in Gary J. Coates (ed.), *Resettling America: Energy, Ecology and Community*. Andover, Mass.: Brick House Publishing Co., 1981.

"Can These Thinkers Help Put Across A Vast New Town?" *House and Home*, December 1964.

Canty, Donald. "A New Approach to New-Town Planning," *Architectural Forum*, August/September 1964, pp. 194–199.

Cautley, Marjorie Sewell, "Planting at Radburn," in *Landscape Architecture*, October 1930, pp. 23–29.

Chapin, F. Stuart, Jr. *Urban Land Use Planning*. Urbana: University of Illinois Press, 1965.

Chase, Richard. *The American Novel and Its Tradition*. Garden City, N.Y.: Doubleday Anchor, 1957.

Cheney, Charles H. "Districting Progress and Procedure in California," *Proceedings of the Ninth National Conference on City Planning*, Kansas City, 1917.

Christensen, Carol A. "Thinking About the Future" and "Revising the Future," in Sandra Chizinsky and Peter Whitten (eds.), *Time's Harvest: Exploring the Future* (2 vols.). Lexington, Mass.: Ginn Publishing for the International University Consortium for Telecommunications in Learning, 1984.

Chudacoff, Howard P. *The Evolution of American Urban Society*. Englewood Cliffs, N.J.: Prentice-Hall, 1975.

Churchill, H.S. "America's Town Planning Begins," *New Republic*, January 3, 1936, pp. 96–98.

Churchill, Henry. "Henry Wright: 1878–1936," in Donald A. Krueckeberg (ed.), *The American Planner*. New York & London: Methuen, 1983.

City Housing Corporation, New York. *Annual Reports*. Nos. 4–10. New York: The Corporation, 1928–1934.

———. "Radburn Garden Homes." New York: The Corporation, 1930.

———. "Radburn, Protective Restrictions and Community Administration." New York: The Corporation, 1929.

Civic League of St. Louis. *A City Plan for St. Louis*. St. Louis, 1907.

Clark, Reuben and Paul J. Mode, Jr., "The Transfer of Power in New Communities," in Shirley F. Weiss, Edward J. Kaiser, Raymond J. Burby, III (eds.), *New Community Development: Planning Process, Implementation, and Emerging Social Concerns*, Vol. II. University of North Carolina: Center for Urban and Regional Studies, New Towns Research Seminar, 1971.

Clemens, Samuel. *The Adventures of Huckleberry Finn*. New York: W.W. Norton & Co., 1961, 1962.

Clinard, Marshall B. *Slums and Community Development*. New York: The Free Press, 1966.

Coates, Gary J. "Future Images, Present Possibilities: Revisioning Nature, Self and Society," in Gary J. Coates (ed.), *Resettling America: Energy, Ecology and Community*. Andover, Mass.: Brick House Publishing Co., 1981.

Columbia Association. *Columbia, Maryland*, January 1985.

Columbia Marketing Department. "Status Report as of March 31, 1985," *Columbia Maryland Quarterly*, Columbia, Maryland.

"Columbia, Maryland," *Building Research*, October/December 1969, pp. 46–49.

"Columbia: Planned to the Nth Degree, It Has Yet to Face its First Real Test," *House and Home*, June 1966, pp. 102–103.

Comey, Arthur C. and Max C. Wehrly, *Planned Communities. Part I of Urban Planning and Land Policies, Vol. II, of the Supplementary Report of the Urbanism Commission to the National Resources Commission*. Washington, D.C.: Government Printing Office, 1939.

Commission on Population Growth and the American Future. *Population and the American Future*. New York: Signet, 1972.

Community Research and Development. *Columbia: A Presentation to the Officials and Citizens of Howard County, Maryland*. Baltimore: Community Research and Development, 1964.

Conger, D. Stuart. *Social Inventions*. Saskatoon, Saskatchewan, Canada: Modern Press for Saskatoon Newstart, 1974.

Conkin, Paul K. *Tomorrow a New World: The New Deal Community Program*. Ithaca, N.Y.: Cornell University Press, 1959.

Cooley, Charles H. *Social Process*. New York: Charles Scribner's Sons, 1918.

Corden, Carol. *Planned Cities: New Towns in Britain and America*. Beverly Hills, Calif.: Sage Publications, 1977.

Crane, Jacob. "Greendale: The General Plan," *Planner's Journal*, July/August 1937, pp. 89–90.

Creese, Walter L. *The Search for Environment, The Garden City Before and After*. New Haven, Conn.: Yale University Press, 1968.

Cullingworth, J.B. *Town and Country Planning in Britain*. Ninth edition. London: George Allen & Unwin, 1985.

"The Critical Path to Columbia," *Business Automation*, August 1967, pp. 40–44.

Davis, J.C. "Utopia and History," *Historical Studies*, April 1968.

Dewey, John. *The Public and Its Problems*. New York: Holt, 1927.

Douglass, Paul, et al. "New Towns: A Comparative Study." Winter Park, Florida: Center for Practical Politics, Rollins College, 1970.

Dreier, John. "Greenbelt Planning; Resettlement Administration Goes to Town," *Pencil Points*, August 1936, pp. 400–19.

Dyckman, John W. "City Planning and the Treasury of Science," in William R. Ewald, Jr. (ed.), *Environment for Man: The Next Fifty Years*. Bloomington: Indiana University Press, 1967.

Eden, W.A. "Ebenezer Howard and the Garden City Movement," *Town Planning Review*, Summer 1947, pp. 123–143.

Eichler, Edward P. and Marshall Kaplan. *The Community Builders*. Berkeley, Calif.: University of California Press, 1967.

Eichler, Edward P. "Why New Communities?" in Bernard J. Frieden and William W. Nash, Jr. (eds.), *Shaping an Urban Future*. Cambridge, Mass.: MIT Press, 1969.

Eldredge, H. Wentworth (ed.). *Taming Megalopolis*. (2 vols.) New York: Anchor, 1967.

Everett, Sherbourne. "Columbia's Neighborhood Centers," *Columbia Today*, June/July 1969.

Fabun, Don. (ed.). *Dimensions of Change*. Beverly Hills, Calif.: Glencoe Press, Macmillan Co., 1971.

"Farm Security Administration Housing Projects," *Architectural Forum*, May 1938, pp. 420–23.

Feiss, Carl. "USA: New Communities—or Their Simulacrum?" *Town and Country Planning*, January 1967.

Ferguson, Marilyn. *The Aquarian Conspiracy: Personal and Social Transformation in the 1980s*. Los Angeles, Calif.: J.P. Tarcher, 1981.

Fernback, Richard. "Greendale," *The Planner's Journal*, November/December 1937.

Finley, William E. "Columbia, Maryland: A New Town for America," in Highway Research Board, *Planned Communities*. Washington, D.C.: National Academy of Sciences - National Research Council, 1965, pp. 18–22.

_____. "New Towns of the Future: Focus on Columbia, Maryland," *Building Research*, January/February 1966, pp. 24–26.

_____. "Techniques of Land Acquisition and Finance for Columbia," *Building Research*, October/December 1969, pp. 32–35.

Ford, P.L. (ed.). *The Works of Thomas Jefferson, Vol. IX*. New York, 1904.

Fraser, Jack B. "New Towns: What Architects Should Know About Them," *Vital Questions*. Washington, D.C.: American Institute of Architects, October 1969.

Freedburg, Michael. "Sweat Equity in New York City," in Gary J. Coates (ed.), *Resettling America: Energy, Ecology and Community*. Andover, Mass.: Brick House Publishing Co., 1981.
Galantay, Ervin Y. *New Towns, Antiquity to the Present*. New York: George Braziller, 1975.
Gans, Herbert J. *The Levittowners*. New York: Vintage Books, 1967.
Gipe, Albert B. "Planning a New City—Columbia," *Institute of Electrical and Electronics Transactions and General Applications*, Vol. IGA-2, #5, September/October 1966, pp. 423–30.
Glaab, Charles N. and Theodore Brown. *A History of Urban America*. New York: The Macmillan Co., 1967.
Glaab, Charles N. *The American City: A Documentary History*. Homewood, Ill.: The Dorsey Press, Inc., 1963.
Goist, Park Dixon. "Seeing Things Whole: A Consideration of Lewis Mumford," in Donald A. Krueckeberg (ed.), *The American Planner*. New York & London: Methuen, 1983, pp. 250–275.
Golany, Gideon. *New Towns Planning and Development: A World-Wide Bibliography*. ULI Research Report 20. Washington, D.C.: The Urban Land Institute, 1973.
Goldrich, Daniel, et al. "Community Controlled Economic Development and Environmental Enhancement: The Case of the Whiteaker Neighborhood, Eugene, Oregon," in Gary J. Coates (ed.), *Resettling America: Energy, Ecology and Community*. Andover, Mass.: Brick House Publishing Co., 1981.
Goodman, Paul and Percival. *Communitas, Ways of Livelihood and Means of Life*. New York: Vintage Books, Random House, 1947, 1960.
Goodman, Paul. "Utopian Thinking," *Commentary*, July 1961, pp. 19–26.
Goodman, Robert. *After the Planners*. New York: Simon & Schuster, 1971.
Green, Constance McLaughlin. *The Rise of Urban America*. New York: Harper & Row, 1965.
"Greenbelt Towns," *Architectural Record*, September 1936, pp. 215–34.
Greendale Decennial Committee. "This is Greendale." Greendale, Wisc.: The Committee, 1948.
"Greentowns All Sold by Federal Government," *American City*, March 1953, p. 113.
Guttenberg, Albert Z. "City Encounter and Desert Encounter: Two Sources of American Regional Planning Thought," *Journal of the American Institute of Planners*, October 1978, pp. 399–411.
Haar, Charles M. (ed.). *The End of Innocence, A Suburban Reader*. Glenview, Ill.: Scott, Foresman & Co., 1972.
"Hail Columbia!" *The Economist*, February 6, 1965.
Hallett, Stanley J. "Planning, Politics and Ethics," in William R. Ewald, Jr. (ed.), *Environment for Man: The Next Fifty Years*. Bloomington: Indiana University Press, 1967.
Hancock, John. "John Nolen: The Background of a Pioneer Planner," in Donald A. Krueckeberg (ed.), *The American Planner*. New York: Methuen, 1983.
Handlin, Oscar and John Burchard (eds.). *The Historian and the City*. Cambridge, Mass.: The MIT Press and Harvard University Press, 1963.
Harman, Willis W. *An Incomplete Guide to the Future*. New York: W.W. Norton, 1976, 1979.
Harris, Thomas G., Jr. "Howard County Plans Its Future: Columbia," *American County Government*, May 1967, pp. 20–23.
Hays, Samuel P. "Business Elite and the Centralization of DecisionMaking," in Bruce M. Stave (ed.), *Urban Bosses, Machines and Progressive Reformers*. Lexington, Mass.: D.C. Heath & Co. 1972.
Henderson, Hazel. *Creating Alternative Futures*. New York: Berkley Windover Books, 1978.
Hofstadter, Richard. *The Age of Reform*. New York: Vintage Books, 1955.
Holloway, Dennis R. "The Appropriate Technology Vision and the Future of Our Communities," in Gary J. Coates (ed.), *Resettling America: Energy, Ecology, and Community*. Andover, Mass.: Brick House Publishing Co., 1981.

Bibliography

Holloway, Mark. *Heavens on Earth, Utopian Communities in America, 1680-1880.* New York: Dover, 1966.

Hoppenfeld, Morton. "The Columbia Process: The Potential for New Towns." Printed in Great Britain by The Garden City Press, Ltd.; reprinted from *The Architects Year Book.* n.d.

———. "A Sketch of the Planning-Building Process for Columbia," *AIP Journal,* November 1967, pp. 398-409.

Howard, Ebenezer. *Garden Cities of Tomorrow: A Peaceful Path to Real Reform.* Cambridge, Mass.: The MIT Press, 1965.

Howard Research and Development Corp. "Visitor's Guide to Columbia." Columbia, Md.: The Corporation, 1973.

Hudson, Robert B. *Radburn: A Plan of Living. A Study Made for the American Association for Adult Education.* New York: American Association for Adult Education, 1934.

Hughes, Michael R. (ed.). *The Letters of Lewis Mumford and Frederick J. Osborn.* Bath: Adams & Dart, 1971.

Hunt, Marshall and David Bainbridge. "The Davis Experience," in Gary J. Coates (ed.), *Resettling America: Energy, Ecology and Community.* Andover, Mass.: Brick House Publishing Co., 1981.

Institute for Urban Studies, University of Pennsylvania. "Accelerating Urban Growth in a Metropolitan Area." (2 vols.) Philadelphia: The Institute, 1954.

Jackson, Wes. "New Roots for Agriculture," in Gary J. Coates (ed.), *Resettling America: Energy, Ecology and Community.* Andover, Mass.: Brick House Publishing Co., 1981.

Jacobs, Jane. *The Death and Life of Great American Cities.* New York: Vintage Books, 1961.

———. *The Economy of Cities.* New York: Random House, 1969.

Johnson, Dale R. "A 'Greenbelt' Blooms," *National Civic Review,* July 1959, pp. 338-42.

de Jouvenel, Bertrand. "Utopia for Practical Purposes," in Frank E. Manuel (ed.), *Utopias and Utopian Thought.* Boston: Beacon Press, 1965, 1966.

Kahn, Herman and Bruce Briggs. "The Long-Term Multifold Trend of Western Culture." Croton-on-Hudson, N.Y.: The Hudson Institute, 1972.

Kantor, Harvey A. "Benjamin C. Marsh and the Fight Over Population Congestion," in Donald A. Krueckeberg, *The American Planner.* New York & London: Methuen, 1983, pp. 58-74.

Kateb, George. "Utopias and Utopianism," *International Encyclopedia of the Social Sciences,* Vol. 16 (1968), pp. 267-70.

Kessler, George E. *A City Plan for Dallas,* 1910.

Kroening, Walter E. "The Story of Greendale, a Government Demonstration in Community Planning and Public Housing," Greendale, Wis.: the author, April 1944.

Krueckeberg, Donald A. (ed.). *The American Planner.* New York & London: Methuen, 1983.

———. *Introduction to Planning History in the United States.* New Brunswick, N.J.: Center for Urban Policy Research, Rutgers University, 1983.

Lalli, Frank. "New Towns: Are They Just Oversized Subdivisions with Oversized Problems?" *House and Home,* June 1966, pp. 93-103.

Laza, Anthony Joseph. *The Planning of Columbia, New Town: From Concept to Implementation.* Unpublished Ph.D. dissertation, Boston College, 1973.

Leopold, Aldo. *A Sand County Almanac.* New York: Oxford University Press, 1949.

Levitt and Sons. "Levitt's Progress" and "Most House for the Money," *Fortune,* October 1952, pp. 151-169.

Levitt, Alfred S. "A Community Builder Looks at Community Planning," *Journal of the American Institute of Planners,* Spring 1951, pp. 80-88.

Levitt, William J. "What! *Live* in a Levittown?" *Good Housekeeping,* July 1958, vol. 147, pp. 47, 175-76.

Liell, John T. *Levittown: A Study in Community Development and Planning.* Unpublished Ph.D. dissertation, Department of Sociology, Yale University, 1952.
Lippman, Thomas W. and Bill Richards. "New Towns: Realities Dim Dreams," *Washington Post,* January 12, 1975.
Lockwood, Maren. "The Experimental Utopia in America," *Daedalus,* Spring 1965.
Lubove, Roy. *Community Planning in the 1920s: The Contribution of the Regional Planning Association of America.* Pittsburgh: University of Pittsburgh Press, 1963.
─────. *The Urban Community, Housing and Planning in The Progressive Era.* Englewood Cliffs, N.J.: Prentice-Hall, 1967.
Marien, Michael. "Which Long-Term Direction for Post-Industrial Society?," in *Future Survey Annual 1983.* Bethesda, Md.: World Future Society, 1984.
Marsh, B. C. "City Planning in Justice to the Working Population," *Charities* xix, February 1, 1908.
Marshall, Douglas Gordon. *Greendale: A Study of a Resettlement Community.* Unpublished Ph.D. dissertation, University of Wisconsin, July 31, 1943.
"Maryland's New Town May Make It Big," *Business Week,* March 9, 1968, pp. 132-136.
"Master Builder with a New Concept," *Business Week,* August 20, 1966.
Mayer, Albert. "Greenbelt Towns for the Machine Age. The Government's Plan to Build Four in this Country Directs Notice to the Successful Ventures Abroad," *New York Times Magazine,* February 2, 1936, pp. 8-9.
─────. "Greenbelt Towns Revisited," *Journal of Housing,* nos. 1, 2, and 3, January, February/March, and April, 1967; pp. 12-26, 80-85, and 151-160.
─────. "Greenbelt Towns: What and Why," *American City,* May 1936, pp. 59-61.
Mayer, Albert, Henry M. Wright and Lewis Mumford, "New Homes for a New Deal, IV: A Concrete Program," *New Republic,* March 7, 1934, pp. 91-94.
McFarland, J. Horace. "The Nationalization of Civic Improvement," *Charities and the Commons,* XVII, 1906.
McKeever, J. Ross. "Private Development by Private Interests," *Urban Land,* April 1965.
McKelvey, Blake. *The Emergence of Metropolitan America: 1915-1966.* New Brunswick, N.J.: Rutgers University Press, 1968.
─────. *The Urbanization of America, 1860-1915.* New Brunswick, N.J.: Rutgers University Press, 1963.
McLanathan, Richard. *The American Tradition in the Arts.* New York: Harcourt Brace and World, 1968.
Meadows, Donella, et al. *The Limits to Growth.* New York: Universe Books for Potomac Associates, 1972.
Meyerson, Martin D. "Utopian Traditions and the Planning of Cities," *Daedalus,* Winter 1961.
Miller, Perry. *Consciousness in Concord.* Boston: Houghton-Mifflin, 1958.
Miller, Zane W. *The Urbanization of Modern America, A Brief History.* New York: Harcourt, Brace, Jovanovich, 1973.
Mitchell, Jonathan. "Low-Cost Paradise," *New Republic,* September 18, 1935.
Moore, Wilbert E. "The Utility of Utopias," *American Sociological Review,* December 1966.
Morris, David. "The Rise of the New City-States," in Gary J. Coates (ed.), *Resettling America: Energy, Ecology and Community.* Andover, Mass.: Brick House Publishing Co., 1981.
Morris, George. "$16,000 Homes for $2,000 Incomes: Greenbelt, Maryland," *Nation's Business,* January 1938.
Morris, Robert L. "New Towns and Old Cities: Part II—What Can the Cities Learn from New Town Experience?" *Nation's Cities,* April 1969, pp. 8-11; May 1969, pp. 19-22; June 1969, pp. 34-41.
Mumford, Lewis. *The Culture of Cities.* New York: Harcourt Brace, 1938.

Bibliography

———. "The Fate of Garden Cities," *Journal of the American Institute of Architects* 15, February 1927.
———. "The Fourth Migration," *Survey Graphic* 7, May 1925, pp. 130–35.
———. "The Garden City Idea and Modern Planning," in Ebenezer Howard, *Garden Cities of Tomorrow*. Cambridge: MIT Press, 1965.
———. "Regional Planning," July 8, 1931 Address to Roundtable on Regionalism, Institute of Public Affairs, University of Virginia. Avery Library, Columbia University.
———. "Regions to Live In," *Survey Graphic* 7, May 1925, pp. 151–52.
———. *The Story of Utopias*. New York: Viking Press, 1922, 1950, 1962.
———. *The Urban Prospect*. New York: Harcourt Brace and World, 1956.
———. "Utopia, the City and the Machine," *Daedalus*, Spring 1965, pp. 271–92.
Myhra, David. "Rexford Guy Tugwell: Initiator of America's Greenbelt New Towns, 1935–36," in Donald A. Krueckeberg (ed.), *The American Planner*. New York & London: Methuen, 1983, pp. 225–249.
Nash, Roderick. *Wilderness and the American Mind*. New Haven, Conn.: Yale University Press, 1973.
"New Town of Columbia Proposes 10 Villages to Accommodate 110,000," *Architectural Record*, February 1965, pp. 128–130.
"The New Town of Columbia Takes Its First Giant Steps," *NAHB Journal of Homebuilding*, August 1968, pp. 63–64.
Newhouse, Eric. "Pollution Problems of Past Plaguing Model City of Future," *Sunday Call-Chronicle*, Allentown, Pa., July 11, 1971.
"New Towns: Industry's Move to Uncongested Land Outside the Cities is Bringing a Planning Dream to Life," *Architectural Forum*, November 1951, pp. 136–142.
Noble, David W. *The Eternal Adam and the New World Garden*. New York: Braziller, 1968.
———. *Historians Against History*. Minneapolis, Minn.: University of Minnesota Press, 1965.
———. *The Progressive Mind, 1890–1917*. Chicago: Rand McNally & Co., 1970.
Nolen, John. *Replanning Small Cities*. New York: B.W. Huebsch, 1912.
Nordhoff, Charles. *The Communistic Societies of the United States*. New York: Schocken Books, 1875, 1965.
Novak, Barbara. *American Painting of the Nineteenth Century; Realism, Idealism, and the American Experience*. New York: Praeger, 1969.
Olkowski, William and Helga. "Beyond Solar: Design for Sustainable Communities," in Gary J. Coates (ed.), *Resettling America: Energy, Ecology and Community*. Andover, Mass.: Brick House Publishing Co., 1981.
Osborn, Frederic. "Britain's Place in Town Planning," in H. Wentworth Eldredge (ed.), *Taming Megalopolis*. Vol. II. Garden City, N.Y.: Anchor Books, Doubleday & Co., 1967.
———. "Preface," in Ebenezer Howard, *Garden Cities of Tomorrow*. Cambridge, Mass.: MIT Press, 1965.
Osborn, Frederic and Arnold Whittick. *The New Towns: The Answer to Megalopolis*. New York: McGraw Hill, 1965.
———. "Sir Ebenezer Howard, the Evolution of His Ideas," *Town Planning Review*, October 1950, pp. 221–235.
Peets, Elbert. "Greendale: The Town Plan." A paper presented at the Milwaukee meeting of the American City Planning Institute, October 24, 1936. The Institute, 1936. Mimeo.
———. "Studies in Planning Texture in Housing in a Greenbelt Town," *Architectural Record*, September 1949, pp. 130–137.
Peng, T.C. and N.S. Verma. *New Town Planning, Design and Development, Comprehensive Reference Materials*. Lincoln, Neb.: University of Nebraska Press, 1971.
Perloff, Harvey S. *New Towns: Why and for Whom*. New York: Praeger, 1973.

———. *Planning the Post-Industrial City.* Washington & Chicago: Planners Press, American Planning Association, 1980.
Perry, Bliss (ed). *The Heart of Emerson's Journals.* Boston, 1937.
"P.B. Reveals Levitt's Building Methods," *Practical Builder,* August 1959, pp. 80–91.
Polak, Frederick L. *The Image of the Future.* Translated and abridged by Elise Boulding. Amsterdam and New York: Elsevier Scientific Publishing Co., 1973.
Pradervand, Pierre. *Development Education—The Twentieth Century Survival and Fulfillment Skill.* Bern, Switzerland: Swiss Federal Department for Foreign Affairs, 1982, 1985.
Redfield, Charles et al. "The Impact of Levittown on Local Government," *Journal of the American Institute of Planners,* Summer 1951, pp. 130–141.
Reeder, Sherwood L. "A Report on the First Two Years of the Greendale Community." Greendale, Wisc.: the author, 1940.
Reiner, Thomas A. *The Place of the Ideal Community in Urban Planning.* Philadelphia: University of Pennsylvania Press, 1963.
———. "The Planner as Value Technician: Two Classes of Utopian Constructs and Their Impacts on Planning," in H. Wentworth Eldredge (ed.), *Taming Megalopolis.* Vol. 1. New York: Anchor Books, 1967.
Reiss, Albert J. Jr. (ed.). *Louis Wirth on Cities and Social Life.* Chicago: University of Chicago Press, 1964.
Reiss, R.L. "American Greenbelt Towns," *Town and Country Planning,* January 1938, pp. 16–18.
Reissman, Leonard. *The Urban Process, Cities in Industrial Societies.* New York: The Free Press, 1970.
Reps, John W. "The Greenbelt Concept," *Town and Country Planning,* July 1960, pp. 246–50.
———. *The Making of Urban America, a History of City Planning in the U.S.* Princeton, N.J.: Princeton University Press, 1965.
Richards, Bill. "Reality Put Damper on Columbia Ideal," *Washington Post,* January 13, 1975.
Riesman, David. *The Lonely Crowd.* New Haven, Conn.: Yale University Press, 1950.
———. "Some Observations on Community Plans and Utopia," *Yale Law Journal,* December 1947, pp. 173–200.
Ritter, Paul. "Radburn Planning: A Reassessment," *Architect's Journal,* November 1960/February 1961.
Robinson, Charles M. *Modern Civic Art.* New York, 1904.
Rosenau, Helen. *The Ideal City in its Architectural Evolution.* London: Routledge and Kegan Paul, 1959.
Rouse, James W. "Cities that Work for Man—Victory Ahead," address before the Lions International/ University of Puerto Rico symposium on "The City of the Future," San Juan, Puerto Rico, October 18, 1967 (offprint).
———. Statement Before the Housing Subcommittee, House Banking and Currency Committee on H.R. 1296, Title II, Land Development and New Communities, March 25, 1966; appearing as "The City of Columbia," in H. Wentworth Eldredge (ed.), *Taming Megalopolis.* New York: Anchor Books, 1967.
———. "Communication in Columbia," *Columbia Life,* July 14, 1971.
———. "A Garden for People to Grow In," *Lawyer's Title News,* January 1966.
———. "Great Cities for a Great Society," *Inland Architect,* May 1965.
———. "How to Build a Whole New City from Scratch," *Savings Bank Journal,* October 1966, pp. 26–32.
———. "New Approach to City Building," *The General Electric Forum for National Security and Free World Progress,* January/March, 1967.
———. Letter to Robert W. Kastenmeier, October 14, 1966.

The Rouse Co. "Columbia, Maryland . . . Where Business Grows," Brochure, Columbia, Maryland, ca. 1984.
———. "Consumer Research: Columbia Residents," Columbia, Maryland, August 1984.
———. *1985–86 Newcomers Guide to Columbia*. Columbia, Maryland, 1985.
———. "The People of Columbia," Brochure, Columbia, Maryland, 1985.
———. "The Plan for Columbia, Columbia Data, Concept and Plan," Columbia: The Rouse Corp., Marketing Dept., December 1969.
———. "What is the Columbia Association?" Columbia, Md.: The Corporation, October 26, 1971.
Schlesinger, Arthur M. "The City in American Civilization," in *Paths to the Present*. Cambridge, Mass.: Riverside Press, 1949, 1964.
Schumacher, E.F. *Small is Beautiful: Economics as if People Mattered*. New York: Harper & Row, Perennial Library, 1973.
Scott, Mel. *American City Planning Since 1890*. Berkeley, Calif.: University of California Press, 1969.
Sennett, Richard. *The Uses of Disorder: Personal Identity and City Life*. New York: Alfred A. Knopf, 1970.
Sherbourne, Everett. "Columbia's Neighborhood Centers," *Columbia Today*, June/July 1969.
Shklar, Judith. "The Political Theory of Utopia: From Melancholy to Nostalgia," *Daedalus*, Spring 1965.
Siegal, Robert L. "Can These Thinkers Help Put Across a Vast New Town?" *House and Home*, December 1964, pp. 82–89.
"Site Plans of 'Greenbelt' Towns, Layouts of the Resettlement Administration's New Suburban Communities Now Under Construction Near Washington, Cincinnati, and Milwaukee," *American City*, August 1936, pp. 56–59.
Sjoberg, Gideon. *The Preindustrial City*. New York: The Free Press, 1960.
Smith, Herbert H. Associates. "Suggested Development Plan, Willingboro Township, New Jersey," prepared for the Willingboro Township Planning Board, May 1964.
Stein, Clarence S. "City Patterns, Past and Future," *New Pencil Points*, June 1942.
———. "Communities for the Good Life," *Architectural Record*, August 1956, pp. 175–77.
———. "Dinosaur Cities," *Survey Graphic* 7, May 1925, pp. 134–38.
———. "Greendale and the Future," in Greendale Decennial Committee, "This is Greendale," Greendale, Wisc., 1948.
———. "Greendale and the Future," *American City*, June 1948, pp. 106–9.
———. "Greendale Revisited," *Layout for Living*, January 1949, pp. 4–7.
———. "Radburn, Greenbelt," *House and Home*, May 1956, pp. 169–73.
———. "Radburn and the Radburn Idea," *Encyclopedia of Housing*, 1949–50.
———. *Toward New Towns for America*. Cambridge, Mass.: MIT Press, 1950, 1957, 1966.
Stein, Clarence S. and Catherine Bauer. "Store Buildings and Neighborhood Shopping Centers," *Architectural Record*, February 1934.
Stephenson, Flora G. "Greenbelt Towns in the United States," *Town and Country Planning*, Winter 1942–43, pp. 121–23.
Sullivan, Louis H. *The Autobiography of an Idea*. New York: Dover Publications, 1924, 1956.
Sussman, Carl (ed.). *Planning the Fourth Migration: The Neglected Vision of the Regional Planning Association of America*. Cambridge, Mass.: The MIT Press, 1976.
Sutter, Ruth E. *The Next Place You Come To, A Historical Introduction to Communities in North America*. Englewood Cliffs, N.J.: Prentice-Hall, 1973.
Tannenbaum, Robert. "Planning Determinants for Columbia, A New Town in Maryland," *Urban Land*, April 1965.

Thernstrom, Stephan. *Poverty and Progress, Social Mobility in a Nineteenth-Century City.* New York: Atheneum, 1972.
Thomas, Ray and Peter Cresswell. *The New Town Idea.* Milton Keynes, U.K.: The Open University Press, 1973.
Thoreau, Henry David. *Excursions, the Writings of Henry David Thoreau,* IX. Boston, 1893.
———. "Where I Lived and What I Lived For," *Walden,* in Norman Foerster (ed.), *American Poetry* and *Prose,* Part I. Boston: Houghton-Mifflin, 1957.
Thrupp, Sylvia. "The City as the Ideal of Social Order," in Oscar Handlin and John Burchard (eds.), *The Historian and the City.* Cambridge, Mass.: MIT Press and Harvard University Press, 1963.
"A Town Built On Dreams." *Newsweek,* May 27, 1985.
"Transportation: Key to 'New Town' Design for Living," *Rural and Urban Roads,* October 1968, pp. 46–50.
Tuan, Yi-Fu. *Topophilia, A Study of Environmental Perceptions, Attitudes, and Values.* Englewood Cliffs, N.J.: Prentice-Hall, 1974.
Tugwell, Rexford G. "Cooperation and Resettlement," *Current History,* February 1937.
———. "Down to Earth," *Current History,* July 1936.
———. "The Meaning of the Greenbelt Towns," *The New Republic,* February 17, 1937.
Turner, Frederick Jackson. "The Significance of the Frontier in American History," in *The Frontier in American History.* Huntington, N.Y.: Robert E. Krieger Publishing Co., 1976.
"A Unique City," *Highway Planning Notes.* Washington, D.C.: Bureau of Public Roads, November 1966, pp. 3–6.
U.S. Congress, 61st, 2nd session, S. Doc. 422, *City Planning,* 1910.
U.S. Congress, 81st, 1st session, House. *Disposition of Greentown Projects.* Report No. 402, 1949.
U.S. Congress, 81st, 1st session, Senate. *Sale of Greentown Suburban Resettlement Projects. Hearings on S 351.* 1949.
U.S. Congress, 81st, 1st session, House. *Suburban Resettlement Projects. Hearings on H.R. 2440, a Bill to Authorize the Public Housing Commissioner to Sell the Suburban Resettlement Projects.* 1949.
U.S. Farm Security Administration. *Greenbelt Communities.* Washington, D.C., 1940.
U.S. Federal Public Housing Authority. *Greenbelt Communities.* Washington, D.C., 1945.
U.S. Housing and Home Finance Agency. "Changing a Racial Policy, Levittown, N.J." in *Equal Opportunity in Housing.* Washington, D.C.: June 1964, pp. 17–27.
U.S. Resettlement Administration. *Greendale, Wisconsin.* Washington, D.C.: 1936.
———. "Greenbelt Towns: A Demonstration in Suburban Planning." Washington, D.C.: Government Printing Office, 1936.
Vance, Mary. *Greendale, Wisconsin.* Exchange Bibliography #4. Urbana, Ill.: University of Illinois, Council of Planning Librarians, 1958.
Vernon, Raymond. *The Myth and Reality of Our Urban Problems.* Cambridge, Mass.: Harvard University Press, 1962, 1966.
"Veterans Seek Purchase of Greendale," *The American City,* January 1949.
Wade, Richard C. "The City in History—Some American Perspectives," in Werner Z. Hirsch (ed.), *Urban Life and Form.* New York: Holt, Rinehart and Winston, 1963.
Ward, John William. *Andrew Jackson—Symbol for an Age.* New York: Oxford University Press, 1953, 1955.
———. "The Politics of Design," in Laurence B. Holland (ed.), *Who Designs America?* New York: Anchor Books, 1966.
Warner, George A. *Greenbelt: The Cooperative Community. An Experiment in Democratic Living.* New York: Exposition Press, 1954.

Warner, Sam Bass, Jr. *Streetcar Suburbs, The Process of Growth in Boston 1870–1900.* New York: Atheneum, 1962, 1973.
———. *The Urban Wilderness, A History of the American City.* New York: Harper and Row, 1972.
Weber, Adna F. "Growth of Cities in the United States," *Municipal Affairs,* June 1901.
Weber, Max. *The City.* New York: Collier Books, 1958.
Webber, Melvin W. "Beyond the Industrial Age and Permissive Planning," Working Paper CES WP 18. London: Centre for Environmental Studies, September 1968.
———. "Order in Diversity: Community Without Propinquity," in Lowdon Wingo, Jr. (ed.), *Cities and Space, The Future Use of Urban Land.* Baltimore, Md.: Johns Hopkins Press for Resources for the Future, 1963.
Weiss, Shirley et al. "New Community Development: A National Study," *Research Previews,* April 1973, pp. 5–15.
Welsh, James. "New Towns: Made to Order, But How Do They Fit?" *Think,* March/April 1968, pp. 17–23.
Werthman, Carl, Jerry S. Mandel, and Ted Dienstfrey. *Planning and the Purchase Decision: Why People Buy in Planned Communities.* Berkeley, Calif.: University of California, Institute of Urban and Regional Development, Center for Planning and Development Research, July 1965.
"What's New About New Towns," *Fortune,* February 1966, pp. 158–160.
White, Morton and Lucia. *The Intellectual Versus the City.* New York: New American Library, Mentor Books, 1964.
Whyte, William H. *The Organization Man.* New York: Simon & Schuster, 1956.
Wiebe, Robert H. *The Search for Order, 1877–1920.* New York: Hill and Wang, 1967.
Wingo, Lowdon Jr. "Urban Space in a Policy Perspective," in Lowdon Wingo, Jr. (ed.), *Cities and Space, The Future Use of Urban Land.* Baltimore: Johns Hopkins Press for Resources for the Future, 1963.
Wirth, Louis. "Urbanism as a Way of Life," *American Journal of Sociology,* July 1938.
Wisconsin Historical Records Survey, Division of Community Service Programs. *Inventory of the Local Government Archives of Wisconsin. Village Series no. 141, Greendale.* Sponsored by the University of Wisconsin and State Historical Society of Wisconsin. Madison, July 1941.
Wood, Edith Elmer. *Housing of the Unskilled Wage Earner.* New York: MacMillan, 1919.
Wright, Henry. "The Autobiography of Another Idea," reprinted from *The Western Architect,* September 1930, by the Regional Planning Association of America.
———. "The Radburn Plan," *National Real Estate Journal,* September 30, 1929, pp. 74–76.
Zehner, Robert B., Raymond J. Burby, III, and Shirley F. Weiss. *Evaluation of New Communities in the United States.* Paper prepared for presentation at the 69th Annual Meeting of the American Sociological Association, Montreal, August 26–29, 1974.

Index

Ackerman, Frederick L., 55, 58; criticism of zoning, 43-44
Adams, Henry, 29
Addams, Jane, 27, 38
Advisory Committee on Housing, 111
Alienation, social, as American theme, 16, 19
Allen, Walter, 19
American Art Union, 16
American Civic Association, 34
American Council to Improve Our Neighborhoods (ACTION), 110
American Historical Association, 10
American Institute of Architects, 40
American Legion Community Development Corporation, 76
Antiurbanism, American: and architecture, influence on, 17-18, 30; and democracy, 15-16; and individualism, 113-14; and nature, attitude toward, 16-17, 22-23; and new towns, 111; Bryan and, 15; Emerson and, 24; in Jacksonian period, 22-23; Jefferson and, 16, 21; Populist movement and, 15; reasons for, 15-16; Thoreau and, 23-24
Appalachian Trail, 55
Arcadian tradition, American, 16, 72
Architecture, American: and technology, slighting of, 18; City Beautiful movement and, 33; Downing and, 17; influence of nature on, and antiurbanism of, 17-18, 30; landscape, influence on urban planning, 31-32; styles of, 17-18; Sullivan and, 18; Wright and, 17-18
"Ariadne Asleep on the Isle of Naxos" (Vanderlyn), 17
Arnold, Joseph L., on greentowns: New Deal, 72-73; cooperative activity in, 84; costs of, and ownership, 75-77; eligibility screening for, 82-83; Resettlement Administration and, 85
Art, civic, 33
Ash Can School (art), 16
Augur, Tracy, 55; on greenbelts, 86-87
Augusta (Georgia), 11
Autobiography of an Idea (Sullivan), 18
Automobile: and policy of urban expansion, 30; and regionalism, 59-60; planning for, and Radburn and "Radburn Idea," 7, 56-57, 59-60

Bacon, Francis
Baker, Edwin M., 111-12
Baldwin Hills Village, 69
Baltimore (Maryland), 38; and Columbia (Maryland), effect of, 121; urban renewal in, 110
"Basic Long-Term Multifold Trend" (Kahn), 129-30
Bassett, Edward M., 42
Bell, Daniel, 116
Bellamy, Edward, 46
Beltsville (Maryland). *See* Greenbelt (Maryland)
Berkeley (California), zoning, 43
Bestor, Arthur, on communitarianism, 6
Bierstadt, Albert, 17
Bigger, Frederick, 55, 86, 88
Bing, Alexander M., 55, 57; and Radburn, ownership in, 59
Blacks: absence of, in Bucks County Levittown, 101; discrimination against, in Levittown (New Jersey), 103; exclusion from greentowns, 82; in Columbia (Maryland), 122; integration of, in Levittown (New Jersey), 103
Boorstin, Daniel, on Jefferson, 22

192 Index

Boston (Massachusetts), 11, 15, 29; parks in, 32, 38; public housing authority, 35; role in Revolutionary War, 12; slums in, 36
Boulding, Elsie, 132
Bound Brook (New Jersey), lawsuit, 74, 76, 80
Britain
—garden cities in, 1; characteristics of, 45–51; influence of Howard on, 1–2, 6, 45–51; urban-rural integration of, 49, 52
—institutional change and social reform in, 6–7
—land ownership: compared to United States, 53; municipal, 6, 53
—New Towns Act (1946), 52–53
—new towns in, 51, 53–54, 105; and urban policy, 1–2, 6; compared with United States, 53; financing of, 52; goals of, 51–52; greenbelt, use of, 52; Howard, influence of, 52–53; Osborn, influence of, 51; ownership of, 52–53; policies of, 51–52; Radburn Idea, influence of, 55; size and population of, 52–53; Thatcher government and, 52
Broadacre City, 7, 18
Bryan, William Jennings, 15, 25; "Cross of Gold" speech, 15
Bucks County (Pennsylvania) Levittown. *See* Levittowns—Bucks County (Pennsylvania)
Burnham, Daniel, 33
Burkhart, Lynn C., on Columbia (Maryland), race and class in, 122–23
Burlington County (New Jersey) (*See also* Levittowns—Levittown (New Jersey)), 95

"Catopaxi" (Church), 17
Chandigarh (India), 55
Charleston (South Carolina), 13, 15
Chase, Richard, on American literature and nature, 19
Chase, Stuart, 55
Cheney, Charles H., on zoning, 43
Chicago (Illinois), 13, 38; as railroad center, and Civil War, 13; Burnhams's Plan of, 33; influence of City Beautiful on, 33; parks in, 32; slums in, 36; Scott on, 33
Chicago World's Fair (1893), White City exhibit, 33
Children: and family, orientation toward, in Columbia (Maryland), 118; concern for, RPAA and, 63; Radburn and, 63–64

Chudacoff, Howard, 12
Church in Radburn, The, 67
Church, Frederick Edwin, 17
CIGNA Corporation, and Columbia (Maryland), 107–8
Cincinnati (Ohio) (*See also* Greenhills (Ohio)), 74
Cincinnati Community Development Corporation, 76
Cities: and reform, social, 14; and welfare, public, 14; Aristotelian view of, 18; as cultural symbol, 5, 18; criticism of, Stein on, 64; expansion of, Stein on threat of, 87; government of, influence of Howard on, 48; history of Schleisinger on, 11, 13; reform, in literary utopianism, 5; social interaction in, Hudson on, 64; Wirth on, 90
City, American: ambivalence toward, 6–10, 113–14, 127–28; and antiurbanism, 15–16, 19, 22–24; and competition and commerce, influence of, 11–13; and interdependence, 18–19, 24; and rise of collective interest, Schlesinger on, 14; and urban planning, holistic view of, 44; and westward expansion, 11–12; Aristotelian view of, contrast to, 18; "boss" in, role of, 25; decline of slavery in, 13; Dewey on, 27; family as basis for, 127; growth of, and policy, 23, 30; in literary utopianism, 4–5; neighborhood as basis of, 116, 127; preindustrial, 89; reform of. *See* Reform—urban
City and Suburban Homes Company, 38
City Beautiful movement, 30, 32–34, 40; architecture of, 33; in Chicago (Illinois), 33; in Washington, D.C., 33; influence of, 33–34; influence of parks on, 32; Marsh on, 39–40
City, "good": and environmental determinism, 6; and "land question," 6; community and, 6; nature as basis for, 119; recreation and, 119; Rouse on, 121
City Housing Corporation (New York), 57, 66; and Radburn (New Jersey), 58–59; and Sunnyside Gardens, 57–58, 67–68; goals of, 57
City-manager, 25; influence of Howard on, 48; in greentowns, 81
"City of the Future, The," 113
City Planning Institute, 40
City Planning Progress, 40
City Scientific, and City Practical: and urban

reform, 40-41; and zoning, 41; Ford on, 40-41
Civic center: and democracy, strengthening of, 35; St. Louis Committee on, 34-35; values of, 34-35
Civic reform. *See* City Beautiful movement; *and* Reform—urban
Civil War: commerce and urban competition, influence of, 13; Schlesinger on, 13
Civilian Conservation Corps, 55
Cleveland, Horace S.W., 32
Clinard, Marshall B., 35, 38
Cole, Thomas, 16
Columbia Maryland, 2, 8, 128
—and community, restoration of, 113-15
—Columbia Interfaith Housing Corporation, 123
—economic integration in, 123
—education, as basis of planning, 116-18
—effect of on Baltimore (Maryland), 121
—employment in, 123-24
—facilities of, 108-10, 117-18
—family and child orientation of, 118
—financing of, 107
—garden city, influence of, 107, 121
—goals of, 113
—government of: and Howard County, 120; and recreation, congruence of, 119-20; Columbia Association, 118-20; community Improvement District, 119; legal and political aspects, 120; village associations, 118
—greenspace, use of, 109, 112-13, 115
—housing: low-income, 123; prices of, 123; types of, 109, 122
—influence of, 110
—influence of Radburn and "Radburn Idea" on, 60, 109-10, 112-13
—land: acquisition of, 108; ownership, 121; use, 109, 112-13, 115
—Meriweather Post Pavilion, 116
—neighborhood as basis of, 108-9, 116-18, 122; and village, 108-9; elementary school as size determinant of, 108, 116-18; Hoppenfeld on, 116-17; pluralism in, Burkhart on, 112-23
—planning of, 115-16; and work group, 115-17; as full city, 111-12, 121; Baker on, 111-12; elementary school in, 108, 116-18; Hoppenfeld on, 116-17; landscaping, 112-13, 115; neighborhood as basis of, 108-9, 116-18, 122; physical and social effects of, 115-17; postindustrialism, and limits as future model, 116, 123-25; Rouse and, 107-17, 122-24; siting of, 107-8; tiered organization of, 108-9, 116-18; transportation, 109, 121; urban core of, 109, 116-18
—population, 122; and size of, 109, 116-17
—racial integration in, 122; and class, Burkhart on, 122-23
—recreation in, 116, 118-19; and government, congruence of, 119-20
—regional integration of, 121
—villages, 116; and neighborhood, 108-9; and schools, as size determinant of, 108, 117; centers, 117-18; Crenshaw on, 118; facilities of, 108-9; separation of, 117-18
—work group and, 115; "Gladstone Papers," 116; Michael and, 115-16; postindustrialism, assumption of, 116, 123-24; recommendations of 115-20, 122; social effects and, 115-17, 122
Columbian Exposition (1893), 31
Commerce, and cities: influence of, and urbanism, 11-13
Commission on Congestion of Population (1911), 42
Committee on Congestion of Population in New York, 39
Communitarian movement, 7; Bestor on, 6; influence on Howard and garden city, 6; social change, and community, 6; utopianism and, 5-6
Community: American ambivalence toward, 7-8, 19; and communitarianism, 6; and "good" city, 6; as consumer product, 105; defined, in new towns, 127-28; Dewey and, 27; diversity in, and new towns, 134; family as model of, 8, 61; in new towns, basis of, 6; neighborhood, as basis of, 64-65; progressivism and, 27-28; Puritan attitudes toward, 20; "Radburn Idea" and, 64-65; Stein on, 65; utopianism and, 5-6
Congestion: and population redistribution, 39; and transportation, 39; as part of "housing problem," 38-39; conferences on, 38-39; relief of, and zoning, 42
Connecticut General Life Insurance. *See* CIGNA Corporation
Consumer Distribution Corporation, and cooperative enterprise, 84-85

Cooley, Charles H., 57; influence of, and family neighborhood, 62-64; and Radburn, 64
Cooperative activity: Arnold on, 84; Consumer Distribution Corporation and, 84-85; decline of, 85; FSA and, 85; Howard and, 84; in greentowns, and Resettlement Administration
Copenhagen (Denmark), 112
Cottage Residences (Downing), 17
Crane, Jacob, and Greendale (Wisconsin), 89, 92
Crenshaw, Richard, on Columbia (Maryland) neighborhood centers, 118
Cybernation: The Silent Conquest (Michael), 115

Dallas (Texas), 41
Darwinism: and urban reform, 1, 6; influence of, 27
de Jouvenal, Bertrand, 131
Democracy: American, and antiurbanism, 15-16; and greentowns, size of, 91-92; civic center, and strengthening of, 35; Dewey, on city and, 27
Demonstration Cities and Metropolitan Development Act, 106
Denver (Colorado), 32
Depression (1930s), and Radburn (New Jersey), as public relief work, 58-59
de Tocqueville, Alexis, 15
Dewey, John, 27, 57, 114; and community, 27; on city, and democracy, 27; influence of, 66
Downing, Andrew Jackson, influence of, 17

Eisenhower, Dwight David, administration, 111
Elementary schools: as neighborhood size determinant, 92, 108, 116-18; decentralized, 116-17; Hoppenfeld on, 118; in Columbia (Maryland), 118; in Levittowns, 98, 100-101, 103; jurisdictional problems of, 101
Eliot, Charles, 32
Emergency Relief Appropriation Act (ERAA, 1935), and greentowns, as public relief, 72-73; guidelines, and conflict with Resettlement Administration, 74-75; lawsuits, 74, 76
Emerson, Ralph Waldo, 23, 29; antiurbanism of, 24

England. *See* Britain
Enlightenment: ideas of, and urban reform, 1; influence of, 20-21
Environmentalism, and urban reform, 6-7

Fabians, 40
Factories, suburban location of, 39-40
Fairlawn (New Jersey), Borough of, 66; conflict with Radburn (New Jersey), 67
Fairless Hills (Pennsylvania), Galbreath and, 99
Family:
—and neighborhood, 62; Cooley on, 62; Hudson on, 63; Radburn and, 62-63; Stein on, 63
—as center of new towns, 61-62
—as community model, 61, 127
—as social foundation, 116
—RPAA, concern for, 62
Farm Security Administration (FSA): and cooperative enterprise, 85; and income maximums, 80
Federal Housing Administration, 30-31
Fifth Avenue Association (New York), 42
Filene, Edward A., 85
Finley, William B., 108
First National Conference on City Planning and the Problems of Congestion (1909), 38
First Radburn Citizens Association, 63-64
Ford, George B., on urban planning, 40-41
Fort Lincoln (D.C.), 106
Fourier, Francois Marie Charles, 6
Frontier: and nationalization, 10-11; as "safety valve," 10, 14; effect on American culture, 10-11; Turner on, 10-13
Functionalism: influence of, 26-27; Sullivan and, 18
Future: and new towns, value of for urbanization, 2-3
Futurists: on industrialism, social effects of, 129-30; Harman on, 130; Kahn on, 129-30

Galbreath, John, 99; and Fairless Hills (Pennsylvania), 99
Gans, Herbert: on Levittown (New Jersey), 102-3
Garden Cities of Tomorrow: A Peaceful Path to Real Reform (Howard), 1, 45-48, 58, 125
Garden cities. *See* Garden city; *and, e.g.,* Columbia (Maryland)

Garden city (*See also* Greentowns; New towns), 71, 107
—American, 2; interpretation of, 2, 44, 54, 69, 87–88, 95, 97, 127–28; and RPAA, 55–57, 60–61; communitarianism, influence of, 6; progressivism, influence of, 3; Radburn and, 2; utopian tradition, influence of, 3
—and rapid transportation, use of, 46, 50
—as legal and political entity, 95, 104
—as model for future, 2–3
—characteristics of, 45–48, 60
—commercial areas in, 83
—cooperative activity in, 84–85
—economy of, 48, 52
—financing of, 50, 52
—government of, 48, 81
—greenbelt and greenspace, function of, 47–49, 52, 85; Stein on, 68–69
—Greendale, as interpretation of, 88
—greentowns, and interpretation of, 77–78
—Howard and, 1–2, 6, 81, 83–84, 121, 124, 127–28, 134; economic integration in, 123; goals of, 45–50, 53, 88; influence on, 45–51; regional integration of, 49, 85, 121; rural-urban integration of, 49, 85
—in Britain, 1, 45; "Industrial Selection Scheme" and, 53; influence of, 52; land ownership of, 53; social balance in, 53
—influence of, 44, 128
—land: acquisition, 53; ownership, 49, 53, 78, 124; reform, 46–47; use, 79
—Mumford on, 47–48, 51, 62
—Osborn on, 51
—rural-urban integration in, 85
—size and population of, 48–49, 52–53
—Town and Country Planning Association on, 47, 50
—zoning in, 48, 59
Garden City Association. *See* Town and Country Planning Association
Geddes, Patrick, 56–57
George, Henry, 40; and land reform, 47
Good Housekeeping, 102
Gould, Elgin, and philanthropic housing, 38
Greenbelt (Maryland), 58, 72, 74–75; cooperative activity in, 84–85; costs of, 75–77; criticism of, 77; Greenbelt Consumer Services, 85; influence of "Radburn Idea" on, 89; land, nonarable, 85–86; population groups, 75, 81–82; population turnover, 80; Resettlement Administration and, 75–76; sale of, 75–76; spatial use, 89

Greenbelt Veterans Housing Corporation, 76
Greenbelt program. *See* Greenbelts; Greentowns
Greenbelts: Augur on, 86–87, 105; and land valuation, effects of, 93; and neighborhood, 68–69; as community foundation, 68; Douglas on, 86; Howard, and use of, 47–48, 68–69, 87; in garden city, 47–48, 85; in greentowns, 71, 86, 91; in Levittowns, 100, 103; in Radburn, 68; Mumford on, 47–48; planners, urban on use of, 86–87; RPAA and, 55; social effects of, 91–93; use and function of, 71, 85–87
Greenbrook Project, 84, 91
Greendale (Wisconsin), 2, 74–75, 84, 87, 89, 91; Citizens Association, 91; cooperative activity in, 84–86; costs of, 75; garden city, interpretation of, 88; Greendale Cooperative Association, 85; Marshall on, 86; neighborhood as basis of, 65, 92; Peets and Crane, on plan and size of, 89, 92; population of, 76, 82; rental in, Marshall on conflicts of, 79; rural-urban integration and, 85–86; sale of, 76; social planning in and "Radburn Idea," 87; Stein on, 65, 87, 90, 93; use of greenbelt in, 86–87, 90, 93
Greenhill Homeowners Association, 76
Greenhills (Ohio), 74–75; cooperative activity in, 85; costs of, 75; greenbelt, social effects of, Mayer on, 91; Greenhills Consumer Services, 85; influence of "Radburn Idea" on, 89; population of, 75; rural-urban integration in, 85–86; spatial use in, 89
Greentowns
—and reform, social, 71–72, 88
—arcadian tradition and, 72
—as legal and political entities, 71; Resettlement Administration and, 80
—as low-income housing, 71–72, 88; and New Deal, public relief projects of, 72–74, 88; and Resettlement Administration, 72–77; Arnold on, 73–76; costs of, and ownership, 75–76
—Blacks, exclusion of, 82
—commercial areas in, 83, 85
—construction standards, 75; Tugwell on, 75
—controversy and criticism, 74, 76–77
—cooperative activity in, and Resettlement Administration, 84–85
—costs of, 77; and population turnover, 75; Arnold on, 77; criticism of, 76–77

—garden city, interpretation of, 77–78
—government, federal: and Resettlement Administration, 80; divestiture of, 76, 93; subsidy of, and socio-economic reform, 88
—government of, 71; and separation of administrative and political, 81; citizens associations and, 90; council-manager, 81; Resettlement Administration and, 81
—greenbelts and greenspace, use of, 71, 86, 91–93; and land valuation, effects of, 93; Stein on, 92
—industry, lack of in, 84
—influence of Howard on, 71, 77–78, 81, 92; and differences of purpose, 83
—influence of "Radburn Idea" on, 88–89
—influence of RPAA on, 88
—influence of Wirth on, 90
—land: ownership, 71, 78, 93; use, 79, 93
—planning of: and rapid transportation, 90; and Resettlement Administration, 81–83, 88; Mayer on, 91; neighborhood as basis of, 91; physical arrangement of, 88–89; preindustrial village as model, 89–93; size, control of, 90–91; social elements, 90–93; Stein on, 91–92; technology, use of, 90–91
—population of: and costs of, 75; and eligibility screening, 82–83; and Resettlement Administration income policy, 80–82, 84; exclusion of Blacks, working wives, 82; turnover in, 79–80
—purposes of, 77, 88; and reform, social, 71–72
—rental and leasing, conflicts of, 79
—Resettlement Administration and, 90; cooperative activity in, 84–85; Douglas on, 86; eligibility screening, 82–83; governance, local, 80; greenbelt, use of, 86; Howard's influence on, 78–79; income parameters of, 81–82, 84; leasing, conflict of, 79; policy statement of, 88; population turnover, 80; revenue problems of, 79; rural-urban integration in, 85–86
—rural-urban integration in, 71–73, 85–86
—selection and criteria of, 73–75
—Tugwell and, 72–74, 88; construction standards, 75–76
—working wives, exclusion of, 82
Growth of Cities of the United States, The (Weber), 39
Guttenberg, Albert, on neighborhood, 64

Hamilton, Wallace, 117
Harman, Willis, on industrialism, 130
Hartford (Connecticut), 32
Harvard University, Department of Landscape Architecture, 32
Hays, Samuel P., and reform, 25
High schools, decentralized, Rouse on, 117
Hofstadter, Richard: on "agrarian myth," 18; on progressivism, 26
Homestead Act (1863), and migration, 14
Hoover, Herbert, 31
"Hoovervilles," 76
Hoppenfeld, Morton, 108; on Columbia (Maryland), 112, 116; on elementary school as design determinant, 118; on neighborhood size, 117; on Rouse, 114; on urban problems, 124
House and Home, on Levittown (Pennsylvania), 99–100
Housing: and capital, RPAA on relationship of, 55, 57; low-income, government policy and, 31, 111; mass production of, and Levittowns, 95–96, 104; Miller on, 31; philanthropic, as slum solution, 38; public, influence of RPAA on, 55; transportation improvements and, 38
Housing Act (1954), 111
Housing of the Working People, The, 38
Housing policy. *See* e.g., Resettlement Administration
Howard, Ebenezer, 7, 45, 52–53, 60, 83, 104, 107, 132
—and garden city, 6, 121, 124, 127–28, 134; American interpretation of, 54, 61; concept of, 49–51; cooperative activity in, 84; economic integration of, 123; goals of, 45–47, 49–50, 53; influence on, 95; land reform and, 46–47, 49, 52; purposes of, 88; regional integration of, 121; revitalization of old metropolitan areas, 121
—and greenbelt, use of, 87
—and new towns, 1–2; as social experiments, 135; influence of, in Britain, 52–54
—and urban reform, 125
—influence of, 56, 58, 69, 128: on city-manager government, 48; on greentowns, 71, 77–79, 81, 83, 92; on urban planning, 45–50, 52–53; purposes of, and differences in, 83, 87
—Mumford on, 46–48, 51

—on land: ownership, 49, 121; reform, and garden city, 46-49, 152
—reform, social, and institutional change, 6
—urban size, control of, 91
—use of technology, 46-47
—use of transportation, 46, 50
—Howard County (Maryland), 122; Columbia (Maryland) in, and Rouse, 107-8, 114; decentralized schools in, 117; jurisdiction of, and Columbia (Maryland), 120; zoning, and Columbia (Maryland), 109
How the Other Half Lives (Riis), 35
HUD, and low-income housing, 111
Hudson, Robert, 59; on church in Radburn, 67; on Radburn and family, 63; on social interaction in cities, 64
Hudson River School (art), 16
Hull House, 35
Hunt, Richard Morris, 30
Husher, Vivian, 87

Illinois, zoning in, 42
Image of the Future, The (Polak), 132
Immigration (*See also* Migration): and urbanization, 36; and slums, 36-37
Improvement of Cities and Towns, The (Robinson), 33
"Indications of the Form of the Future" (Stein), 61
Individualism: and planning, urban, 113-14; influence of Rouse and, 113
Industrialism: futurists on, 128-29; Harman on, 130; Howard on, 46
Industry: inclusion of, in Levittowns, 96-97, 100, 102-3; lack of, in greentowns, 84
Irvine Rance (CA), 106; financing of, 107

Jackson, Andrew, 13, 23; and Jacksonian period, antiurbanism of, 22, 29
Jacobs, Jane, 5
Jefferson, Thomas: and Jeffersonian period, and nature, 29; antiurbanism of, 16, 21; Boorstin on, 22
Johns Hopkins University, 121
Journal of Housing, The, 91
Journal of the American Institute of Architects, 55
Journal of the American Institute of Planners, 97

Kahn, Herman: on high-tech society, 129-30; on postindustrialism, 130
Kansas City, parks in, 31-32
Kateb, George, on utopianism, 4
Keith, Nathaniel, 110
Kent, William, 38
Kessler, George E., 31; on zoning, 41
Kitimat (British Columbia), 55

Lake Havasu City (Arizona), financing of, 107
Land
—American attitudes toward, 21-22
—Jefferson on, 22
—ownership: as wealth, Howard and, 46-47; in garden city, 78, 121; in greentowns, 71, 78, 93, 121; municipal, 6, 49, 52-53; private, 21, 53; reform, Mill on, 47; RPAA on, 59
—reform of, and social reform, 6
—use of, in greentowns, 79, 93
—valuation of: control of, 121; effects of, on greenbelts, 93
Landia (Long Island, New York). *See under* Levittowns—Landia (New York)
Landscape architecture. *See* Architecture, American
Landscapes (art): in America, and B. Novak on, 16-17, 20
Landscaping. *See, e.g.,* Greenbelts; Greentowns; *and under* Levittowns
Lansell, John, 73
League of New Community Developers, 106
Le Corbusier (Charles Edouard Jeanneret-Gris), 18
L'Enfant, Pierre Charles, 33
Letchworth (Britain), 45, 50
Levitt, Abraham, 102; and housing, mass production of, 95-96
Levitt, Alfred S., 97, 102; and Landia (New York) plan, 98-99
Levitt & Sons, 2, 95, 101; and housing, mass production of, 95-96; and Landia (New York) plan, 97-98; and Levittown (New Jersey), 101-2; and Levittowns, 95-96
Levitt, William, 102; and Levittown (New Jersey), 102-4; on Levittown (Pennsylvania), 99-100
Levittowns, 95

—Bucks County (Pennsylvania): Blacks, absence of in, 101; buyers of, 103; commercial facilities, 100; community facilities, 100; elementary school as basis of, 100-101; greenbelt, use of, 100; *House and Home* on, 99-100; industry, inclusion of, 100; infrastructure of, 100; jurisdictional problems of, 101; land acquisition, 99; landscaping of, 100; neighborhood, as basis of, 100-101; plan of, 99-100, 102; residents of, 100-101; W. Levitt on, 99-100
—focus on houses, 95-96, 104
—influence of Landia (New York) plan on, 96-97
—Landia (Long Island, New York): A.S. Levitt on, 98-99; as planned community, 96-98; houses, design of, 97; influence of, 96-97; influence of "Radburn Idea" on, 98; infrastructure of, 97-98; Landia Association, and community maintenance, 98; landscaping, 97; not built, 97, 99; planning of, 96-100
—landscaping in, 97, 100, 103
—Levittown (New Jersey), 2, 95-96; Blacks, discrimination against, 103; buyers of, 103-4; commercial facilities of, 102; community facilities, 103; differences from other Levittowns, 101-4; FHA/VA, and buyers, 104; Gans on goals of, 102; house types, mixing of, 103; industry in, 102-3; influence of garden city on, 95; integration of, 103; jurisdictional area of, 104; land acquisition and site of, 101-2; landscaping of, 103; legal and political entity, 95, 104; Levitt and planning of, 102, 104; marking of, 104; neighborhood as basis of, 102; plan of, 96, 102-3; racial integration of, 102; residents of, Gans on, 103; schools, subsidy of, 103
—Levittown (New York): commercial facilities, 96; plan of, 96; recreational facilities, 96; subdivision style of, 96
Lewis, R.W.B.: on American literary hero, 19; on nature and "Adamic Myth," 18
Lexington (Massachusetts), 12
Literature, America: and nature, attitudes toward, 19; city, view of, 19; Lewis on hero of, 19
Locke, John, on natural law, influence of, 20-21

Lonely Crowd, The (Reisman), 111
Long Island (New York), Levittown. *See under* Levittowns
Looking Backward (Bellamy), 46
Low-income housing: and New Deal, public relief projects, 72, 74, 88; greentowns and, 71-72; HUD and, 111; policy, Zane on, 31
Loyola College, 121

McFarland, J. Horace, on urban beautification, 33-34
MacKaye, Benton, 55
Marien, Michael, on postindustrial society and production, 130-33
Marsh, Benjamin C.: criticism of City Beautiful, 39; on factory location, 39-40
Marshall, Douglas, on Greendale: rental conflicts in, 79; rural and urban factors, 86
Marx, Karl, 6; and land reform, 47
Massachusetts Bureau of Statistics of Labor, 36
Mayer, Albert, on greentown planning, 91
Michael, Donald, 115; and Columbia work group, 115-16
Migration (*See also* Immigration): in U.S., 14, 73; rural to urban, and suburbs, development of, 26, 73; Mumford on, 56
Mill, John Stuart, and land reform, 47
Miller, Zane, 11-12; on low-income housing policy, 31
Milwaukee (Wisconsin) (*See also* Greendale (Wisconsin)), 74
Milwaukee Community Development Corporation, 76
Minneapolis (Minnesota), parks, 32
Minnesota, zoning in, 42
"Model Street" (St. Louis, Missouri), 34
Modern Civic Art, 33
More, Thomas, and utopia, 3
Morgenthau, Henry, 38
Mumford, Lewis, 4, 121; and regionalism, 55; and RPAA, 55; on garden city, and fertility, 62; on Howard and garden city, 46-48, 51; on migration in U.S., 56

Nash, Roderic, on Olmsted and parks, 32
National Association of Real Estate Boards, 77
National Capital Planning Commission, 108
National City Planning Conference (1917), 43

Nation's Business, criticism of greentowns, 76-77
Nature, American attitude toward, 9-10, 16-17; and antiurbanism, 9, 16-17; as counterforce to urbanism, 29-30, 32; exalted, in Transcendentalism, 19-20, 23; Hofstadter on, 18; in art, 16-17, 20; individualism and, 18-19; influence of, on urban planning, 9; in Jacksonian period, 23, 29; in Jeffersonian period, 22-23, 29; in literature, 19-20; Lewis on, 18; Noble on, 19; Puritans and, 20
Neighborhood and "neighborhood concept," 55; and family, 61-62; as basis of city, 116, 127; as basis of greentowns, 65, 91-92, 108, 116, 122; Cooley on, 62-64; elementary school and, 7, 92, 100-101, 117; Guttenberg on, 64; Hudson on, 63; Levittowns and, 96, 98, 100-102; Park on, 64; parks and, 68-69, 88; Perry on, 64; Radburn and, 61-65; Stein on, 63-65; suburban, social simplification in, Sennett on, 65-66; Wirth on, 64
New Atlantis (Bacon), 5
New Communities Act, 106; and Title VII, 107
New Deal, and greentowns, 2, 72, 74, 88
New Deal in the Suburbs, The (Arnold), 72
Newport (Rhode Island), 11
New towns (*See also* Garden city; greentowns; Levittowns), 1; American interpretation of, 2; and antiurbanism, 8, 111; and urban planning, 2; arcadian influence on, 7-8; as models, 2-3, 131-35; British, 1-2, 51-54; community and, 6, 8, 127-28, 134; cultural influence on, 2; differences between, 106; economics of, and decentralization, 132-33; expansion of in 1960s, 105; family and individual, as center of, 8, 61-62; financing, government, 105-7; financing, private, 106-7; goals of, Stein on, 61; Howard, influence of, 1, 52-54, 128, 135; institutions in, minimized, 8, 66, 120, 127, 134; land use in, 127; New Towns Act (Britain, 1946), 52; Osborn, influence of, 51; planning of, 6-7, 133-34; political mechanisms, as tools for, 67-68; progressivism, influence of, 3; Radburn and "Radburn Idea," influence of, 7, 55, 67; size of, as democratic influence, 92; Stein on, 67, 69, 128; structural reform, lack of in, 127-28, 132; U.S. and Britain, compared, 53
New York City, 11-13, 38; board of Estimate, 42; Central Park, 31; Commission on Building Districts and Restrictions, 42-43; Commissioner's Land Plan (1811), 36; parks, 38; philanthropic housing in, 38; tenement reform, failure of, 36-37; zoning, and Scott on, 42-43
New York State Commission on Housing and Regional Planning, 57
Noble, David: on nature, American attitude towards, 19; on progressivism, 27-28
Nolen, John, 44
Norfolk (Virginia), 11, 96
No Slums in Ten Years (Rouse and Keith), 110
Novak, Barbara, on American landscape painting, 16, 20

Olmsted, Frederick Law, 31; and parks, 32; influence of, 69; Nash on, 32
Organization Man, The (Whyte), 111
Osborn, F.J.: influence of on new towns, 51; on Howard and garden city, 45, 51
Owen, Robert Dale, 6

Panorama (art), popularity of, 17
Park, Robert, on neighborhood, 64
Parks: and regional planning, 32; and urban planning, 31-32; as neighborhood backbone, 88; in Boston, 38; in Chicago, 38; in New York City, 31, 38; influence on City Beautiful movement, 32
Peets, Elbert, 76; and Greendale, 89, 92
Perry, Clarence, 55
Philadelphia (Pennsylvania), 11-12, 16, 38, 99, 101; slums in, 36
Pittsburgh Civic Commission, 41
"Plan for the Year 2000" (Finley), 108
Planners, urban: and greenbelts, use of, 86-87, 92-93; and greentowns, 88, 90-93, 119
Planning, regional, influence of parks on, 32
Planning, urban
—and City Practical/Scientific, 40-41
—and cultural values, influence of, 2-3, 9, 131; individualism and community, tension of, 28, 113-14
—and greentowns: goals of, 91; greenbelt,

use of, 91; neighborhood in, 65, 91-92, 108, 116, 122
—and garden city, 2, 7-8; goals of, 45-47; influence of, 2, 33, 44, 128; influence of Howard on, 45-51; in Britain, 45-47; land ownership in, 49, 52
—and social reform, 7-8, 35-36
—arcadian tradition and, 72, 77
—Columbia (Maryland): and limitations of, 124-25; influence of, 110, 113-14
—courses in, 32
—Ford on, 40-41
—origins of, 28, 31-32
—parks and, 31-32
—population dispersion and, 39
—Radburn and "Radburn Idea," influence of, 7, 55, 57, 77
—Rouse and social effects of, 125
—social planning, Stein on, 69
—total city and, 44
—transportation and, 38-39, 46, 50, 73
Plumber and Sanitary Engineer, The, 37
Polak, Frederick, 3, 132
Poor: and reform, effects of, 25; urban migration of, 14, 26
Pope, Robert Anderson, 39
Populist movement, and antiurbanism, 15
Portsmouth, 11
Post-industrialism: assumption of, and Columbia (Maryland) plan, 116, 123-24; Kahn on, 130; social implications of, 124
"Post-Industrialism-as-a-More-Self-Reliant-Society" (Marien), 130-31
Progressivism and progressive movement: and community, 27; concern with family, 37; Hofstadter on, 26; ideals of, and zoning, 43; individualism and, 25-26; influence of, 3; Noble on, 27-28; Weibe on, 26
Prohibition, 25
Providence (Rhode Island), 11
Public health, and social reform and urban planning, 35-36
Puritans, attitudes toward nature, and influence of, 20

Quincy (Massachusetts), 29

Radburn (New Jersey), 2, 77, 83, 88, 100, 104, 110-11, 115, 119; and Radburn Citizens Association, 66; arcadian tradition and, 68, 72; as model, 65, 128; CHC and, 58; children, concern for, 63-64; church of, 58; conflict with Fairlawn, 67; elementary school, and neighborhood, 7, 63, 116-18; garden club, 69; goals of, 57, 59, 62-64; governance, 66-67, 98; greenspace, Stein on, 68-69; influence of, 7, 92, 110, 112-13; influence of RPAA on, 55-56, 59, 63; land ownership in, 59; legal and political aspects, 120; neighborhood, and family, 62, 64-66, 116; planning of, 58, 61; political institutions, lack of, 66, 68; Radburn Association and, 66-67, 98; Radburn Idea and, 59; recreation in, 66-67, 69; size, of neighborhoods, 108; Stein on, 61-62, 67-69, 99
Radburn Association: and church, 67; and governance of Radburn, 66-67; and recreation, 66-67
Radburn Citizens Association, 66
"Radburn Idea, The," 7, 55, 98; advantages of, 59-60; and development of Radburn, 59; arcadian premise of, 68, 72; automobile, planning for, 59-60; economies of, 60; elements of, 60; influence of, 55, 60, 87-89, 98, 109-110; neighborhood, as community basis of, 61, 64; RPAA and, 59; spatial organization and, 60; Stein on, 61
Railroad flats. *See* Tenements
Railroads, urban influence on development of, 12-13
Rancocas (New Jersey), 101
Reconstruction Finance Corporation, 31
Recreation (*See also* Parks: *and, e.g.,* Levittowns—community facilities): in "good" city, 119; in greentowns, 66-67, 69, 116, 118-19
Reform
—civic. *See* City Beautiful movement
—housing: economic factors, 36-37; tenement as focus of, 35-37
—land: and municipal ownership, 49, 52; and social reform, 6; and urban planning, 46-47, 49; garden city and, 46-47, 49
—social, 114; and land reform, 6; and urban reform, 1, 7-8, 14; antiurbanism and, 72; arcadian tradition and, 72; greentowns and, 71-72; institutional change and, 6-7; public health and, 35-36; utopianism and, 4
—urban, 33-34; and American Civic Association, 34; and City Practical or Scientific,

40–41; and Greentowns, government subsidy of, 88; and ownership, municipal, 49; and social reform, 1, 6–7; Dewey and, 27; effects of, 1; environmentalism and, 6; Howard and, 45–47, 125; in nineteenth century, 25–27; St. Louis Committee on, 34–35; utopianism and, 4

Regional Planning Association of America (RPAA), 2, 55, 68, 86, 110, 121; and anti-urbanism, 111; and capital and housing, relationship of, 57; and children, concern for, 63–64; and "Fourth migration," 56; and garden city, interpretation of, 55–57, 60–61; and Radburn and "Radburn Idea," 55–61, 63–64; and regionalism and automobile, 56–57, 59–60; and Sunnyside Gardens, 57; Dewey and, 64, 66; influence of, 55, 59, 88; membership of, 55; social goals of, 62

Regional Planning Association of New York, 97

Regionalism: and automobile, 59–60; Mumford and, 56; RPAA and, 56–57

Reisman, David, 111

Resettlement Administration, and greentowns, 72–75, 84; and rural-urban integration, 85–86; cooperative activity in, 84–85; costs of, 77; criticism of, by *Nation's Business*, 76–77; eligibility screening, 82–83; government and management of, 76, 81; greenbelts, use of, 86; income parameters and, 79, 82, 84; influence of Howard on, 78; lack of industry in, 84; leasing, conflicts of, 79; local governance, 80; merger with Department of Agriculture, 85; policy statement of, 78, 80, 88; political and legal aspects of, 80; population of, 75–76, 79–80; purpose of, 73, 90; selection criteria, and conflict with ERAA, 74; Suburban Division of, 72–80; Tugwell and, 75, 80

Reston (Virginia), 106; financing of, 107

Revolutionary War: and Enlightenment, influence of, 11; role of cities in, 11–12

Riis, Jacob, 35

Robinson, Charles Mulford, 33; on urban beautification, 34

"Rocky Mountains, The" (Church), 17

Roosevelt, Franklin D., 31, 88; and greentowns, as public relief programs, 72–73, 76, 88

Rouse Company, 107, 111, 117; and Columbia (Maryland), 107, 111

Rouse, James, 124; and Columbia (Maryland), 107–10, 112–17, 122, 124; and economic integration of cities, 123; and individual, growth of, 113–14; and market valuation of land, 121; and racial integration in Columbia (Maryland), 122; and regional integration of Columbia (Maryland), 121; and urban planning and renewal, 110, 121, 125; civic activities of, 110–111; influence of "Radburn Idea" on, 110; on school decentralization, 117

Rousseau, Jean Jacques, influence of, 21

Royce, Josiah, 27

Rural Electrification Administration, 55

Rural-urban integration: and garden city, 49, 52, 85; and greentowns, 71–73

St. Louis (Missouri), 13, 74; "Model Street," 34

St. Louis Committee, on civic center and reform, 34–35

Salem (Massachusetts), 11

Savannah (Georgia), 11

Schlesinger, Arthur, 11; on cities and Civil War, 13; on cities and collective interest, 14

Scott, Mel, 42; on Burnham's Plan of Chicago, 33; on New York zoning, 42–43

Sennett, Richard, on suburban neighborhood, 65

"Significance of the Frontier in American History, The" (Turner), 10

Size: control of, in greentowns, 90; small, in cities, democratic influence of, 90–92; Stein on, 91

Slavery, decline of in cities, 13

Slums: and immigration, 36–37; as result of congestion, 38–39; economic factors, 38; in New York, 36–37; perception of, and social statistics, 37–38; philanthropic housing and, 38; "problem" and solutions, 37–39

Smith, Al, 57

Smith, Geddes, 57

Social reform. *See* Reform: social

Soul City, 106

Spence, Herbert, and land reform, 47

Standard State Enabling Act (1924), 43

Statistics, social: and perception of slums, 37-38
Stein, Clarence, 55-58, 88, 100, 110-12; influence of, 97, 116-17; on cities, 64, 87; on family and neighborhood, 62-66; on garden city, 68; on greespace, use of, 68-69, 87, 92-93; on Greentowns, size of, 91-92; on new towns, 61, 67, 69, 128; on Radburn and "Radburn Idea," 59-60, 62-66; on Tugwell, 78
Suburbanization: as result of government policy, 30-31; as result of improved transportation, 30; "sprawl," criticism of, 111; Warner on, 38
Suburbs: and nature, 29-30; and transportation, improvement of, 30, 73; development of, and migration trends, 73; location of factories in, 39-40; Tugwell on population of, 84
Sullivan, Louis, on functionalism, 18
Sunnyside Gardens, 57; City Housing Corporation and, 57-58, 67-68; RPAA and, 57

Taylor, Frederick Winslow, and functionalism, 26
Technology: and nature as counterforce to, 30; Howard's use of, 46; in greentowns, use of, 90; social elements of, 91
Tenement: as focus of housing reform, 35-36; types of, 36-37
Tennessee Valley Authority, 55
Thernstrom, Stephan, 14
"This is Greendale" (Husher), 87
Thoreau, Henry: and antiurbanism of, 23-24
Title IV, "Land Development and New Communities" 106
Title VII, Housing Act (1970), and New Communities Act, 107
Tivoli Gardens (Denmark), 112
Town and Country Planning Association, 45; on garden city, 47, 50
Towson State University, 121
Transcendentalism: Emerson and, 23-24; exaltation of nature in, 19-20, 23; Thoreau and, 23-24
Transportation: and philanthropic housing, 38; and population redistribution, 39; Howard's use of, 46, 50; rapid, and suburbs, development of, 73
Tugwell, Rexford Guy, 72; and greentowns, 72-73, 75-76, 80, 88; on city dwellers' income, 82; on suburban population, 84; Stein on, 78
Turner, Frederick Jackson, 10, 12; frontier view of, influence, 10-11, 13; challenged, 12-14

United States: antiurbanism in, 15-18, 21-23, 30, 72, 111, 113-14; city, influence of, 11-13; frontier, influence of, 10-11; garden cities, interpretation of, 2, 53-56, 60-61, 88; greentowns, divestiture of, 93; land ownership, compared to Britain, 53; migration in, 14, 26, 56, 73; Mumford on migration in, 56; New Deal, and new towns, as public relief, 31, 72, 105-7; new towns, 72, 105-7; progressivism in, 24-25; Public Works Administration, Housing Division, 73; suburbanization, and government policy, 30-31; trade patterns, and Civil War, 13; urban-rural conflict, 23, 25; urbanization, 9-10, 22-23; westward expansion, influence of cities of, 11-12; Works Progress Administration, 72-73
United States Housing Authority, 31
United States Steel, Bucks County (Pennsylvania) plant, 99; Fairless Works, 99, 101
University of Maryland, The, 121
University of Pennsylvania, Institute for Urban Studies, 100-101
Urban America, 111
Urban beautification (*See also* City Beautiful), 33-34
Urban Land Institute, 2, 105
Urban planning. *See* Planning, urban
Urbanization, American: and attitude toward nature, 24; and conflict with individualism, 25; and immigration, 36-37; expansion, 9-10, 22-23
Utopia and utopianism: agrarian, economic basis of, 16; and institutional change, 5, 7; arcadian, influence of, 16; community and, 5-6; decline of, 6; environmental emphasis of, 4-5; holistic aspects of, 4; Kateb on, 4; secular emphasis, 3-4; spatial. *See* City, "good"

Vallingby (Sweden), 55
Vanderlyn, John, 17
Veblen, Thorstein, 57
Veiller, Laurence, 43

Veterans Administration, housing policy of, 30
Village: preindustrial, as greentown model, 89–91, 93; schools, as size determinant of, 117; social interaction in, Wirth on, 90; Stein, on use of greenbelt in, 92

Wade, Richard, 11–12
Ward, John, 23
Warner, Sam Bass, Jr., on suburbanization, 30
Washington, D.C.: influence of City Beautiful, 33; L'Enfant plan of, 33; urban renewal in, 110
Washington Symphony Orchestra, 116
Weber, Adna F., 39
Welfare, public: cities and, 14; influence of functionalism, 26–27
Welwyn (Britain), 45, 50–51
Whitacre, Charles Harris, 55, 59
Wiebe, Robert, on progressivism, 26
Wilderness and the American Mind (Nash), 32
Willingboro (New Jersey). *See* Levittowns—Levittown (New Jersey)

Wirth, Louis: influence of on greentowns, 90; on neighborhood, 64
Wisconsin, zoning, 42
Wives, working, exclusion from greentowns, 82
Wood, Edith Elmer, 55; on population redistribution, 39
Works Progress Administration, Housing Division, 80
Worldwatch Institute, 133
Wright, Frank Lloyd, 7; design philosophy of, 17–18
Wright, Henry, 55, 57
Wurster, Catherine Bauer, 55

Zoning: Ackerman, criticism of, 43–44; and factories, suburban location of, 39; and housing problems, solution of, 39–40; and progressivism, ideals of, 43; appeal of, and segregation of land use, 41, 43; garden city and, 48; in Berkeley (California), 43; in Minnesota, 42; in New York City, 42–43; in Wisconsin, 42; Kessler on, 41; spread of, 43